UNLEASH YOUR INNER AUTHORPRENEUR
DIY MARKETING STRATEGIES WRITERS NEED TODAY

RAE A. STONEHOUSE

Live For Excellence Productions

INTRODUCTION

Welcome to **Unleash Your Inner Authorpreneur: DIY Marketing Strategies Writers Need Today**.

I'm Rae Stonehouse and the author of some 30+ self-help, personal/professional self-development books of my own and nonfiction books for my clients.

While my **Successful Self-Publisher Series: How to Write, Publish and Market Your Book Yourself**, focuses on different aspects of writing and self-publishing, this publication will focus on marketing strategies for self-published authors.

One of my biggest lessons in my own self-publishing journey has been that it could easily take 30% of your time to write your book and 130% to market it. In fact, the marketing portion may even be quite a bit more than that if you hope to achieve a positive return on your investment in publishing.

In one of my other publications **Blow Your Own Horn! Personal Branding for Business Professionals,** I promote personal branding focusing on business professionals.

INTRODUCTION

This book focuses on self-publishing authors. A common factor among many business professionals and authors is that many feel self-promotion is bragging and we were taught at a young age that nobody likes a braggart.

This can be a limiting belief if we don't move past it. I am fond of a quote by Walt Whitman, American cowboy poet, that goes "if you done it... it ain't braggin!"

The quote is probably taken out of context, but I think it works for us. If you want the world to know about your publication and you as an author, well... You'll need to blow your own horn, but that's another book.

Figuring out the best ways to market your writing is important if you want to make it in the writing world. It doesn't matter if you're already a well-known author trying to grow your audience, or if you're starting out and want to kick off your writing career. Having solid marketing tactics is key. That's why in this motivational yet practical guide, we'll equip you with the proven DIY tactics you need to take charge of promoting your work. You'll learn how to create a compelling author brand, leverage social media engagement, generate buzz for your latest book, and more—all without breaking the bank.

With insights from successful author entrepreneurs and step-by-step guidance on optimizing your online platforms, website, and content, this book will help unleash your inner marketing guru. You'll gain the confidence and tools to connect with readers, grow your audience, and build the writing career you love through strategic self-promotion.

Whether you're published traditionally or self-published, this book will empower you to become your own best advocate. You'll be able to effectively broadcast your message and stories to the world—and watch your book sales rise in response. Are you ready to unlock the authorpreneur within and propel your writing to new heights? Then this book is for you!

INTRODUCTION

THE IMPORTANCE OF AUTHOR BRANDING:

Now, when everyone can share their thoughts and ideas easily, and content is important, making a unique identity for yourself as an author is super important. This means creating a special image, persona, and reputation that sets you apart from other writers. It's all about making sure people recognize and remember who you are and what you stand for in your writing.

One might wonder why author branding is important. First, branding helps to build trust and credibility with readers. When an author consistently delivers high-quality content and maintains a consistent image, readers are more likely to trust and invest in their work. Through branding, authors can establish themselves as experts in their niche, leading to increased readership and a loyal following.

Second, author branding lets writers establish their distinct voice and style. Each author has a unique perspective and way of storytelling. By creating a brand around this individuality, authors can attract readers who resonate with their particular approach and are more likely to become dedicated fans. A clear brand identity can make a writer's work easily recognizable among a sea of content and help them stand out in a crowded marketplace.

Author branding is instrumental in effective marketing and promotion. Building a strong brand will make it easier for authors to target their ideal audience through targeted marketing campaigns. It lets authors connect with their readers on a deeper level, helping with a sense of community and engagement. Through effective branding, authors can foster a relationship with their readers, resulting in increased book sales, positive word-of-mouth, and ongoing success in the industry.

Another significant benefit of author branding is the ability to diversify income streams. A recognizable and trusted brand can expand beyond writing books, letting authors branch out into other areas such as speaking engagements, merchandise, and collaborations. By leveraging their brand, authors can explore new opportunities to reach a broader audience and enhance their financial stability.

Last, author branding is essential for long-term career growth. In a competitive industry, where new authors emerge every day, it is important to develop a brand that can evolve and adapt. A well-established author brand can lay the foundation for a successful and enduring writing career, enabling authors to sustain their relevance and impact for years to come.

Author branding plays an important role in today's publishing landscape. It is an effective tool for building trust, establishing a unique identity, and connecting with readers. Successful branding can lead to increased readership, greater marketing opportunities, and diversified income streams. Ultimately, author branding is a powerful asset that can pave the way for long-term success and recognition in the writing industry.

Rae A. Stonehouse

Author

January 2024

COPYRIGHT

ISBN:

Ebook: 978-1-998813-56-8

Paperback: 978-1-998813-57-5

Audiobook: 978-1-998813-58-2

〜

SECTION ONE: THE AUTHORPRENEUR MINDSET - BUILDING YOUR AUTHOR BRAND

UNDERSTANDING THE CONCEPT OF AN AUTHORPRENEUR:

An AUTHORPRENEUR IS A RELATIVELY new term that has gained popularity in the publishing industry. It refers to an author who not only writes books but also takes on the role of an entrepreneur to build a sustainable business around their writing. Essentially, an authorpreneur combines their creative writing talents with a business mindset to establish a successful and profitable career as an author.

The idea of authorpreneurship recognizes that being a successful author goes beyond simply writing a great book. It involves taking responsibility for all parts of the writing career, including marketing, branding, and even self-publishing. Authors who embrace the role of an authorpreneur understand that they must wear multiple hats and actively promote their work to reach a wider audience.

Here are a few key parts of the authorpreneur concept:

Business mindset: An authorpreneur thinks like an entrepreneur. They understand the market and target audience for their work, and they develop strategies to effectively monetize their writing. This may include exploring different publishing options, building a brand, or creating multiple streams of income.

Marketing and promotion: An authorpreneur takes charge of marketing and promoting their work. They develop a marketing plan, build an author platform, engage in social media marketing, and use various strategies to create visibility and attract readers.

Building a brand: Branding is a crucial part of being an authorpreneur. Creating a recognizable brand helps establish trust and loyalty among readers. This includes building a strong author website, having a consistent author image, and delivering a clear and compelling message through various marketing channels.

Entrepreneurial skills: An authorpreneur understands the business side of writing and develops the skills to succeed. This can include financial management, negotiation skills, project management, and networking. They also stay updated with industry trends and learn new skills to stay ahead of the competition.

Multiple income streams: An authorpreneur recognizes that relying only on book sales may not sustain a writing career. They diversify their income by exploring other avenues such as speaking engagements, coaching, teaching workshops, licensing rights, and merchandise.

By embodying the role of an authorpreneur, writers have more control over their writing careers. They are not limited to traditional publishing models and can leverage self-publishing platforms and digital marketing strategies to reach a larger audience. However, being an authorpreneur also requires a significant investment of time and effort beyond writing, as authors need to balance their creative pursuits with the demands of running a business.

Understanding the idea of an authorpreneur is important for authors looking to make a living from their writing. By embracing a business mindset, focusing on marketing, and branding, and seeking multiple income streams, authors can transform their passion for writing into a sustainable and profitable career.

∾

THE RISE OF THE AUTHORPRENEUR:

A COOL NEW trend has popped up recently: the rise of the "authorpreneur." These creative go-getters use their writing skills and smart business sense to not just write, but also to run successful businesses in the publishing world. They're not just writers; they're business owners who know how to make the most of their talents in the industry.

Gone are the days when writers had to rely solely on traditional publishing houses to bring their work to the world. With the advent of self-publishing platforms and the growing popularity of ebooks, authors now have more control and freedom than ever before. This has opened up opportunities for aspiring writers to take charge of their own work and build their own brands.

The term "authorpreneur" refers to authors who not only write books but also take charge of the entire publishing process and monetize their creativity in various ways. They have a deep understanding of the market and use their entrepreneurial skills to connect with their target audience, develop marketing strategies, and navigate the ever-changing landscape of the publishing industry.

One of the key characteristics of authorpreneurs is their ability to diversify their income streams. They no longer rely solely on book sales, but instead explore alternative revenue streams such as speaking engagements, merchandise, online courses, and coaching. By leveraging their expertise and credibility as authors, they create multiple income streams around their brand, ultimately building a sustainable business rather than relying on a single book release.

Authorpreneurs also embrace the power of digital marketing and social media platforms to establish their personal brand and connect with their readership. They understand the importance of building a loyal community of followers who not only buy their books but also serve as ambassadors for their brand. Through blog posts, podcasts, vlogs, and active social media engagement, authorpreneurs build a strong online presence and prove themselves to be authorities in their niche.

Additionally, authorpreneurs are proactive in seeking out partnerships and collaborations. They understand the power of networking and strategic alliances, whether it be collaborating with other authors on joint projects or partnering with influencers and organizations that align with their brand values. By combining forces with like-minded individuals or organizations, authorpreneurs can reach new audiences and expand their influence.

While the path of the authorpreneur is undoubtedly rewarding, it is not without its challenges. Building a successful authorpreneurial career requires a unique combination of creativity and business skills. It requires dedication, perseverance, and a willingness to adapt to the changing demands of the market. However, those who embrace this new model are empowered to shape their own destinies, pursue their passion for writing, and build a business around their creativity.

The rise of the authorpreneur signals a new era in the publishing industry, where writers can take control of their own careers and build thriving businesses from their passion for writing. As technology continues to advance and new opportunities arise, the authorpreneur is poised to continue to rise, challenging traditional publishing norms and reshaping the way we consume and experience literature.

DEFINING YOUR AUTHOR PERSONA:

YOUR AUTHOR PERSONA is the public and professional image you cultivate as a writer. It goes beyond your writing style and encompasses your brand, values, and overall presence as an author. Developing a strong author persona can help you connect with your audience, build credibility, and establish your identity in the literary world. Here are a few steps to help you define your author persona:

Identify your audience: Consider who your target readership is. Are you writing for young adults, mystery enthusiasts, fantasy lovers, or a specific niche? Understanding your audience's preferences, interests, and demographics will help you shape your author persona to better resonate with them.

Define your writing style: Your writing style is an essential part of your author persona. Are you lighthearted and humorous, poetic, and introspective, or perhaps edgy and provocative? Determine the tone, voice, and genre that best reflect your writing style, as it will set the foundation for your overall author persona.

Embrace your values and passions: Think about what matters to you as a writer and as an individual. What themes, causes, or values do you wish to convey through your writing? Incorporating these parts into your author persona will give you a distinct identity and connect you with readers who share similar beliefs.

Establish an online presence: Having an online presence is imperative for authors. Consider creating a website or a blog where you can share your writing, engage with your readers, and establish yourself as an authority in your chosen genre. Social media platforms like Twitter, Facebook, and Instagram can also help you connect with readers, network with other writers, and promote your work.

Be authentic and consistent: Your author persona should authentically represent who you are as a writer and a person. It should not be a fabricated image or persona you struggle to maintain. Be true to yourself and let your unique voice shine through in your writing, interactions with readers, and public appearances. Consistency is also essential in maintaining your author persona. Make sure your online presence and public image reflect the same values, tone, and interests across all platforms.

Engage with your audience: Interacting with your readers and fellow writers is an excellent way to refine your author persona and build a loyal following. Respond to comments, participate in writing communities, go to literary events, and consider setting up book signings or virtual Q&A sessions. This engagement will help you better understand your audience and establish your author persona as accessible, approachable, and relatable.

Remember that your author persona is not set in stone and can evolve as you grow and develop as a writer. It is an ongoing process that requires reflection, authenticity, and adaptation. By defining your author persona and cultivating a strong public image, you can connect with your audience on a deeper level and prove yourself to be a respected and recognized author in the literary world.

EMBRACING THE DUAL ROLES OF WRITER AND MARKETER:

As a writer, it's easy to get lost in the creative process, lost in the world of words and storytelling. We strive to create compelling narratives, to engage readers, and to share our unique perspectives with the world. But as the digital landscape continues to evolve, writers are being asked to take on a new role – that of a marketer.

Traditionally, writers have relied on publishers and literary agents to handle the marketing parts of their work. However, with the rise of self-publishing and the increasing demand for digital content, writers are now being expected to actively promote their own work. This shift has led to a merging of roles, where writers must embrace both the creative process and the practical side of marketing.

Embracing this dual role can seem overwhelming at first, as it involves acquiring new skills and understanding the algorithms of social media platforms. But it also presents exciting opportunities. As writers, we have the unique advantage of knowing our work intimately; we understand the themes, characters, and messages we want to convey. This deep understanding lets us authentically market our work, connecting with readers who will resonate with our stories.

To embrace the dual roles of writer and marketer, it is essential to understand the target audience. Identifying who our readers are and where they spend their time online lets us craft tailored marketing strategies. We can use social media platforms, such as Instagram and Twitter, to engage with potential readers, share behind-the-scenes insights, and create a sense of community. Using email newsletters, we can keep our audience informed about upcoming releases, book signings, or exclusive content.

We must learn to leverage the power of storytelling in our marketing efforts. As writers, we understand the impact of a captivating narrative. By weaving storytelling techniques into our marketing campaigns, we can create an emotional connection with our audience. Whether through blog posts, video content, or podcast interviews, we can share our own story as writers, letting readers see the person behind the words.

Collaboration is also important in this new landscape. By partnering with fellow writers, bloggers, influencers, or book clubs, we can expand our reach and tap into new audiences. Cross-promotion and guest blogging are effective ways to work together and mutually benefit from each other's platforms.

Embracing the dual roles of writer and marketer is about finding a balance. It's about recognizing that marketing is not separate from the creative process, but an essential part of it. By embracing this new landscape and understanding the power of marketing, writers can make sure their work reaches its intended audience and resonates with readers in a meaningful way. So let us not shy away from the challenge, but instead, embrace it, and let our words reach the hearts and minds of those who need them most.

Understanding the Importance of Personal Branding in the Author's Journey

In today's highly competitive publishing industry, personal branding is more important than ever for authors. It not only helps to establish their unique identity and voice but also plays an important role in their journey toward success.

Personal branding refers to the way authors present themselves to the world, highlighting their skills, values, and knowledge. It is essentially their reputation and the impression they create in the minds of readers, fellow authors, agents, and publishers. With the rise of social media and the ease of online self-publishing, personal branding has become indispensable in attracting an audience and standing out from the crowd.

One of the main benefits of personal branding is its ability to create a sense of trust and credibility. To engage readers and build a following, authors must establish themselves as experts in their chosen genre or subject matter. By consistently delivering high-quality content and aligning their personal brand with their writing style, authors can develop a level of trust with their audience, making sure readers continue to choose their books and recommend them to others.

Personal branding is not only important for readers but also for industry professionals, such as agents and publishers. With limited resources and countless manuscripts to review, agents and publishers are more likely to notice authors with a strong personal brand. A well-crafted brand shows an author's commitment, professionalism, and marketability, making it easier for agents and publishers to see the potential for success.

Personal branding gives authors a platform to connect with readers directly. Through social media, blogs, and newsletters, authors can engage with their audience, share insights into their writing process, and build a community around their work. By cultivating a loyal fan base, authors can create a network of supporters who will not only buy their books but also spread the word to others.

Personal branding should not be mistaken for self-promotion or a deceptive marketing tactic. It is about authentically representing oneself and building a genuine connection with readers. By show-casing their unique voice and perspective, authors can attract readers who resonate with their message and writing style, leading to long-term success and impact.

· · ·

Personal branding is an essential part of an author's journey toward success. It helps to establish credibility, build trust with readers and industry professionals, and create a direct connection with their audience. By investing time and effort into developing a strong personal brand, authors can differentiate themselves from the competition, attract a loyal fan base, and ultimately meet their goals in the publishing industry.

NAVIGATING THE WORLD OF AUTHOR BRANDING AND SELF-PROMOTION IN PUBLISHING:

AUTHORS NOW HAVE MORE on their plate than writing compelling stories. They also need to focus on building their brand and promoting themselves in the publishing world.

With the rise of self-publishing and online platforms, it has become even more crucial for authors to establish their unique author brand and actively engage in self-promotion. Here are strategies to help authors navigate the world of author branding and self-promotion in publishing.

Define Your Author Brand:

Before diving into self-promotion, it's essential to clearly understand your author brand. What are the unique qualities, themes, or messages that define your writing? Consider your target audience, genre, and personal interests. Your brand should reflect your writing style, values, and the emotional experience readers can expect from your work.

Establish a Stellar Online Presence:

In the digital age, authors must have a strong online presence to connect with readers and industry professionals. Create an author website or blog, use social media platforms like Twitter, Facebook, and

Instagram to engage with your audience. Be consistent across all platforms, using a professional profile picture, a compelling bio, and regular updates to showcase your work and interact with readers.

Engage with Your Audience:

Remember that building a brand is about connecting with people. Engage your audience by responding to comments, messages, and reviews. Host Q&A sessions, giveaways, or virtual book clubs. Show genuine interest in your readers and build a community around your writing. These interactions will not only build loyal fans but also encourage positive word-of-mouth promotion.

Collaborate with Influencers:

Reach out to influencers in your niche, such as book bloggers, podcasters, or established authors, and propose collaboration opportunities. Consider offering guest posts, interviews, or giveaways on their platform. Collaborations can help expand your reach and tap into a wider audience base, increasing your visibility in the publishing industry.

Leverage Social Media Advertising:

While organic engagement and content creation are important, social media advertising can significantly boost your visibility. Use paid advertisements on platforms like Facebook, Instagram, or Goodreads to reach potential readers who may not be aware of your work. Target your ads based on genre, interests, or demographic data to maximize their impact.

Go to Author Events and Conferences:

Participate in writing conferences, book festivals, and other author events to network with industry professionals, fellow authors, and readers. These events provide opportunities for book signings, panels, and speaking engagements where you can promote your work face-to-face. Capture these moments through photos, videos, or live streams to share them on your online platforms.

Leverage Book Reviews and Online Influencers:

Positive reviews play an important role in attracting potential readers. Encourage readers to leave honest reviews on platforms like Amazon, Goodreads, or book blogs. Additionally, consider sending advance copies of your book to influential reviewers or bloggers who specialize in your genre. A positive review from a respected source can significantly boost your credibility and encourage readers to explore your work.

Embrace Email Marketing:

Build an email list of interested readers who want updates, behind-the-scenes content, or exclusive offers from you. Regularly send newsletters with updates about your writing, upcoming releases, events, or exclusive content. Personalize these emails to make your readers feel valued and appreciated.

Leverage Traditional Media:

While digital platforms are important, don't overlook traditional media opportunities. Contact local newspapers, radio stations, or bookstores for potential interviews, reviews, or events. Traditional media can provide a different avenue for promoting your work and reaching readers who may not be as active online.

Be Authentic and Consistent:

Throughout your author branding and self-promotion journey, remember to stay true to yourself and your writing. Authenticity is key to building trust and lasting connections with readers. Be consistent in your messaging, quality of content, and engagement. Over time, your brand will gain recognition and attract a loyal fan base.

Remember, author branding and self-promotion are ongoing processes that require dedication, creativity, and adaptability. By promoting your work and engaging with your audience, you can navigate the publishing world and maximize your chances of success in the competitive market.

～

THE NEW PUBLISHING LANDSCAPE - WHY AUTHORS MUST MARKET THEMSELVES:

THE PUBLISHING INDUSTRY has undergone significant changes in recent years, thanks to advances in technology and the rise of self-publishing platforms. While these changes have opened up opportunities for authors to reach a wider audience, they have also created a highly competitive environment.

Gone are the days when authors could solely rely on their publishers to handle all parts of book marketing and promotion. In today's publishing landscape, authors must market themselves and their work. Here are a few reasons this is essential:

Increased competition: With the flood of new books being published every day, authors face fierce competition for readers' attention. Standing out in such a crowded marketplace is difficult, and relying only on traditional publishing channels may not be enough. Authors must actively engage with potential readers through various marketing channels to build a loyal fan base.

Changing reader behavior: Readers today have different habits and preferences when discovering new books. While traditional media like newspapers and magazines still play a role, more readers are turning to online platforms, social media, and book review blogs for book recommendations. By marketing themselves, authors can leverage these platforms to reach a wider audience and build a strong online presence.

Direct connection with readers: Marketing yourself as an author lets you directly connect with your readers. By engaging with them on social media or through newsletters, you can build a relationship with your audience, gain valuable feedback, and develop a loyal fan base. This direct connection can lead to increased book sales, as readers who feel a personal connection with an author are more likely to buy their books and recommend them to others.

Financial independence: With self-publishing platforms, authors have greater control over their work and can earn higher royalties. However, this independence comes with the responsibility of marketing your own book. By investing time and effort into marketing, authors can increase their chances of success and financial stability. Effective marketing can lead to increased book sales, which can generate passive income and potentially open doors to other opportunities like speaking engagements or book tours.

Long-term career building: As an author, you're not just selling a single book; you're building a career. Effective marketing can lead to positive reviews, word-of-mouth recommendations, and a strong author brand. By consistently promoting yourself and your work, you can create a platform for future books and prove yourself to be a trusted voice in your genre or niche.

The new publishing landscape requires authors to market themselves. By embracing marketing strategies and connecting directly with readers, authors can stand out in a competitive industry, increase their book sales, and build a successful and sustainable writing career.

THE EVOLUTION OF AUTHORSHIP IN THE DIGITAL AGE:

THE DIGITAL AGE has revolutionized many parts of our lives, and the world of literature is no exception. The evolution of authorship in the digital age has brought about significant shifts in the way authors create, publish, and interact with their readers. From digital writing tools to self-publishing platforms, the digital age has opened up exciting opportunities for authors while also posing new challenges.

One of the most prominent changes in the digital age is the way authors write and create their works. Authors traditionally relied on typewriters or pen and paper to draft their manuscripts. However, with the introduction of word processing software and online writing tools, authors now have access to a range of digital writing platforms that help streamline the writing process. These tools let authors easily edit, organize, and collaborate on their work, enhancing their productivity and efficiency.

Another significant development in the digital age is the ease of self-publishing. Authors had to submit their manuscripts to publishing houses and face the hurdle of rejection. However, with the rise of self-publishing platforms such as Amazon Kindle Direct Publishing, Smashwords, and Lulu, authors now have the opportunity to bypass traditional publishing channels and directly publish their works to a global audience. This has democratized the publishing industry, letting aspiring authors share their stories with no traditional publishing deal.

Social media and online communities have also played an important role in shaping the evolution of authorship in the digital age. Authors now have direct access to their readership through platforms like Twitter, Facebook, and Instagram. They can engage with readers by sharing updates about their writing process, hosting virtual book clubs, and participating in online discussions. This direct interaction has bridged the gap between authors and readers, fostering a sense of community and enabling authors to build a dedicated fan base.

However, the digital age also brings challenges for authors. With the rise of ebooks and digital reading platforms, the market has become saturated with a lot of content. Standing out in such a crowded marketplace requires authors to not only write captivating stories but also understand marketing and promotion strategies. Authors must actively engage in self-promotion, using social media, author websites, and online advertising to reach potential readers.

The digital age has raised concerns about copyright infringement and intellectual property rights. With the ease of digital reproduction, protecting an author's work from piracy has become a pressing issue. Authors must be vigilant in tracking and preventing unauthorized distribution of their content to ensure they can continue to benefit from their creativity.

The evolution of authorship in the digital age has brought both opportunities and challenges. Digital writing tools, self-publishing platforms, and social media have empowered authors, enabling them to write, publish, and connect with readers in unprecedented ways. However, the large amount of content and the need for self-promotion require authors to adapt and develop new skills to succeed in the rapidly evolving landscape of the digital age.

~

THE BLENDING OF CREATIVITY AND COMMERCE:

THE BLENDING of creativity and commerce is a harmonious union with the power to mold industries, spur innovation, and redefine the boundaries of what is possible. This fusion of artistic expression and economic entrepreneurship has become an essential part to success in today's rapidly evolving world.

Creativity is the force that fuels imagination, enabling individuals to envision new possibilities and inspire others. It is the impetus behind groundbreaking inventions, captivating works of art, and thought-provoking literature. The creative mind dares to challenge conventions, break through barriers, and redefine norms. It is the driving force behind the birth of industries and the catalyst for cultural revolutions.

But commerce serves as the practical conductor that transforms creative ideas into physical realities. It provides the infrastructure, resources, and framework necessary to turn dreams into commodities. Commerce brings order and structure to the chaos of creativity, turning ideas into products, services, and experiences that can be shared with the world. Without the power of commerce, many creative visions would remain trapped within the minds of their creators, unable to manifest into the lives of others.

The blending of creativity and commerce can be seen in various industries, such as fashion, technology, entertainment, and design. These sectors thrive on their ability to harness creativity to create innovative and appealing products and experiences, while also leveraging commerce to package and monetize their ideas. Fashion designers transform their artistic visions into wearable garments that captivate consumers and drive sales. Technological innovators develop revolutionary devices that merge functionality with aesthetic appeal. Filmmakers craft compelling stories that resonate with audiences and generate box office success. Industrial designers blend functionality and aesthetics to create user-friendly and aesthetically pleasing products.

However, the harmonious blending of creativity and commerce is not without its challenges. In the pursuit of commercial success, there is always the risk of compromising artistic integrity or sacrificing unique creative visions for market demand. Balancing the pursuit of profit with the preservation of creativity requires a delicate equilibrium. It calls for visionary leaders who understand the value of creativity and the importance of nourishing it within the realm of commerce.

As we move forward in an increasingly globalized and interconnected world, the blending of creativity and commerce will continue to shape industries and push boundaries. Through this synergy new industries emerge, old ones evolve, and society progresses. By embracing the potential of creativity to drive commerce and commerce to enable creative expression, we create a world where innovation thrives, diversity flourishes, and human potential is unleashed to its fullest.

HISTORICAL CONTEXT AND THE SHIFT IN THE PUBLISHING INDUSTRY:

THE PUBLISHING INDUSTRY has gone through significant shifts throughout history, reflecting changes in technology, politics, and society. These transformations have had a profound impact on how books are produced, distributed, and consumed, ultimately reshaping the industry itself.

Historical context is important in understanding the evolution of the publishing industry. Before the invention of the printing press by Johannes Gutenberg in the 15th century, books were primarily copied by hand, making them expensive and rare. The printing press revolutionized the industry by enabling mass production of books, leading to an increase in literacy rates and the spread of knowledge. This marked the beginning of a new era for publishing, as it allowed for the wider dissemination of ideas and the democratization of information.

During the 19th and early 20th centuries, the publishing industry flourished with the rise of industrialization. Improved printing technologies, such as lithography and steam-powered presses, made book production faster, cheaper, and more efficient. This led to the growth of large publishing houses and the establishment of a commercial market for books. Introducing paperback books in the mid-19th century made books even more accessible and affordable to a wider audience.

In the mid-20th century, the publishing industry faced another turning point with television and other forms of mass media. This era saw a decline in book sales as people turned to other forms of entertainment. However, the rise of paperback novels and book clubs helped to revive the industry by catering to different consumer preferences and creating new distribution channels.

The late 20th century saw a major shift with the emergence of the internet and digital technologies. The digital revolution disrupted the traditional publishing model, as ebooks and online platforms offered new ways to create, distribute, and consume content. This led to challenges and opportunities for both traditional publishing houses and self-published authors. Online retailers like Amazon revolutionized book sales by offering a vast choice of books and reaching a global audience.

The rise of social media also played a significant role in transforming the publishing landscape. Platforms like Goodreads and Wattpad provided spaces for authors and readers to connect and share their work. Additionally, social media platforms let authors engage directly with their audience, thus influencing marketing strategies and promoting self-publishing initiatives.

The publishing industry has confronted demands for diversity and inclusivity. As societies have learned of underrepresented voices and perspectives, there has been a growing demand for diverse literature. Publishers have had to adapt to this shift by seeking out and promoting authors from marginalized communities.

The publishing industry has constantly evolved throughout history due to changing technologies, shifts in consumer behavior, and societal demands. From the Gutenberg printing press to the rise of digital publishing, each transformation has changed how books are created, distributed, and consumed. As the industry continues to navigate these changes, it is vital for publishers to adapt to new trends and technologies to remain relevant in an increasingly digital and intercon-nected world.

SUCCESS STORIES OF AUTHORPRENEURS:

J.K. ROWLING - J.K. Rowling is one of the most successful authorpreneurs of our time. After facing many rejections, Rowling's book "Harry Potter and the Philosopher's Stone" was finally accepted by Bloomsbury Publishing in 1996. The book became a worldwide sensation, launching a highly successful series and a multi-billion-dollar franchise including books, movies, merchandise, and even a theme park. Rowling's success as an authorpreneur has made her one of the most influential and wealthiest authors in the world.

Stephen King - Stephen King is known for his horror and suspense novels, with over 350 million copies of his books sold worldwide. While he faced initial rejections and financial struggles early in his writing career, King persevered and found success with his breakout novel "Carrie" in 1974. Since then, he has published many bestsellers, many of which have been adapted into successful movies and TV shows. King's ability to not only write compelling stories but also build a strong brand has made him a highly successful authorpreneur.

Elizabeth Gilbert - Elizabeth Gilbert is best known for her memoir "Eat, Pray, Love", which became a global bestseller and inspired millions of readers to seek personal transformation and self-discovery.

Gilbert's success as an authorpreneur stems from her ability to connect with her audience through compelling storytelling and vulnerability. She has since published several other successful books, including "Big Magic: Creative Living Beyond Fear", where she provides insights and guidance for aspiring artists and creatives.

Tim Ferriss - Tim Ferriss is not only an author but also a highly successful entrepreneur, investor, and podcast host. His book "The 4-Hour Workweek" gained widespread acclaim for its unconventional advice on productivity and lifestyle design. Ferriss has since published several more best-selling books, focusing on topics such as personal development, health, and performance. He has also built a strong personal brand, leveraging his books and podcasts to create a successful online business empire.

Danielle Steel - Danielle Steel is one of the most prolific authors of our time, having written over 190 novels that have sold over 800 million copies worldwide. Steel's success as an authorpreneur comes from her ability to consistently produce engaging stories across genres like romance, drama, and historical fiction. She has built a dedicated fan base and her books have been a mainstay on bestseller lists for decades. Steel's business acumen and relentless work ethic have made her a true success story in the world of authorpreneurs.

These success stories of authorpreneurs highlight the power of perseverance, creativity, and entrepreneurial spirit in turning a passion for writing into a thriving business. Through their talent, determination, and ability to connect with their audience, these authors have achieved both critical acclaim and financial success, inspiring and paving the way for aspiring authorpreneurs around the world.

EMBRACING THE DUAL ROLES OF WRITER AND MARKETER:

As a writer, it can often be a challenge to embrace the dual roles of writer and marketer. Many writers usually focus only on their craft, pouring their heart and soul into the words they write. However, it is essential to also understand the importance of marketing your work.

Embracing the role of a marketer does not mean compromising your artistic integrity or selling out. It simply means recognizing that for your work to reach its intended audience and have the impact it deserves, you need to actively promote it.

One way to embrace both roles is to cultivate a mindset shift. Instead of viewing marketing as a necessary evil or a distraction from your writing, think of it as an opportunity to connect with your readers on a deeper level. Marketing lets you share your work with a wider audience, engage with readers, and build a community around your writing.

Another way to embrace both roles is to educate yourself about marketing strategies and techniques. This doesn't mean you have to become an expert in marketing overnight, but having a basic understanding of key concepts can go a long way. Learn about social media marketing, email marketing, content creation, and other relevant tools and platforms that can help you reach your target audience.

It is also important to adopt a consistent and strategic approach to marketing. Set goals for yourself, create a marketing plan, and develop a schedule for promoting your work. Consistency is key when marketing, as it helps to build brand awareness and trust with your audience.

However, find a balance between writing and marketing. You still need to dedicate time and energy to honing your craft and producing high-quality content. Without compelling and engaging writing, your marketing efforts will fall flat.

Last, embrace the feedback and insights you receive from your readers and the marketing data you gather. Pay attention to which types of content resonate most with your audience, and use that information to inform your future writing and marketing decisions.

Embracing the dual roles of writer and marketer can be challenging, but it is necessary in today's publishing landscape. By approaching marketing with a positive mindset, educating yourself, and finding a balance, you can effectively promote your work and connect with your audience in a meaningful way.

SECTION ONE KEY TAKEAWAYS AND ACTION ITEMS

KEY TAKEAWAYS:

1. **Understanding the Authorpreneur Concept:** Recognize that being a successful author today means blending creative writing with entrepreneurial skills.
2. **Business Mindset:** Adopt an entrepreneurial approach, understanding market trends and strategies to monetize your writing.
3. **Marketing and Promotion:** Take charge of marketing your work to increase visibility and connect with readers.
4. **Branding:** Develop a strong, recognizable brand that establishes trust and loyalty among your audience.
5. **Entrepreneurial Skills:** Learn key business skills like financial management, negotiation, and networking.
6. **Diversifying Income:** Explore multiple income streams beyond book sales, like speaking engagements and workshops.
7. **Direct Reader Connection:** Utilize digital platforms for direct interaction with your audience.
8. **Author Persona Development:** Create a public image that resonates with your target readership and reflects your values.

9. **Writer-Marketer Balance:** Understand the importance of balancing your writing with marketing responsibilities.
10. **Personal Branding:** Focus on establishing a strong personal brand to enhance credibility and reader trust.
11. **Self-Promotion Strategies:** Leverage social media, collaborations, and traditional media for effective self-promotion.
12. **Adapting to Digital Changes:** Embrace the challenges and opportunities presented by the digital age in publishing.
13. **Creative and Commerce Blend:** Recognize the importance of merging creativity with business skills.

Action Items:

1. **Develop a Business Plan:** Create a strategy encompassing marketing, branding, and income diversification.
2. **Build Your Brand:** Work on your author website and social media profiles to reflect your author persona.
3. **Enhance Marketing Skills:** Take courses or go to workshops on digital marketing and social media engagement.
4. **Engage With Readers:** Schedule regular interactions with your audience through social media, blogs, or webinars.
5. **Explore Income Opportunities:** Identify and pursue additional income sources related to your writing.
6. **Create Marketing Content:** Develop marketing materials that align with your brand and engage your target audience.
7. **Network and Collaborate:** go to industry events and seek collaborative opportunities with other authors and influencers.
8. **Stay Updated:** Keep up with the latest trends in digital publishing and marketing.
9. **Manage Your Time:** Allocate specific times for writing and marketing to ensure a balanced approach.

10. **Seek Feedback:** Regularly solicit and incorporate feedback from your audience to refine your author brand and marketing strategies.
11. **Use Analytics:** Monitor the effectiveness of your marketing strategies using digital analytics tools.
12. **Protect Your Work:** Stay informed about copyright laws and protect your intellectual property.

In our next Section...

Get ready to step up your game in the exciting realm of author marketing! In our upcoming section, we'll dive into advanced strategies and innovative tactics that will help authors make a splash in the digital world. We'll cover the ins and outs of using social media to its full potential, mastering the art of email campaigns, and the importance of collaborations and partnerships in expanding your reach.

We'll also explore the nuances of online advertising, leveraging book reviews and influencer marketing, optimizing your author website, and the significance of building a strong author community. Additionally, we'll dig into creative merchandising, public speaking, and interviews to broaden your exposure. This section is packed with actionable tips and insights, perfect for both budding and experienced authors eager to amplify their presence and turn their writing passion into a flourishing career. Stay tuned for these exciting insights!

SECTION TWO: SELF-PROMOTION AND MARKETING STRATEGIES

NAVIGATING THE WORLD OF AUTHOR BRANDING AND SELF-PROMOTION IN PUBLISHING:

IN THE FAST-PACED and competitive world of book publishing, it's no longer enough for authors to simply write a great book and hope for success. With the rise of social media, online platforms, and a growing emphasis on author branding, self-promotion has become an integral part of an author's journey. Here are tips for authors on how to navigate the world of author branding and self-promotion in publishing.

Develop Your Author Brand:

Author branding is about creating a distinct identity that sets you apart from other authors and helps readers recognize and connect with you. Start by defining your target audience, understanding their interests and preferences, and crafting a unique brand message that aligns with them. Consider your values, themes, and writing style to develop a brand that is authentic and resonates with your readers.

Build a Strong Online Presence:

Today, having a strong online presence is important for an author's success. Start by creating a professional website that showcases your books, features an engaging author bio, and provides a platform for blog posts, interviews, and updates. Additionally, create profiles on social media platforms such as Facebook, Twitter, Instagram, or LinkedIn, to engage with readers and fellow authors. Regularly update these platforms with exciting content, such as sneak peeks, book launch announcements, behind-the-scenes insights, and exclusive giveaways.

Collaborate and Network:

Building relationships with fellow authors, bloggers, and influencers can greatly enhance your author brand and self-promotion efforts. Join writing communities or go to book conferences and workshops to connect with like-minded individuals. Collaborate by exchanging guest blog posts, participating in joint author interviews or organizing virtual book tours. Partnering with influencers or leveraging book review blogs can help increase your book's visibility and reach a wider audience.

Engage with Your Readers:

Reader engagement is a powerful tool for author branding and self-promotion. Respond to comments and messages promptly, showing genuine interest and building connections with your readers. Encourage reader feedback and reviews and consider hosting Q&A sessions or virtual book clubs to foster interaction. Use newsletters to keep your readers updated about upcoming releases, exclusive content, or limited-time offers. By creating a loyal readership, you'll gain invaluable word-of-mouth promotion.

Harness the Power of Content Marketing:

Content marketing involves creating and sharing relevant content that showcases your expertise, interests, and writing style. This can be as blog posts, articles, podcasts, or videos. By providing valuable content, you prove yourself to be an authority in your niche, attract more readers, and foster a sense of trust and loyalty. Optimize your content for search engines to increase its discoverability and reach.

Use Book Marketing Services:

While authors need to be proactive in self-promotion, using professional book marketing services can be highly beneficial. These services provide guidance in book launch strategies, social media management, advertising campaigns, and media outreach. They can help you reach a wider audience, create compelling book trailers, secure book reviews, and negotiate promotional opportunities with influential media outlets.

Remember, author branding and self-promotion require consistent effort and adaptability. Stay updated with industry trends, experiment with different promotional techniques, and don't be afraid to seek support or guidance when needed. Embrace the challenge of navigating the world of author branding and self-promotion and enjoy the journey toward building a successful writing career.

THE ROLE OF SELF-PROMOTION IN THE MODERN PUBLISHING LANDSCAPE:

THE ROLE of self-promotion in the modern publishing landscape has become increasingly important for authors. In an industry that is highly competitive and constantly evolving, authors can no longer rely only on traditional publishing houses to market their books. With advancements in technology and the rise of the digital age, self-promotion has become an essential tool for authors to effectively reach their target audience and succeed.

One of the main reasons self-promotion is important in the publishing landscape is the changing dynamics of book sales. Publishers would invest heavily in marketing and promotion for their authors, but with the rise of online booksellers and digital platforms, the responsibility has shifted to authors themselves. Authors are now expected to build their own personal brand, engage with their readers directly, and actively promote their books through means like social media, personal websites, and author events.

Self-promotion enables authors to have greater control over their own careers. Instead of relying on publishers to handle all parts of promotion, authors can now take charge of their own marketing strategies and tailor them to their specific needs and target audience. This control lets authors be more involved in the success of their books and allows them to build a dedicated fan base that will support their future work.

In addition, self-promotion provides authors with the chance to showcase their unique voice and perspective. By engaging with readers directly, authors can share their personal stories, insights, and behind-the-scenes experiences. This connection with readers fosters a sense of authenticity and builds trust, leading to a stronger and more loyal fan base. Self-promotion lets authors differentiate themselves from the thousands of books that are published each year and to stand out in a crowded market.

However, note that self-promotion does not replace the value of traditional publishing or the knowledge of professionals. Authors still benefit from the editing, design, and distribution support that traditional publishing houses offer. Self-promotion is a complementary strategy that works hand in hand with traditional publishing channels. Effective self-promotion requires a balance between leveraging personal efforts and using the resources of the publishing industry to maximize success.

Self-promotion has become an integral part of the modern publishing landscape. Authors must actively engage in marketing and promotion to reach their audience, build their personal brand, and succeed a highly competitive industry. By embracing self-promotion, authors can take control of their careers, connect with readers, and differentiate themselves in a crowded market.

STRATEGIES FOR EFFECTIVE SELF-PROMOTION:

IDENTIFY **your strengths and unique qualities:** Take some time to reflect on your skills, experiences, and accomplishments. Understand what sets you apart from others and focus on showcasing those qualities in your self-promotion efforts.

Establish clear goals: Determine what you want to achieve through self-promotion. Whether it's gaining more visibility, attracting new clients, or advancing in your career, having clear goals will help you create focused strategies.

Build a strong personal brand: Your personal brand represents how you are perceived by others. It includes your values, knowledge, and the overall impression you make. Invest time in crafting a compelling personal brand that aligns with your goals and reflects your authentic self.

Develop an online presence: Having an online presence is important for self-promotion. Create a professional website or a portfolio showcasing your work. Leverage social media platforms to share relevant content, engage with others in your industry, and network with potential clients or employers.

Network strategically: Go to industry events, join professional organizations, and participate in online communities relevant to your field. Networking provides valuable opportunities to connect with like-minded individuals, exchange ideas, and build relationships that can lead to future collaborations or opportunities.

Seek testimonials and endorsements: Ask for feedback and testimonials from satisfied clients or colleagues who can vouch for your skills and expertise. These endorsements provide social proof that can greatly enhance your credibility when promoting yourself.

Share your expertise through content creation: Position yourself as an authority in your field by sharing your knowledge through blog posts, articles, or videos. This helps establish your credibility and attracts an audience interested in what you offer.

Leverage social proof: Share success stories, awards, or notable achievements to show your track record of delivering results. Highlighting positive experiences and showing your value can be an effective way to build trust and attract new opportunities.

Take advantage of speaking engagements or media opportunities: Look for opportunities to speak at conferences, webinars, or podcasts. These platforms not only showcase your expertise but also expose you to a wider audience and increase your visibility within your industry.

Continuously learn and adapt: Stay current with industry trends, technology advancements, and best practices. Learning and adapting to changes in your field will keep you ahead of the curve and enable you to continually improve your self-promotion strategies.

Remember, effective self-promotion is about authentically showcasing your skills and value. By implementing these strategies and staying consistent, you can increase your visibility, attract new opportunities, and ultimately meet your goals.

∾

THE NEW PUBLISHING LANDSCAPE - WHY AUTHORS MUST MARKET THEMSELVES:

THE PUBLISHING LANDSCAPE has undergone a massive transformation in recent years, and authors must adapt to this new environment to succeed. Gone are the days when publishers handled the majority of an author's marketing efforts. Now, authors are expected to take on a much larger role in promoting their own work.

One of the biggest reasons authors must market themselves is the rise of self-publishing. With platforms like Amazon Kindle Direct Publishing and Smashwords, anyone can become a published author. While this has opened up opportunities for many aspiring writers, it has also flooded the market with an overwhelming number of books. To stand out, authors must go above and beyond to reach their target audience.

Another factor is the decline in traditional bookstores. With the rise of ebooks and online retailers, physical bookstores have struggled to survive. This means that authors can no longer rely on traditional book tours and signings to generate buzz around their work. Instead, they must turn to social media, book blogs, and other online platforms to connect with readers.

The emergence of social media has changed the way people consume content. Authors can now engage directly with their readers through platforms like Twitter, Instagram, and Facebook. Building a strong online presence not only helps authors connect with their audience, but it also lets them build a personal brand and prove themselves to be experts in their field.

In addition, the rise of book bloggers and booktubers has revolution-ized book marketing. These influencers have enormous reach and can make or break a book's success. By connecting with these individuals and building relationships with them, authors can gain valuable expo-sure and support for their work.

Ultimately, authors must market themselves because the publishing landscape has evolved to require it. With the rise of self-publishing, the decline of traditional bookstores, the importance of social media, and the emergence of book influencers, authors simply cannot rely on publishers alone to promote their work.

Marketing oneself as an author is a multifaceted endeavor that includes building an online presence, engaging with readers, connecting with book bloggers and influencers, and constantly adapting to the changing landscape of publishing.

While this may seem daunting, it also presents authors with new opportunities and creative freedom. By taking charge of their own marketing efforts, authors can directly influence the success of their work and connect with readers in ways that were previously unimaginable.

Authors must market themselves in the new publishing landscape to stand out, connect with readers, and ultimately succeed in an increas-ingly competitive industry. Embracing self-promotion and using the power of social media and online platforms is no longer an option, but a necessity for authors looking to thrive in the modern publishing world.

∼

CHANGES IN TRADITIONAL
VS. SELF-PUBLISHING:

IN RECENT YEARS, there have been significant changes in the world of publishing, particularly concerning the methods of publishing books. Traditional publishing and self-publishing have both experienced transformations that have shifted the landscape of the industry. Let's explore some of these changes:

Access to publishing: One of the most significant changes is the accessibility of publishing for aspiring authors. Traditional publishing used to be the dominant choice, with only a few authors being selected by publishing houses. However, self-publishing platforms, such as Amazon's Kindle Direct Publishing, have emerged, allowing anyone with a manuscript to publish their work at a minimal cost. This has opened doors for a diverse range of voices to be heard.

Time to market: Traditional publishing often involves a long process from submitting a manuscript to the publication of the book. This includes finding an agent, negotiating contracts, and going through rounds of edits. But self-publishing lets authors publish their book almost instantly. This shortened timeline enables authors to share their work in a timelier way, which is especially beneficial for those wanting to address current events or trends.

Creative control: Traditional publishing typically involves a collaborative approach, where the author's manuscript is reviewed and edited by professionals within the publishing house. While this ensures a high-quality end product, it may also result in changes to the author's original vision. Self-publishing gives authors complete creative control. From the cover design to the content itself, authors have the freedom to execute their vision exactly as they see fit.

Revenue and royalties: In traditional publishing, authors often receive an advance against royalties, and their earnings are based on the number of copies sold. However, the percentage of royalties authors receive from each book sale is generally lower than in self-publishing. Self-published authors have the potential to earn a higher percentage of the royalties, sometimes ranging from 35% to 70%, depending on the platform and pricing structure.

Marketing and promotion: Traditional publishing houses have established networks and resources for marketing and promoting books. They have relationships with influential reviewers, bookstores, and media outlets, allowing for greater exposure. But self-published authors are responsible for their own marketing efforts, which can be time-consuming and require a deep understanding of online platforms, social media, and book promotion strategies. However, self-publishing platforms now offer various marketing tools and resources to support authors in getting their work noticed.

Perceived credibility: Traditional publishing has long been associated with legitimacy and credibility. A book published by a renowned publishing house is often viewed as having passed a rigorous selection process and is considered of higher quality. Self-published books have sometimes been stigmatized as lacking in these areas. However, with the increasing number of successful self-published authors and improvements in quality control, this perception is gradually changing.

Both traditional and self-publishing have their advantages and disadvantages, and the decision between the two depends on an author's goals, preferences, and circumstances. The changes in the publishing industry have brought more options and opportunities for authors, democratizing the process and ultimately empowering them to share their stories with the world.

CREATING A COMPELLING AUTHOR BIO:

CREATING a compelling author bio is an essential part of establishing your presence as a writer. It is an opportunity to introduce yourself to readers, showcase your skills, and pique their interest in your work. Here are steps to help you write a compelling author bio:

Keep it concise: Your author bio should be a summary of who you are as a writer. Aim for a length of around 100-200 words to maintain reader interest.

Highlight your expertise: Mention your writing background, credentials, or any significant achievements related to your writing career. This could include degrees in writing, awards or accolades you've received, or publications you've been featured in.

Showcase your unique voice and style: Use your author bio as an opportunity to convey your writing style and personality. This will give readers a taste of what to expect from your work.

Connect with your readers: Include personal information to create a connection with your audience. Share a hobby or an interest outside of writing that adds depth to your bio.

Mention your genre or niche: Mention the genre or niche in which you primarily write. This will help readers identify if your style aligns with their preferences.

Include a hook or interesting fact: Consider adding a hook or an intriguing element about yourself that will grab readers' attention. This could be a quirky fact or a unique experience that relates to your writing.

Use a professional tone: Though it's important to showcase your personality, maintain a professional tone in your author bio. This will reflect your commitment to your craft and help establish trust with readers.

Update regularly: As your writing career progresses, keep your author bio updated. Add any new publications, awards, or experiences relevant to your writing journey.

Get feedback: Share your author bio with trusted friends or writing colleagues and ask for their feedback. They may provide valuable insights on how to improve or clarify certain parts.

Proofread and edit: Ensure your author bio is error-free and well-written. It should engage, be concise, and free of grammatical mistakes.

Remember, your author bio is an introduction to who you are as a writer. It should capture readers' attention, build their curiosity, and make them want to explore your work further. By following these steps, you'll create a compelling author bio that showcases your skills and entices readers to dive into your writing.

DESIGNING AN EYE-CATCHING AUTHOR LOGO:

DESIGNING an eye-catching author logo is an important step in creating a strong personal brand. It should not only reflect your unique style and personality but also grab the attention of potential readers and enhance your overall professional image. Here are tips to help you design an eye-catching author logo:

Understand your brand: Before starting the design process, take some time to define your brand identity. Consider your writing genre, target audience, and the emotions or messages you want to convey through your books. This will give you valuable insights for creating a logo that aligns with your brand.

Choose the right colors: Colors play a significant role in logo design as they can evoke specific emotions and create a visual impact. Select colors that resonate with your brand and genre. For example, if you write mystery or thriller novels, darker and moody color schemes might be more appropriate. But if you write children's books, brighter and more playful colors could work better.

Typography matters: Selecting the right typography can make a huge difference in the impact of your logo. Consider fonts that are legible, reflect your writing style, and evoke the right emotions. Experiment with different font pairings but avoid using too many fonts as it can clutter your logo.

Incorporate relevant symbols or elements: Adding unique symbols or elements related to your genre or writing style can make your logo stand out. For example, if you write fantasy novels, consider incorporating a magical creature or symbol. These visual elements can create a strong association with your brand and help your logo communicate your author identity effectively.

Keep it simple and scalable: An eye-catching logo should be simple and easily recognizable, even when scaled down or viewed in different mediums. Avoid overcrowding your logo with too many details or intricate designs that may not translate well into smaller sizes. Remember, a clean and uncomplicated design will leave a lasting impression on your audience.

Experiment and iterate: Don't be afraid to experiment with different layouts, color combinations, and typography choices. Try out various ideas and gather feedback from others to refine your design. Iterate on your ideas until you feel confident that your logo effectively represents your brand and captures the attention of potential readers.

Hire a professional designer if needed: If you're not confident in your design skills or want to ensure a polished and professional result, consider working with a graphic designer who specializes in logo design. They can provide valuable insights and expertise to bring your vision to life.

Remember, an eye-catching author logo should reflect your brand and writing style. It should be memorable, visually appealing, and resonate with your target audience. By following these guidelines, you can create a logo that captures attention and helps establish your unique author identity.

∼

SECTION TWO KEY TAKEAWAYS AND ACTION ITEMS

1. **Importance of Author Branding**: Author branding is essential in setting yourself apart and connecting with readers.
2. **Digital Presence**: A strong online presence is important for an author's success.
3. **Networking**: Building relationships with other authors, bloggers, and influencers can significantly boost your brand and promotional efforts.
4. **Engaging Readers**: Actively engaging with your readers strengthens your brand and fosters loyalty.
5. **Content Marketing**: Using content marketing to showcase expertise and attract more readers.
6. **Using Professional Services**: Professional book marketing services can be beneficial for broader reach and effective promotion.
7. **Self-Promotion in Modern Publishing**: Self-promotion is essential due to changes in the publishing industry dynamics.

8. **Control and Authenticity**: Self-promotion gives authors control over their career and helps in showcasing their unique voice.
9. **Personal Branding and Goals**: Developing a personal brand and clear goals is key for effective self-promotion.
10. **Adapting to the Publishing Landscape**: Adapting to self-publishing and the decline of traditional bookstores requires authors to be proactive in marketing.
11. **Leveraging Influencers**: Connecting with book bloggers and influencers for promotion.
12. **Changes in Publishing Methods**: Understanding the shifts in traditional and self-publishing is crucial for strategy development.
13. **Author Bio and Logo**: Crafting a compelling author bio and designing an eye-catching logo are important for branding.

Action Items:

1. **Develop Your Author Brand**: Define your target audience and craft a unique brand message.
2. **Build an Online Presence**: Create a professional website and active social media profiles.
3. **Engage in Networking**: Join writing communities and collaborate with peers and influencers.
4. **Interact with Readers**: Respond to comments, host Q&A sessions, and use newsletters for regular updates.
5. **Implement Content Marketing**: Create and share relevant content to establish authority.
6. **Seek Professional Marketing Help**: Consider using book marketing services for wider reach.
7. **Set Clear Self-Promotion Goals**: Determine what you aim to achieve through self-promotion.
8. **Build a Personal Brand**: Craft a compelling personal brand that reflects your unique qualities.

9. **Engage with Influencers**: Connect with book bloggers and social media influencers.
10. **Stay Updated**: Keep abreast of the latest trends and changes in the publishing industry.
11. **Write a Compelling Author Bio**: Focus on your expertise, writing style, and a personal connection.
12. **Design an Author Logo**: Create a logo that reflects your brand identity and genre.
13. **Evaluate Publishing Options**: Understand the pros and cons of traditional vs. self-publishing for your work.
14. **Use Feedback and Endorsements**: Collect and showcase testimonials from satisfied readers or colleagues.
15. **Adapt and Learn**: Continuously update your skills and strategies in line with industry changes.

In our next Section...

In our next section, "Expanding Your Reach - Advanced Strategies for Author Brand Development," we'll explore sophisticated techniques to broaden your influence and strengthen your author brand. This section is designed to build on the basics of personal branding and online presence, introducing you to more dynamic strategies for enhancing your authorial identity.

Key areas we'll cover include mastering social media for deeper engagement with readers, innovative content marketing methods, and the power of collaboration and networking. Additionally, we'll dig into using multimedia for cross-promotion, advanced SEO (Search Engine Optimization) tactics for authors, and navigating the complexities of book deals and publishing contracts. Finally, the section will provide insights into tapping into new markets, leveraging author analytics for strategic decisions, and ensuring sustainable growth of your author brand. This comprehensive guide aims to equip you with essential skills and knowledge for lasting success and recognition in the competitive world of publishing.

SECTION THREE: EXPANDING YOUR REACH - ADVANCED STRATEGIES FOR AUTHOR BRAND DEVELOPMENT

UNDERSTANDING THE IMPORTANCE OF PERSONAL BRANDING IN THE AUTHOR'S JOURNEY:

IN THE HIGHLY COMPETITIVE publishing industry, authors must do more than just write a great book. They also need to develop a strong personal brand to stand out from the crowd and effectively market their work. Personal branding is the process of defining and promoting oneself as a unique and valuable author, and it plays an important role in an author's journey.

One of the main reasons personal branding is important for authors is that it helps to establish credibility and trust with readers. As potential readers browse through countless books online or in bookstores, they are more likely to be attracted to authors with a strong personal brand. A well-crafted brand communicates professionalism, knowledge, and a unique voice, making readers more inclined to give an author's work a chance.

Personal branding also lets authors differentiate themselves from other writers in the same genre. Instead of blending in with the many authors producing similar content, a strong personal brand helps authors to carve out their own niche and attract a specific audience. By identifying and showcasing their unique strengths, perspectives, and writing style, authors can cultivate a loyal following who will eagerly expect their next release.

Personal branding extends beyond the author's books—it encompasses their entire online presence. Today, authors are expected to have a strong online presence and engage with readers through platforms like social media, blogs, and websites. This is where personal branding shines, as it helps to create a consistent and cohesive image across all channels. Readers can easily identify an author's work, style, and values, fostering a deeper connection and making sure they remain engaged and loyal followers.

Additionally, personal branding opens up opportunities for authors beyond just book sales. With a strong personal brand, authors become recognized experts within their field, and this can lead to speaking engagements, collaborations, and other professional opportunities. By positioning themselves as authorities in their genre, authors can expand their reach and influence, further establishing their brand and gaining wider recognition.

Finally, personal branding also plays a critical role in building meaningful relationships with readers. By sharing personal stories, insights, and experiences, authors can create emotional connections with their audience. This engagement fosters trust, loyalty, and a sense of community, encouraging readers to become advocates for an author's work.

Personal branding is an essential part of an author's journey in today's competitive publishing industry. It helps authors to establish credibility, differentiate themselves from other writers, cultivate a loyal following, and build meaningful connections with readers. By investing time and effort into developing a strong personal brand, authors can pave the way for a successful career and leave a lasting impact in the literary world.

IDENTIFYING AND ASSESSING YOUR UNIQUE AUTHOR IDENTITY & VOICE ACROSS PLATFORMS

IDENTIFYING and assessing your unique author identity and voice across different platforms is important for building a successful and consistent brand. This process involves evaluating your niche, knowledge, and target audience to create a cohesive and authentic author persona. By establishing a strong author identity, you can effectively engage with your audience and prove yourself to be an expert in your field.

Here are steps to help you identify and assess your unique author identity and voice across platforms:

Define Your Niche: Start by clearly defining your niche – the specific area or topic you want to focus on as an author. This could be a genre of writing, subject matter, or a combination of both. Understanding your niche will help you position yourself and differentiate yourself from other authors.

Assess Your Expertise: Take time to evaluate your knowledge in relation to your chosen niche. Reflect on your qualifications, experiences, and knowledge that make you unique and credible in your field. Consider what sets you apart from others and what value you can bring to your audience.

Understand Your Target Audience: Identifying your target audience is essential for tailoring your author identity and voice to their needs and preferences. Determine who your ideal readers are – their demographics, interests, motivations, and challenges. This will help you create content that resonates with them and build a loyal following.

Craft Your Author Persona: Based on your niche, expertise, and target audience, develop a clear author persona. Think of this as the personality or image you want to project to your readers. Consider the tone, style, and approach you want to adopt in your writing – whether it's formal, humorous, empathetic, or authoritative. Your author persona should authentically represent you but also align with your target audience's expectations.

Be Consistent Across Platforms: Ensure consistency in your author identity and voice across all platforms you use, such as your website, blog, social media, and any other channels you engage with your audience. The same tone, language style, and core messaging should be maintained throughout your online presence. This consistency helps establish trust and recognition among your readership.

Seek Feedback and Adapt: Actively seek feedback from your audience and peers to continually refine your author identity and voice. Pay attention to what resonates with your readers and what they find valuable. Adapt and adjust your approach while staying true to your unique attributes.

Remember, building a strong author identity and voice takes time and effort. Consistently refining and reassessing your approach will help you grow and evolve as an author, making you more relatable and relevant to your audience.

BUILDING A VISUAL IDENTITY AND ONLINE PRESENCE:

When building a visual identity and online presence for your brand, there are several important elements to consider. These include creating a catchy tagline, writing a compelling bio, selecting impactful photos, and designing a well-designed website. Let's explore each element in more detail:

Tagline: Your tagline is a concise and memorable phrase that captures the essence of your brand. It should convey the unique value proposition of your business and resonate with your target audience. Think of famous taglines like Nike's "Just Do It" or Apple's "Think Different" – they are short, powerful, and instantly recognizable.

Bio: Your bio should communicate your brand's story, values, and mission. It should be written in a compelling and authentic way that connects with your target audience. Your bio should showcase what sets you apart from competitors and why people should choose your brand. Keep your bio concise and easy to read.

Photos: High-quality and visually appealing photos are important for creating a strong brand identity. These photos should reflect your brand's personality, values, and target audience. Ensure consistency in the style and tone of your photos to create a cohesive visual identity.

Whether it's product images, team photos, or lifestyle shots, make sure they align with your brand's messaging.

Website: Your website is the online hub of your brand. It should have a clean and user-friendly design that reflects your brand identity. Use consistent fonts, colors, and imagery across your site to maintain a cohesive look. Make sure your website is responsive and optimized for different devices. Include relevant information about your brand, products, services, and contact details.

Social media presence: Establishing a strong presence on relevant social media platforms is important for building an online presence. Optimize your profiles by using your brand logo, tagline, and bio. Regularly share engaging and relevant content that reflects your brand's voice. Interact with your audience, respond to comments, and use social media analytics to track and understand your audience's preferences.

Consistency is key: It's essential to maintain consistency across all brand elements. This includes using the same colors, fonts, and visual style. Consistency helps in creating brand recognition and trust. Make sure your brand identity is reflected consistently across all channels, from your website to social media to offline marketing materials.

By focusing on these important brand elements – tagline, bio, photos, website, and consistency – you can build a strong visual identity and online presence for your brand. Remember to keep your messaging authentic, engaging, and in line with your brand values to resonate with your target audience.

CASE STUDIES OF SUCCESSFUL AUTHOR BRANDS:

CASE STUDY 1: J.K. Rowling - The Harry Potter Series

J.K. Rowling's author brand has become synonymous with the Harry Potter series, which has sold over 500 million copies worldwide. What started as a fantasy novel for children quickly became a global phenomenon, leading to a successful author brand. Rowling's brand is built on several key factors:

Strong Connection with Readers: Rowling interacts with her fans regularly, often responding to their messages on social media platforms. She has created a sense of community and engagement around her brand, making her readers feel valued and connected.

Memorable Characters and World-Building: The Harry Potter series introduced iconic characters and a richly detailed magical world. Rowling's storytelling abilities resonated with readers of all ages, fostering a deep emotional connection. This immersive experience and the memorable characters have contributed to the longevity of her brand.

Philanthropy and Social Causes: Rowling's author brand is not limited to her books; she uses her platform and wealth to support various philanthropic initiatives. Her founding of Lumos, a charity focused on ending institutionalization of children, showcases her commitment to social causes, further enhancing her brand image.

Case Study 2: Stephen King - The Master of Horror

Stephen King is known as the master of horror, having written many best-selling novels that have captivated readers for decades. His author brand is built on several key elements:

Consistent Quality: King's brand is closely tied to the consistent quality of his work. Readers expect unique, engaging, and terrifying stories from him. King's dedication to delivering high-quality horror fiction has created a loyal fan base that eagerly awaits his new releases.

Prolific Output: King's prolific writing career, with over 60 novels and hundreds of short stories, has contributed significantly to his author brand. Fans trust they will always have something new to read from him, ensuring his continued success and relevance.

Multimedia Adaptations: Many of King's books have been adapted into successful films, television series, and even graphic novels. These adaptations have expanded his brand beyond the written word, attracting new fans and cementing his reputation as a horror icon.

Case Study 3: James Patterson - Master of Thrillers

James Patterson has established a successful author brand in the thriller genre, consistently delivering gripping and suspenseful novels. Patterson's brand is known for:

Collaborations: Patterson has successfully partnered with other authors to co-write several of his books. This collaboration lets him release multiple books each year, connecting with different readership demographics while maintaining a consistent brand presence.

Series Structure: Patterson's brand is built on several long-running series with recurring characters. This formula has created a sense of familiarity for readers, who eagerly expect new installments. The series structure also helps with cross-promotion and keeps readers engaged with the author's brand.

Engagement with Readers: Patterson actively engages with his readers through social media, book tours, and fan events. He values reader feedback and often incorporates it into his writing process, making sure his books resonate with his audience.

These case studies highlight the importance of various elements in establishing successful author brands, such as engaging with readers, creating memorable characters and worlds, supporting social causes, consistent quality, prolific output, multimedia adaptations, collaborations, series structure, and engagement with readers.

SECTION THREE KEY TAKEAWAYS AND ACTION ITEMS

Key Takeaways:

1. **The Power of Personal Branding**: Personal branding is crucial for authors to establish credibility, stand out from others, and effectively market their work.
2. **Differentiation in Genre**: A strong personal brand helps authors carve out a unique niche, attracting a specific audience with distinct preferences and interests.
3. **Beyond Books**: Personal branding extends to an author's online presence, enhancing engagement across platforms like social media, blogs, and websites.
4. **Opportunities Beyond Sales**: A well-established personal brand can open doors to speaking engagements, collaborations, and other professional opportunities.
5. **Building Relationships with Readers**: Personal branding lets authors connect emotionally with readers, fostering trust, loyalty, and a sense of community.

Action Items:

1. **Define Your Niche and Expertise**: Clearly understand and outline the specific area or topic you want to focus on as an author.
2. **Craft Your Author Persona**: Develop a consistent tone, style, and approach in your writing that aligns with your audience's expectations.
3. **Establish Consistency Across Platforms**: Ensure a uniform author identity and voice on your website, social media, and other channels.
4. **Engage and Adapt**: Regularly seek feedback from your audience and refine your approach, maintaining authenticity and relevance.
5. **Focus on Key Brand Elements**: Create a compelling tagline, write a strong bio, choose impactful photos, and design an engaging website.
6. **Learn from Successful Author Brands**: Analyze case studies of successful authors like J.K. Rowling, Stephen King, and James Patterson to understand their strategies in building a strong brand.
7. **Leverage Your Unique Identity**: Use your unique voice and knowledge to engage with your audience and prove yourself to be an authority in your field.

In our next Section...

In our next section, we'll dig into the art of effective book promotion and sales strategies in the digital age. We will explore cutting-edge techniques for digital marketing, including social media campaigns, email marketing, and leveraging online communities to increase book visibility and sales. This segment will offer practical advice on how to harness the power of digital platforms to connect with readers and promote your book successfully. We'll also discuss the importance of an engaging online author persona, and how to create content that resonates with your audience, driving both engagement and book sales.

Additionally, we will cover the significance of analytics in measuring the success of your promotional efforts. By understanding key metrics such as website traffic, social media engagement, and conversion rates, authors can gain insights into the effectiveness of their marketing strategies and make data-driven decisions. This section aims to equip authors with the knowledge and tools needed to navigate the complex landscape of digital marketing, ensuring their book reaches its full potential in the competitive world of publishing.

SECTION FOUR: YOUR BOOK, YOUR BUSINESS

TREATING YOUR BOOK AS A PRODUCT:

WHEN TREATING your book as a product, it means considering various marketing strategies and applying business principles to maximize its potential success. Below are steps and tips on how to do that:

Define your target audience: Clearly identify who your book is intended for. Consider demographics, interests, preferences, and buying habits of potential readers. This will help you shape your marketing efforts more effectively.

Research the competition: Study similar books in your genre to understand market trends, pricing, and positioning. Identify what sets your book apart and emphasize those unique selling points.

Develop a compelling brand: Create an attractive and memorable brand for your book. Design an eye-catching cover that reflects the content and appeals to your target audience. Develop consistent branding elements like author logos, fonts, and color schemes that align with your book's genre and theme.

Build a strong online presence: Establish an author website or a dedicated website for your book. Optimize it for search engines and make it easy for potential readers to find and buy your book. Consider creating a blog or regularly posting engaging content related to your book's topic to attract and engage readers.

Leverage social media: Utilize social media platforms to build an audience and interact with readers. Create profiles on platforms that your target audience frequents and share enticing content related to your book. Engage with your followers by responding to comments, hosting Q&A sessions, and running contests or giveaways.

Generate buzz: Build anticipation for your book through pre-launch marketing. Offer sneak peeks, behind-the-scenes content, or release a sample chapter to generate excitement among potential readers. Get endorsements or testimonials from influencers in your genre to add credibility and attract attention.

Use book reviews: Positive reviews play an important role in convincing potential readers to buy your book. Encourage readers to leave reviews by offering incentives such as early access to future books or exclusive content. Use reputable book review websites and platforms to extend your reach.

Pricing and promotion: Analyze pricing strategies in your genre and set a competitive yet profitable price for your book. Consider running promotional discounts or limited-time offers to incentivize readers to buy. Collaborate with other authors or relevant businesses for joint promotions or cross-promotions.

Communicate with readers: Engage with your readers through various channels like email newsletters, social media, or online forums. Offer exclusive content, updates, and discounts to keep readers interested and connected with your brand.

Analyze results and adapt: Track and analyze marketing efforts to understand what works and what doesn't. Monitor sales, website traffic, social media engagement, and reader feedback. Make data-driven decisions to refine your marketing strategies and continuously improve.

Treating your book as a product means applying marketing principles to ensure its visibility, appeal, and success. By implementing these strategies, you can increase your book's chances of reaching your target audience and achieving your desired outcomes.

UNDERSTANDING YOUR TARGET AUDIENCE AND MARKET:

UNDERSTANDING your target audience and market is a crucial part of running a successful business. This knowledge lets you tailor your products, services, and marketing strategies to meet the needs and preferences of your customers. By understanding your target audience and market, you increase your chances of capturing a larger share of the market, achieving higher customer satisfaction, and ultimately driving profitability.

To understand your target audience and market, consider these steps:

Conduct market research: Start by conducting comprehensive market research to gain insights into the demographics, psychographics, and behaviors of your target audience. Identify features such as age, gender, income level, geographic location, lifestyle, interests, and buying habits common among your ideal customers. This will help you create buyer personas and segment your market effectively.

Analyze competition: Study your competitors to determine their target audience and market positioning. Identify what sets you apart from your competitors and how you can capitalize on the gaps or weaknesses in their offerings to attract your target audience effectively.

Gather customer feedback: Actively seek feedback from your existing customers to understand their needs, preferences, and pain points. This feedback can be gathered through surveys, focus groups, social media interactions, or direct communication. Use this information to refine your products or services and improve customer satisfaction.

Track industry trends: Stay up to date with industry trends, technological advancements, and cultural shifts that may affect your target audience and market. This knowledge will let you adapt your strategies to meet changing customer demands proactively.

Use data analytics: Leverage data analytics tools to collect and analyze data related to customer behavior, engagement, buying patterns, and other relevant metrics. By integrating data analytics into your decision-making processes, you can make data-driven decisions, identify patterns, and forecast market trends more accurately.

Create buyer personas: Develop detailed buyer personas that represent your target audience. A buyer persona is a fictional representation of your ideal customer, including their demographics, goals, motivations, and challenges. These personas help you empathize with your customers, understand their needs, and create targeted marketing campaigns that resonate with them.

Test and iterate: Continuously test and iterate your products, services, and marketing strategies based on customer feedback and market trends. By tracking the success of your initiatives and adjusting based on data and insights, you can improve your offerings and position yourself to better fulfill the needs of your target audience.

Remember that understanding your target audience and market is an ongoing process. It requires a commitment to gathering and analyzing data, staying informed about industry trends, and adjusting your strategies. By maintaining a deep understanding of your target audience and market, you will be well-equipped to adapt to changing circumstances and maintain a competitive edge in your industry.

SECTION FOUR KEY TAKEAWAYS AND ACTION ITEMS

KEY TAKEAWAYS:

1. **Defining the Target Audience:** Identify the demographics, interests, and buying habits of your book's potential readers to shape effective marketing efforts.
2. **Researching the Competition:** Understand market trends and what sets your book apart.
3. **Brand Development:** Create a compelling brand with an eye-catching cover and consistent branding elements.
4. **Online Presence:** Establish and optimize an author website for search engines and reader engagement.
5. **Social Media Utilization:** Engage with readers on platforms where your audience is active, using engaging content related to your book.
6. **Generating Buzz:** Use pre-launch marketing to build anticipation and leverage endorsements to attract attention.
7. **Leveraging Book Reviews:** Encourage readers to leave reviews and use book review platforms to extend reach.
8. **Effective Pricing and Promotions:** Set a competitive price and run promotional discounts or offers.

9. **Reader Communication:** Maintain engagement through channels like newsletters and social media.
10. **Adapting to Feedback:** Analyze marketing results and adapt strategies based on data.

Action Items:

1. **Identify Your Audience:** Conduct research to define your book's target market.
2. **Competitive Analysis:** Study similar books to understand your unique position.
3. **Brand Creation:** Design a compelling cover and develop a consistent branding strategy.
4. **Website Development:** Build a website and ensure its SEO-friendly and engaging.
5. **Social Media Strategy:** Create and maintain profiles on key platforms, sharing relevant content regularly.
6. **Pre-Launch Marketing:** Implement a marketing plan before your book's release.
7. **Seek Reviews:** Encourage and incentivize readers to leave reviews on various platforms.
8. **Pricing Strategy:** Determine competitive pricing and plan promotional activities.
9. **Engage with Readers:** Regularly communicate with your audience through various mediums.
10. **Continuous Improvement:** Monitor feedback and sales data to refine and improve your marketing strategies.

In our next Section...

In our next section, we'll dig into the art of mastering social media and email marketing for authors. Social media platforms and email newsletters are powerful tools for authors to connect with their audience, promote their work, and build a loyal readership. We'll explore effective strategies for engaging with followers on platforms like Twitter, Facebook, Instagram, and Goodreads. This will include tips on creating compelling content, scheduling posts, and interacting with fans to build a vibrant community around your writing.

Additionally, we'll discuss the importance of email marketing in an author's toolkit. This segment will guide you through building and maintaining an email list, crafting engaging newsletters, and using email campaigns to announce new releases, share exclusive content, and keep your readers informed and excited about your work. We'll provide practical advice on how to balance promotional content with valuable insights and stories, ensuring your emails are a welcome addition to your subscribers' inboxes.

～

SECTION FIVE: CREATING COMPELLING AUTHOR BIOS AND PROFILES

CRAFTING A COMPELLING AUTHOR WEBSITE:

AN AUTHOR WEBSITE is an essential platform for showcasing your work, connecting with readers, and building a solid online presence. It serves as a hub for your brand, letting you share your writing, provide updates on your latest projects, and engage with your audience. Here are key steps to help you create a compelling author website:

Define your brand: Before you start building your website, take some time to define your brand. Consider your writing style, genre, and unique selling points. Think about how you want to be perceived by readers and what makes you stand out as an author. This will help you create a cohesive and consistent website design and content.

Choose a user-friendly platform: There are various website-building platforms available, such as WordPress, Squarespace, or Wix. Research and choose one that aligns with your needs, technical skills, and budget. Look for a platform that offers customizable templates, easy navigation, and responsive design for mobile devices.

Design your website: Your website design should reflect your brand and entice visitors to explore further. Use colors, fonts, and imagery that align with your writing style. Choose a clean and intuitive layout that lets readers easily find information about your books, upcoming events, and contact details. Include an author bio and high-quality author photos to create a personal connection with readers.

Showcase your work: Create dedicated pages for each of your books, including cover images, book descriptions, and links to buy or download. Consider adding sample chapters or excerpts to give readers a taste of your writing. Make sure your book pages are visually appealing and easy to navigate.

Provide a blog or news section: A blog or news section on your website is a great way to engage with your audience and provide updates on your writing journey. Share behind-the-scenes insights, writing tips, and news about your upcoming projects. Regularly update your blog to keep readers coming back for new content.

Include an events calendar: If you participate in book signings, speaking engagements, or other literary events, create an events calendar to inform readers about your upcoming appearances. Include details such as dates, locations, and links for registration. This will help connect with readers who want to meet you in person.

Offer a newsletter sign-up: Building an email list is important for staying in touch with your readers. Include an opt-in form on your website that lets visitors subscribe to your newsletter. Offer incentives such as exclusive content, giveaways, or discounts on your books to encourage sign-ups.

Engage with social media: Integrate your social media profiles with your website to make it easy for visitors to follow you on platforms like Facebook, Instagram, Twitter, or Goodreads. Display social media icons prominently and link them to your respective profiles. This will expand your online presence and let readers connect with you on multiple platforms.

Optimize for search engines: Consider SEO while creating your website. Use relevant keywords in your headings, page titles, and content to improve your website's visibility in search engine results. Regularly update your website with fresh and engaging content to attract search engine traffic.

Test and refine: Once your website is ready, test it thoroughly on different devices and browsers to ensure a seamless user experience. Ask for feedback from friends, fellow authors, or potential readers to identify any areas for improvement. Regularly review your website's analytics to gather insights on visitor behavior and make necessary refinements to enhance your website's effectiveness.

Remember, your author website is a representation of your brand and a powerful tool for engaging with readers. Invest time and effort into creating a compelling website that showcases your writing and connects with your target audience.

CRAFTING A COMPELLING AUTHOR BIO:

As an author, one of the most important tools at your disposal is your author biography, also known as an author bio. This summary of who you are and what you have done can have a significant impact on how readers view and connect with your work. A compelling author bio can help you establish your credibility, build trust with your audience, and even increase your book sales. Here are tips to help you craft a compelling author bio:

Introduce yourself: Start your bio by introducing yourself and briefly summarizing your background. Mention your name and any relevant qualifications or experience that make you an authority in your field. Keep it concise and focused on the most impressive or relevant information.

Highlight your achievements: This is where you can showcase your accomplishments as an author. Include any awards you have won, books you have published, or notable accolades you have received. Focus on the highlights to grab the attention of your readers and leave a lasting impression.

Connect with your audience: Your author bio should resonate with your target audience. Consider including personal anecdotes or experiences that will help readers relate to you. If you write in a specific genre or niche, let readers know why you are passionate about that topic and what sets your work apart from others.

Include your credentials and expertise: If you have any relevant qualifications or expertise in your field, mention them in your author bio. This can help establish your credibility and position you as an authority in your niche. Whether you have a degree in a related field or have spent years researching and writing on a particular subject, let readers know why they should trust your knowledge and expertise.

Consider your tone and voice: Your author bio should reflect your writing style and the tone of your work. If you write humorous novels, consider injecting some wit and humor into your bio. If you write serious nonfiction, adopt a more professional and authoritative tone. The goal is to give readers a taste of what to expect from your writing style.

Keep it updated: As you achieve new milestones or publish new works, remember to update your author bio regularly. Readers appreciate staying up to date with an author's progress, and an outdated bio can make you seem stagnant or unreliable.

Engage with your readers: Finally, remember that your author bio is an opportunity to engage with your readers. Consider including a call to action, such as inviting readers to connect with you on social media or sign up for your newsletter. This not only encourages reader engagement but also helps you grow your author platform.

Crafting a compelling author bio is an essential part of your overall author brand. It should reflect your expertise, achievements, and writing style while also connecting with your target audience. Refine and update your author bio to ensure it effectively represents who you are as an author and sparks interest in your work.

~

SECTION FIVE KEY TAKEAWAYS AND ACTION ITEMS

KEY TAKEAWAYS:

1. **Author Website as Brand Hub:** Your author website is a central platform for showcasing work, engaging with readers, and establishing an online presence.
2. **Brand Definition:** Defining your brand is important for creating a cohesive and consistent website.
3. **User-Friendly Platform Selection:** Choose a website-building platform that suits your technical skills and budget.
4. **Design and Content:** Ensure the website design is clean, intuitive, and reflective of your writing style. Include detailed pages for each book and a personal author bio.
5. **Regular Updates and Engagement:** Keep your website updated with fresh content, blog posts, and upcoming events to engage readers.
6. **Newsletter and Social Media Integration:** Offer newsletter sign-ups and integrate social media for broader engagement and reach.
7. **SEO Importance:** Implement SEO strategies to enhance visibility in search engine results.

8. **Feedback and Refinement:** Regularly refine your website based on feedback and analytics.
9. **Crafting a Compelling Author Bio:** A well-crafted bio helps establish credibility and connects with the audience.
10. **Personal Connection and Achievement Highlighting:** Share personal anecdotes and highlight achievements to resonate with readers.

Action Items:

1. **Brand Development:** Define your brand, focusing on your writing style, genre, and unique aspects.
2. **Platform Research and Selection:** Research and choose a suitable website-building platform.
3. **Website Design and Content Creation:** Design the website to reflect your author brand and regularly update with engaging content.
4. **Blog and News Section Maintenance:** Maintain an active blog or news section for ongoing reader engagement.
5. **Events Calendar Management:** Keep an up-to-date events calendar for reader interaction opportunities.
6. **Newsletter Strategy:** Develop a strategy to grow your email list through newsletter sign-ups.
7. **Social Media Activity:** Regularly update and engage with your audience on social media platforms.
8. **SEO Optimization:** Implement basic SEO practices for your website.
9. **Website Testing and Refinement:** Continuously test and refine your website based on user feedback and analytics.
10. **Author Bio Updation:** Regularly update your author bio to reflect recent achievements and milestones.

In our next Section…

In our next section, we'll dig into the advanced techniques of digital marketing for authors. We'll explore how to effectively use various digital marketing tools and platforms to further amplify your online presence and book sales. This will include in-depth discussions on targeted advertising, email marketing campaigns, and leveraging analytics for strategic planning. We'll also touch on the importance of SEO for authors, providing practical tips on how to optimize your website and content to rank higher in search engine results, thus increasing visibility and attracting a wider audience.

Additionally, we'll focus on the power of networking and collaboration in the digital space. This will involve strategies for forming partnerships with fellow authors, bloggers, and influencers in your genre, as well as tips for effective cross-promotion and guest appearances on various digital platforms. The goal is to provide a comprehensive guide to expanding your digital footprint and harnessing the full potential of online marketing tools to create a strong, sustainable brand as an author.

SECTION SIX: MASTERING SOCIAL MEDIA FOR AUTHORS

ENGAGING WITH READERS ON SOCIAL MEDIA OVERVIEW:

ENGAGING with readers on social media is a crucial part of building an active and dedicated online community. It involves creating meaningful interactions, responding to comments and messages, and fostering a sense of belonging among your audience.

Here is an overview of how to effectively engage with readers on social media:

Create valuable content: Share high-quality and relevant content that resonates with your target audience. Whether it's blog posts, articles, videos, or graphics, make sure your content adds value and sparks interest.

Be consistent: Establish a consistent posting schedule to keep your readers engaged. Regular updates will keep your audience connected and build anticipation for your next post.

Respond to comments: Encourage readers to leave comments and respond to them promptly. Engaging with comments shows your audience that you value their opinions and are interested in their thoughts.

Ask questions: Pose questions in your posts to encourage readers to engage with your content. Asking for opinions or advice not only increases the likelihood of comments but also fosters a sense of community among your readers.

Use polls and surveys: Conducting polls and surveys on social media platforms is an excellent way to actively involve your audience. It lets you gather feedback, gain insights, and spark discussions.

Encourage user-generated content: Encourage readers to create and share their content related to your brand or industry. This not only adds variety to your social media feed but also builds a connection with your audience.

Show appreciation: Acknowledge and appreciate your readers' contributions and support. Regularly highlight user-generated content, give shout-outs, or run contests to show your gratitude for their engagement.

Humanize your brand: Show the personal side of your brand by sharing behind-the-scenes content, team stories, or even personal anecdotes. This humanizes your brand and makes it more relatable and approachable to readers.

Track social media mentions and tags: Keep an eye on social media mentions and tags related to your brand. Responding to these mentions shows you are attentive and value feedback even when it is not directly communicated to you.

Share exclusive content: Reward your loyal readers with exclusive content or offers. This could be sneak peeks, discounts, or early access to new releases. Exclusive content makes readers feel special and appreciated.

Remember, engaging with readers on social media should be a two-way conversation. Listen to your audience, understand their needs, and respond empathetically. By building a genuine connection with your readers, you can create a loyal and active community that supports and promotes your brand.

~

CHOOSING AND LEVERAGING THE RIGHT PLATFORMS FOR BRAND BUILDING:

CHOOSING AND USING the right platforms effectively is key for businesses to build their brand, especially with how digital everything is now. With so many platforms available, it's overwhelming to decide which ones are the best fit for your brand. Here are steps to help you make informed decisions and effectively build your brand on the right platforms.

Define your brand goals: Before selecting platforms, it's essential to identify your brand goals. Are you looking to increase brand awareness, engage with your target audience, drive sales, or all of the above? Clearly understanding your goals will guide you in choosing the proper platforms that align with those goals.

Research your target audience: Who is your target audience? Understanding their demographics, interests, and online behavior is important in determining which platforms they are most active on. Conduct market research, analyze consumer data, and use social listening tools to gain insights into where your target audience spends their time online.

Choose the right social media platforms: Different platforms cater to different demographics and content types. Consider these platforms and their strengths:

Facebook: With its wide user base, Facebook is suitable for brands targeting a broad audience. It offers various advertising options and provides opportunities for community building through groups and pages.

Instagram: Great for visually appealing content, Instagram is popular among younger audiences. If your brand relies on visual elements like fashion, art, or food, this platform is ideal for showcasing your products or services.

X [formerly known as Twitter]: Ideal for timely updates and discussions, Twitter is known for its fast-paced nature. If your brand's content is focused on news, current events, or thought leadership, Twitter can be an effective platform to engage with your audience.

LinkedIn: Primarily a professional networking platform, LinkedIn is perfect for brand building in B2B industries. It lets you establish thought leadership, share industry insights, and connect with potential business partners or clients.

YouTube: Video content is becoming increasingly popular. If your brand can provide educational, entertaining, or informative videos, building a presence on YouTube can help you reach a wider audience.

Consider other digital platforms: Social media isn't the only platform for brand building. Depending on your industry and target audience, other platforms may be relevant, such as:

Blogs: Maintaining a blog on your website can help establish your brand as an authority in your industry. It lets you provide in-depth content, share your knowledge, and engage with your audience through comment sections.

Podcasts: Podcasts are growing in popularity and are an effective way to showcase your brand's personality and expertise. Create engaging audio content that resonates with your target audience.

Influencer marketing: Collaborating with influencers in your industry can help extend your reach and build brand trust. Identify influencers who align with your brand values and have an engaged following to leverage their influence.

Monitor and analyze performance: Once you've chosen the platforms, monitor their performance using analytics tools. Measure key metrics like engagement rates, conversions, and reach to assess which platforms are most effective in achieving your brand goals. Adapt your strategy to optimize performance.

Choosing and leveraging the right platforms for brand building requires a strategic approach. Define your goals, research your target audience, choose the proper platforms, and regularly analyze performance to ensure your brand is building a strong online presence.

CONTENT STRATEGIES AND COMMUNITY ENGAGEMENT:

CONTENT STRATEGIES and community engagement go hand in hand in building a strong and active online community. A well-thought-out content strategy is essential for attracting and retaining community members, while community engagement helps to foster a sense of belonging and participation among community members. Here are key points to consider when developing content strategies and community engagement initiatives:

Define your target audience: Before developing content or engaging with your community, it is important to clearly understand who your target audience is. What are their interests, demographics, and motivations? This knowledge will help you tailor your content and engagement efforts to meet their needs and preferences.

Set clear goals: Clearly define what you aim to achieve with your content strategy and community engagement initiatives. Is it to increase website traffic, generate leads, or foster customer loyalty? Having measurable goals will help you assess the effectiveness of your efforts and make necessary changes.

Develop a content calendar: Create a content calendar to plan and organize your content production. This ensures consistent and regular content updates to keep your community engaged. The calendar should include a mix of different content types, such as blog posts, videos, infographics, and social media posts, to cater to different preferences.

Provide valuable and relevant content: Your community members are more likely to engage if they find your content valuable and relevant to their interests. Conduct thorough research to identify topics and themes that resonate with your target audience. Incorporate educational, entertaining, and informative content to keep your community engaged and coming back for more.

Encourage user-generated content: User-generated content is a powerful way to engage your community and build a sense of belonging. Encourage your community members to contribute their own content, such as testimonials, reviews, photos, or videos. This not only fosters engagement but also helps to establish trust and authenticity among your community members.

Foster two-way communication: Engagement is a two-way street. Actively listen to your community members' feedback, comments, and suggestions, and respond promptly. This shows you value their opinions and are committed to building a meaningful relationship with them. Create opportunities for dialogue, such as Q&A sessions, polls, or online forums, to foster open communication.

Organize contests or challenges: Organizing contests or challenges can be an effective way to engage your community members and incentivize participation. Offer prizes or rewards to encourage community members to actively engage with your content or perform certain actions. This generates excitement, encourages sharing, and boosts overall engagement.

Collaborate with influencers: Engaging with influencers in your industry can help amplify your content and reach a wider audience. Identify influencers who resonate with your brand and have a strong following among your target audience. Collaborate with them to create content or host community events, which can significantly boost engagement and community reach.

Analyze and adapt: Continuously track and analyze the effectiveness of your content strategies and community engagement initiatives. Use analytics tools to track key metrics, such as website traffic, social media engagement, and community growth. Use these insights to adapt your strategies and optimize future efforts.

Developing a strong content strategy and fostering community engagement are important for building a strong online community. By understanding your audience, providing valuable content, encouraging user-generated content, fostering two-way communication, and continuously analyzing and adapting, you can create an active and engaged community that supports your brand's goals.

SECTION SIX KEY TAKEAWAYS AND ACTION ITEMS

KEY TAKEAWAYS:

1. **Value-Driven Content Creation:** Focus on sharing high-quality, relevant content that resonates with your target audience. Ensure it adds value and sparks interest.
2. **Consistency is Key:** Maintain a regular posting schedule to keep your audience engaged and looking forward to your updates.
3. **Active Engagement:** Promptly respond to comments and messages, showing readers that their opinions matter.
4. **Encourage Interaction:** Use questions, polls, and surveys to involve your audience and stimulate discussion.
5. **User-Generated Content:** Motivate readers to share their own content related to your brand, enhancing variety and connection.
6. **Personal Touch:** Humanize your brand by sharing personal stories or behind-the-scenes content.
7. **Platform-Specific Strategies:** Tailor your approach for different platforms like Facebook, Instagram, Twitter, LinkedIn, YouTube, blogs, and podcasts.

8. **Track and Analyze:** Regularly track performance using analytics tools and adapt your strategy for ideal results.
9. **Foster a Community:** Implement strategies to build a sense of belonging among your audience, through contests, shout-outs, and regular interaction.
10. **Adaptation and Improvement:** Continuously refine your approach based on feedback and changing market trends.

Action Items:

1. **Craft and Share Engaging Content:** Develop a content calendar and consistently post material that resonates with your audience.
2. **Regularly Engage with Comments and Queries:** Make it a priority to interact with your audience on social media platforms.
3. **Implement Interactive Features:** Use polls, surveys, and questions to foster active audience participation.
4. **Encourage and Showcase User Contributions:** Highlight and appreciate content created by your readers.
5. **Add a Personal Dimension to Your Brand:** Share personal anecdotes and behind-the-scenes glimpses to connect with your audience.
6. **Select and Focus on Suitable Platforms:** Determine which platforms are most effective for your brand and concentrate your efforts there.
7. **Use Analytics Tools:** Monitor social media and website analytics to understand audience behavior and preferences.
8. **Host Community-Building Events:** Organize online events, contests, and challenges to keep your community engaged.
9. **Seek and Act on Feedback:** Regularly ask for and incorporate feedback from your audience to improve your strategies.
10. **Stay Informed and Adaptive:** Keep up with social media trends and adapt your strategies to stay relevant and effective.

. . .

In our next Section…

In our next section, we'll dig into "Maximizing Online Visibility and Reader Engagement." This critical part of an author's journey focuses on harnessing digital platforms to enhance visibility and connect more deeply with readers. We'll explore advanced techniques for optimizing your online presence, including leveraging SEO strategies to increase the reach of your website and blog content. Additionally, we'll discuss innovative ways to use social media analytics to understand your audience better and tailor your content to their preferences.

SECTION SEVEN: MAXIMIZING ONLINE VISIBILITY AND READER ENGAGEMENT

WRITING ENGAGING BLOG POSTS TO AMPLIFY YOUR VOICE:

ARE you looking to make an impact with your writing? Do you want to amplify your voice and share your thoughts with the world? A powerful way to meet these goals is by writing engaging blog posts. Blogging lets you express your ideas, connect with like-minded individuals, and build a loyal readership. In this chapter, we will explore strategies to help you write captivating blog posts that will resonate with your audience.

Know Your Target Audience: Understanding your readership is important to writing engaging blog posts. Research your target audience's interests, preferences, and needs. This will help you tailor your content specifically to them. Are your readers students, professionals, parents, or hobbyists? What are their common struggles, aspirations, and goals? By answering these questions, you can create content that speaks directly to your audience.

Craft Attention-Grabbing Headlines: In the fast-paced online world, catchy headlines are essential to capture your reader's attention. Aim to create headlines that are informative, thought-provoking, and promise value. Using numbers, asking questions, or using intriguing words can be effective strategies to pique your audience's curiosity.

However, avoid clickbait tactics and ensure your content delivers on its promise.

Start with a Hook: A compelling introduction is key to engaging your readers from the start. Begin your blog post with a hook that captures their interest. It could be an intriguing story, a shocking fact, or a thought-provoking quote. The goal is to make your audience want to read more and not just skim through your content.

Tell Personal Stories: People love to connect with real experiences and emotions. Sharing personal stories, anecdotes, or insights can help readers relate to your content on a deeper level. Whether it's a struggle you've overcome, a lesson learned, or a success achieved, weaving personal stories into your blog posts will make them more relatable and memorable.

Use Visuals: Visuals can significantly enhance the engagement of your blog posts. Incorporate relevant images, infographics, or videos to break up text and provide visual appeal. Visual content also makes your post more shareable on social media platforms.

Write in an Informal Tone: Blogging lets you connect with your readers in a conversational way. Write in a friendly and relatable tone, as if you are having a casual conversation with a friend. Avoid using overly technical jargon or complex language that might alienate your audience. Keep your sentences concise and use bullet points or subheadings to break up your content for easy readability.

Encourage Interaction and Discussion: Engaging blog posts should stimulate conversation and interaction with your readers. Encourage comments, ask questions, or provoke thoughts at the end of your post. Prompting readers to share their opinions or experiences will foster a sense of community and connection, as well as invite them to become actively involved in the conversation.

Proofread and Edit: Neglecting grammar mistakes, typos, or poor formatting can undermine your credibility and distract your readers. Proofread your blog posts carefully before publishing them. Consider using editing tools and getting feedback from others to ensure your posts are polished and error-free.

Promote Your Blog: Writing engaging posts is only part of the equation; promoting your blog is equally important. Share your posts on social media platforms, participate in relevant online communities, and engage with other bloggers in your niche. By promoting your blog, you will expand your reach and attract more readers to your content.

Writing engaging blog posts requires knowing your audience, captivating them with attention-grabbing headlines and hooks, incorporating personal stories, using visuals, adopting a conversational tone, encouraging interaction, and promoting your content. By following these strategies, you will amplify your voice, connect with your readers, and make a lasting impact with your blog. So, start writing and let your words resonate with the world!

CRAFTING ENGAGING CONTENT FOR AUTHOR BRANDING:

In TODAY's competitive publishing industry, authors must establish a strong brand to stand out and attract readers. One of the most effective ways to build your author brand is by creating engaging content that resonates with your target audience. Here are tips for crafting captivating content that will help you develop and enhance your author brand:

Know your target audience: Understand who your ideal readers are and what they are interested in. Conduct market research to gather insights about their preferences, demographics, and reading habits. This information will guide you in creating content that speaks directly to your audience, making it more engaging and relatable.

Develop a content strategy: Create a content plan that aligns with your author's brand and goals. Determine the themes, topics, and formats you will focus on. This could include blog posts, videos, social media updates, and more. Strategize how your content will resonate with your audience and reinforce your brand message.

Be authentic and genuine: Readers appreciate authenticity, so strive to be genuine in all your content. Share personal stories, experiences, and insights that highlight who you are as an author. Your unique voice and perspective will set you apart and make your brand more memorable.

Provide value to your audience: People are more likely to engage with content that provides value to them. Offer helpful tips, advice, or information relevant to your audience's interests. This could include writing advice, book recommendations, behind-the-scenes looks at your writing process, or exclusive sneak peeks at upcoming projects.

Encourage audience interaction: Foster a sense of community by encouraging your audience to interact with your content. Include calls to action that invite readers to leave comments, ask questions, or participate in discussions. Engage with your audience by responding to their comments and feedback, showing you value their input.

Maintain consistency: Consistency is key in developing your author brand. Regularly produce new content and stick to a consistent posting schedule. This helps to build anticipation and keeps your audience engaged. Additionally, make sure your content aligns with your established brand message and values.

Use multimedia: Don't limit yourself to just one type of content. Mix things up by incorporating various types of multimedia. For example, share photographs, videos, and infographics that complement your written content. This will make your brand more dynamic and visually appealing.

Use social media platforms: Social media is a powerful tool for author branding. Identify the social media platforms that your target audience is most active on and leverage them to share your content. Use hashtags and engage with other authors and readers in the community to expand your reach and gain exposure.

Collaborate with others: Partnering with other authors or industry professionals can help expand your audience and enhance your brand. Collaborate on guest blog posts, interviews, or podcasts to share your knowledge and gain visibility with a different audience.

Analyze and adapt: Monitor the performance of your content using analytics tools and metrics. Pay attention to which types of content receive the most engagement and adjust your content strategy. Stay flexible and open to experimenting with different approaches to continuously improve your content and grow your author brand.

By crafting engaging content that resonates with your target audience, you can establish and enhance your author brand, ultimately attracting more readers and gaining recognition in the publishing industry.

CONTENT IDEAS AND SEO BASICS FOR AUTHORS:

BOOK REVIEWS: Write detailed and fair reviews of books that are within your genre or that have influenced your writing.

Author Interviews: Interview authors whose work you admire or who have had success in your genre. Ask them about their writing process, inspirations, and any advice they have for aspiring authors.

Writing Tips and Advice: Share your own tips and advice on various parts of writing, such as character development, plot structure, or dialogue. These can be as blog posts, videos, or social media posts.

Behind-the-Scenes: Give your readers a glimpse into your writing process by sharing behind-the-scenes content. This could include photos of your writing space, updates on your current work in progress, or insights into your research process.

Writing Prompts: Provide writing prompts to spark creativity in your readers. You can share these as blog posts, social media posts, or even create a dedicated section on your website for writing prompts.

Book Recommendations: Share your favorite books within your genre or books that have inspired your writing. This could be as reviews, lists, or even book clubs where you can discuss and recommend books to your readers.

Author Events and Readings: If you have any upcoming author events, book signings, or readings, promote them and explain your website and social media platforms.

SEO BASICS FOR AUTHORS:

KEYWORD RESEARCH: Conduct keyword research to identify popular search terms related to your book or writing niche. Use these keywords strategically in your website content, blog posts, and social media updates to improve discoverability.

Title and Meta Descriptions: Craft compelling and keyword-rich titles and meta descriptions for your web pages and blog posts. These elements appear in search engine results, so make sure they accurately represent your content and entice readers to click.

Quality Content: Focus on creating high-quality, engaging, and informative content that appeals to your target audience. This will not only resonate with readers but also improve your chances of ranking higher in search engine results.

Internal and External Linking: Include internal links within your website content to connect related pages. This helps search engines understand your website's structure and improves user navigation. Additionally, consider contacting other relevant websites or bloggers for backlinking opportunities, which can boost your website's credibility and authority.

Image Optimization: Optimize images on your website by including relevant keywords in the file names and alt text. This helps search engines understand the content of the images and can improve your ranking in image search results.

Social Media Engagement: Utilize social media platforms to connect with your audience and promote your content. Engage in conversations, share your writing journey, and encourage readers to share and comment on your posts. This can help improve your online visibility and increase traffic to your website.

Regular Updates: Consistently create and update your website content. Regularly publishing new blog posts or sharing relevant updates makes sure search engines continuously crawl and index your website, keeping it fresh in search results.

BUILDING A STRONG ONLINE PRESENCE THROUGH WEBSITE:

HAVING a strong online presence is important for both businesses and individuals, given how much we rely on digital connections these days. One of the most effective ways to establish and grow your online presence is by creating a professional and engaging website. A well-designed and user-friendly website can significantly improve your reach, visibility, and credibility in the online world. Here are steps to building a strong online presence through your website:

Define your purpose and target audience: Start by identifying your goals for the website and determining your target audience. What do you want to achieve with your website? Do you want to generate leads, promote your products or services, or provide valuable information? Knowing your purpose and target audience will guide the design and content creation process.

Choose a domain and hosting provider: A domain is your website's address, such as www.yourbusinessname.com. Choose a domain that is concise, memorable, and relevant to your brand. Additionally, select a reliable hosting provider that ensures your website is secure, loads quickly, and has minimal downtime.

Optimize your website for search engines (SEO): Implementing basic SEO tactics will help your website rank higher in search engine results. Research relevant keywords and incorporate them into your website's content, meta tags, headings, and URLs. Create valuable and informative content easy to read and share.

Design an appealing and user-friendly layout: Your website's design should reflect your brand's identity and values. Use a clean and professional layout that makes navigation intuitive for visitors. Make sure your website is mobile-friendly, as the majority of internet users access websites through their smartphones or tablets.

Create informative and engaging content: Content is king in the online world. Regularly update your website with high-quality and relevant content that appeals to your target audience. A blog section can be a great way to provide valuable information and engage with your audience. Include compelling visuals like images and videos to enhance the user experience.

Include clear calls to action (CTAs): Guide your website visitors toward the actions you want them to take. Whether it's signing up for a newsletter, buying a product, or contacting you for more information, make sure your CTAs are clear and prominent on your website.

Integrate social media and share buttons: Social media platforms have become an integral part of building an online presence. Connect your website to your social media profiles and include social media share buttons on your content pages. This encourages visitors to share your content, increasing your brand's visibility and reach.

Regularly monitor and analyze your website's performance: Use website analytics tools to track your website's performance. Monitor metrics like traffic, bounce rate, and conversions to understand how users interact with your website. Make necessary improvements based on these insights to enhance your online presence.

Building a strong online presence through your website is an ongoing process. Continuously update and optimize your website to reflect your brand's growth and adapt to changing user preferences. By following these steps, you will be well on your way to establishing a strong and impactful online presence.

LEVERAGING BOOK BLOGGERS AND INFLUENCERS:

IN THE DIGITAL AGE, book bloggers and influencers have become powerful voices in the literary world. They can reach a wide audience and generate valuable buzz around books. For authors and publishers, leveraging these bloggers and influencers can be a key strategy in promoting and marketing their books. Here's how you can effectively collaborate with book bloggers and influencers to maximize your book's exposure:

Research and identify relevant bloggers and influencers: Start by researching book bloggers and influencers with a strong following in your genre or niche. Look for those who regularly review and promote books like yours. Consider their reach, engagement rate, and the quality of their content.

Build genuine relationships: Once you have identified potential bloggers and influencers, start building genuine relationships with them. Follow their blog or social media accounts, engage with their content, and leave thoughtful comments. This will help you establish a connection and showcase your genuine interest in their work.

Personalize your pitch: When contacting bloggers and influencers, personalize your pitch. Show you have taken the time to understand their interests and values. Mention specific reasons you think they would enjoy your book and how it aligns with their content or niche. This will increase the chances of them being interested in collaborating with you.

Provide an easy way to access your book: Make it simple for bloggers and influencers to access your book. Offer them a digital copy or provide a physical copy if preferred. Include all relevant information, such as a book synopsis, author bio, and high-quality cover images. This will save them time and make the collaboration process smoother.

Encourage honest reviews: While it may be tempting to only seek positive reviews, it is essential to respect the integrity of bloggers and influencers. Encourage them to provide honest reviews, even if there are parts they may not have enjoyed. Authenticity is important in building trust with their audience, and readers value honest opinions.

Offer exclusive content or incentives: To incentivize bloggers and influencers, consider offering exclusive content related to your book. This could be a bonus chapter, author interview, or behind-the-scenes material. Additionally, you can provide small incentives like give-aways or book swag to encourage them to share their review or promotional content on their platforms.

Engage with their followers: By actively engaging with the bloggers and influencers' followers, you can further increase your book's exposure. Respond to comments on their posts, interact with their audience, and participate in relevant discussions. This will help you establish your presence as an author and attract potential readers.

Express gratitude and maintain relationships: Once the collaboration is over, express your gratitude to the bloggers and influencers for their support. Thank them publicly on their blog or social media platforms. Continue to have your relationship by supporting their future work and staying engaged with their content. Who knows, they could become valuable advocates for your future projects.

By leveraging book bloggers and influencers, you can tap into their wide audience and gain valuable exposure for your book. Remember, it's essential to approach bloggers and influencers with respect, authenticity, and genuine interest in their work. Cultivating these relationships can pave the way for successful book promotion and marketing.

~

CREATING COMPELLING BOOK TRAILERS AND TEASERS:

BOOK TRAILERS and teasers have become an essential marketing tool for authors and publishers to promote their books to a wider audience. Like movie trailers, book trailers are short videos that aim to capture the essence of a book and entice viewers to read it. With the rise of social media and online platforms, book trailers and teasers can be shared and viewed by millions of people, making them a powerful promotional tool. Here are tips for creating compelling book trailers and teasers:

Understand the essence of your book: Before creating a trailer or teaser, it is important to have a deep understanding of your book's themes, tone, and target audience. This will help you craft visuals and narratives that accurately represent your book and appeal to potential readers.

Keep it short and captivating: Book trailers and teasers should be short and attention-grabbing, aiming to capture the viewer's interest within the first few seconds. Keep the length to 1-2 minutes and focus on showcasing the most captivating parts of your book.

Use compelling visuals: Visuals are key in book trailers and teasers. Consider using stunning imagery, animations, or even video snippets to create a visually engaging experience. Use high-quality images that reflect the mood and atmosphere of your book, as well as specific scenes or characters that will intrigue viewers.

Choose the right music: Music plays a significant role in creating the right mood and atmosphere for your book trailer. Select a track that complements the theme of your book and enhances the emotional impact of the visuals. Make sure the music doesn't overpower the voiceover or dialogue if you include them.

Incorporate quotes and reviews: If your book has received positive reviews or has standout quotes, consider incorporating them into your trailer or teaser. These testimonials can help build credibility and generate interest among potential readers.

Craft a compelling narrative: A well-crafted narrative is essential for a successful book trailer. Decide on the storyline you want to tell through your visuals and use voiceover or text to guide the viewer through it. Make sure the narrative is concise, clear, and leaves viewers wanting to know more.

Include a CTA: At the end of your book trailer or teaser, include a CTA that encourages viewers to take the next step, such as visiting your website, buying the book, or signing up for a mailing list. This will help convert viewers into readers and potential fans.

Optimize for mobile viewing: As most people consume content on their mobile devices, make sure your book trailer or teaser is optimized for mobile viewing. Make sure the video plays smoothly across different platforms, and the key visuals and messages are clear even on smaller screens.

Share and promote: Once your book trailer or teaser is ready, share it across multiple platforms such as your website, social media channels, YouTube, and other relevant book communities. Engage with your audience by encouraging comments, sharing behind-the-scenes tidbits, or hosting giveaways related to your book trailer or teaser.

Creating compelling book trailers and teasers is an art form that requires careful consideration of your book's unique qualities and target audience. By following these tips, you can create engaging and captivating videos that ignite curiosity and drive readers to discover your book.

SECTION SEVEN KEY TAKEAWAYS AND ACTION ITEMS

Key Takeaways:

1. **Know Your Audience**: Understanding your readers' interests and needs is important for creating content that resonates with them.
2. **Attention-Grabbing Headlines**: Use catchy and informative headlines to draw readers in.
3. **Compelling Introductions**: Start with a hook to grab the reader's attention from the beginning.
4. **Personal Stories**: Share real experiences and emotions to connect with readers on a deeper level.
5. **Use Visuals**: Enhance your posts with relevant images, infographics, or videos for visual appeal and shareability.
6. **Informal Tone**: Write in a conversational way for a more relatable and engaging reading experience.
7. **Encourage Interaction**: Stimulate conversation and community by inviting readers to comment and share their thoughts.
8. **Proofread and Edit**: Ensure your posts are polished and error-free to maintain credibility.

9. **Promote Your Blog**: Actively share your posts on social media and in relevant online communities.
10. **Authentic and Genuine Content**: Be true to yourself and your experiences to create a unique voice and perspective.
11. **Regular Updates and Consistency**: Maintain a consistent posting schedule and keep your content aligned with your brand message.
12. **Multimedia Usage**: Diversify Your Content With Different Types of Multimedia to Engage a Broader Audience.
13. **Social Media Integration**: Connect your blog to social media for increased visibility and engagement.
14. **Collaborate and Network**: Partner with other authors and influencers to expand your reach.
15. **Use Analytics**: Track the performance of your content and adapt your strategy based on insights.
16. **SEO Basics**: Implement SEO tactics like keyword research and optimized titles for better discoverability.
17. **Book Trailers and Teasers**: Create engaging visual content to generate excitement for your books.
18. **Leverage Book Bloggers and Influencers**: Collaborate with bloggers and influencers for authentic promotion and increased exposure.

Action Items:

1. **Research Your Audience:** Conduct market research to understand your readers' preferences.
2. **Create Catchy Headlines:** Craft headlines that are both informative and intriguing.
3. **Develop Engaging Introductions:** Practice writing hooks that immediately capture interest.
4. **Incorporate Personal Elements:** Include personal stories or experiences in your blog posts.

5. **Select and Create Visuals:** Use or create visuals that complement your blog's content and theme.
6. **Adopt a Conversational Writing Style:** Write as if speaking to a friend, keeping language simple and relatable.
7. **Foster Reader Engagement:** End posts with a question or CTA to encourage reader interaction.
8. **Rigorously Edit Posts:** Proofread your content or use tools to check for errors and readability.
9. **Build a Social Media Strategy:** Plan and schedule regular blog promotions across your social media channels.
10. **Stay True to Your Brand:** Ensure all content aligns with your brand and represents your authentic voice.
11. **Plan Your Content Calendar:** Develop a schedule for regular content creation and updates.
12. **Experiment with Different Media Formats:** Try incorporating various multimedia elements into your content.
13. **Optimize for SEO:** Learn and apply SEO basics to improve your blog's search engine ranking.
14. **Design Book Trailers:** Create and share book trailers or teasers to build anticipation for your releases.
15. **Engage with Bloggers/Influencers:** Identify and contact bloggers and influencers for collaboration opportunities.
16. **Track Content Performance:** Use analytics tools to understand which types of content perform best.
17. **Stay Updated with SEO Trends:** Regularly update your SEO knowledge and apply new tactics to your content.
18. **Distribute and Promote Book Trailers:** Share your trailers across various platforms and engage with viewers.

In our next Section...

The section will cover the pivotal role of email marketing in building and maintaining reader relationships. We'll offer practical advice on crafting engaging email content, growing your email list, and leveraging newsletters as a powerful tool for promoting new releases and author events. These strategies are designed to not only expand an author's reach but also to cultivate a dedicated and interactive community of readers, enhancing both the author's brand and their connection with their audience.

SECTION EIGHT: EMAIL MARKETING FOR AUTHORS

BUILDING AND MAINTAINING AN EMAIL LIST OF BOOK LOVERS:

BUILDING AND MAINTAINING an email list of book lovers can be a highly effective way to promote and market your books. Here are steps to help you create and maintain an email list of book lovers:

Identify your target audience: Determine the specific demographic of book lovers you want to target. Are they fans of a certain genre or authors? Understanding your target audience will help you tailor your email content to their interests.

Create an incentive: Offer something valuable to encourage people to sign up for your email list. It could be a free ebook, exclusive content, or access to a private online book club. Make sure your incentive aligns with the interests of book lovers.

Create an opt-in form: Design a simple and user-friendly opt-in form that lets people sign up for your email list on your website or social media pages. Make sure the form communicates the benefits of joining your list.

Use social media and website integration: Promote your email list on your social media platforms and website. Include links to your opt-in form in your social media bios, posts, and website banners.

Offer exclusive content: Send exclusive book excerpts, author interviews, or book recommendations to your email list. This will help to build trust and keep your subscribers engaged.

Regularly send newsletters: Send out regular newsletters to your email list featuring book recommendations, author updates, and exclusive content. This will help keep your subscribers interested in your emails and provide value.

Engage with your subscribers: Encourage your subscribers to respond to your emails and participate in discussions. Respond to their comments and feedback promptly to maintain a personal connection.

Segment your email list: As your list grows, segment your subscribers based on their interests. This will let you send targeted emails based on specific genres, authors, or book preferences.

Creating compelling book trailers and teasers can also help you engage and attract book lovers. Here are tips for creating compelling book trailers and teasers:

Start with a hook: Begin your book trailer or teaser with an attention-grabbing line or scene that intrigues the viewer and entices them to continue watching.

Keep it short and impactful: Make sure your trailer or teaser is concise and focuses on the most exciting and captivating parts of your book. Ideally, it should be no longer than 1-2 minutes.

Use visuals and imagery: Incorporate visually appealing images and scenes into your trailer or teaser that represent the mood, setting, or key moments of your book. This will help create an emotional connection with the viewer.

Include compelling text: Use text overlays or voiceovers that highlight the key themes, plot points, or endorsements of your book. This will further engage the viewer and pique their interest.

Use music and sound effects: Choose background music or sound effects that complement the tone and atmosphere of your book. This can help create a more immersive experience for the viewer.

Call to action: End your trailer or teaser with a strong CTA, such as directing viewers to your website or social media pages to learn more about the book or make a purchase.

Share on multiple platforms: Once your book trailer or teaser is ready, share it on various platforms, including your website, social media, and video-sharing platforms like YouTube and Vimeo.

Remember, building an email list and creating compelling book trailers and teasers are ongoing processes. Continuously engage with your email subscribers and update your trailers to keep them fresh and appealing to your target audience.

CRAFTING EFFECTIVE NEWSLETTERS AND EMAIL CAMPAIGNS:

CRAFTING effective newsletters and email campaigns is essential for engaging your audience and driving conversions. Here are guidelines to help you create compelling content that resonates with your subscribers:

Define your goals: Before starting the newsletter or email campaign, establish clear goals. Are you aiming to increase sales, build brand awareness, or provide valuable information? Defining your goals will help shape the content and design of your newsletters.

Understand your audience: Segment your mailing list based on demographics, interests, or past interactions to deliver targeted content. The more you know about your subscribers, the better you can personalize your messages and meet their needs.

Create a captivating subject line: The subject line is the first thing people see, so make it attention-grabbing. Use action words, personalization, and a hint of curiosity to entice recipients to open the email.

Personalize your content: Tailor the content to suit the interests and preferences of your subscribers. Use their name in the greeting and ensure the content feels personalized and relevant. This could include personalized product recommendations, relevant industry news, or exclusive offers.

Keep it concise and scannable: People have limited time and prefer scanning emails quickly. Keep paragraphs short, use bullet points or numbered lists, and include bold or highlight key points to make the email easy to skim. Use subheadings to break up the content and guide readers through the email.

Engaging and visually appealing design: Use a visually appealing design that aligns with your brand. Keep your layout clean and organized, using whitespace effectively. Incorporate high-quality visuals, such as images and videos, to capture attention. Ensure your email is mobile-responsive, as more subscribers read emails on their smartphones.

Include a clear call to action (CTA): Every newsletter or email should have a clear purpose and desired action. Whether it's to make a purchase, download a resource, or sign up for an event, your CTA should stand out and guide readers toward the desired action.

Test and optimize your emails: Continually test different elements of your emails, such as subject lines, CTAs, and designs. Split testing can help you understand what resonates best with your audience and optimize future campaigns based on the results.

Consistency and regularity: Establish a regular schedule for your newsletters or email campaigns. Consistency builds trust with your subscribers and helps them expect and look forward to your emails. However, be mindful not to overload their inboxes; finding the right frequency is important.

Monitor and analyze results: Use analytics tools to monitor the performance of your newsletters and campaigns. Look at open rates, click-through rates, and conversions to assess their effectiveness. Analyzing the results will provide insights into what works and let you refine your strategies.

By following these guidelines, you can craft effective newsletters and email campaigns that engage your audience and drive the desired action. Remember to continually adapt and optimize based on your subscribers' preferences and behaviors.

SECTION EIGHT KEY TAKEAWAYS AND ACTION ITEMS

KEY TAKEAWAYS:

1. **Target Audience Clarity**: Understanding the specific demographics and preferences of your target audience is important for creating effective content.
2. **Incentive-Based Engagement**: Offering value-driven incentives is key to attracting subscribers to your email list.
3. **Effective Communication**: Consistent, engaging newsletters play an important role in maintaining subscriber interest and loyalty.
4. **Personal Touch**: Personalization in emails fosters a stronger connection and relevance to your audience.
5. **Engagement Strategies**: Prompt responses and interactions with subscribers enhance the sense of community and engagement.
6. **Visual Content Impact**: Utilizing visually appealing elements in emails and book trailers significantly increases engagement.

7. **Email Campaign Goals**: Defining clear goals for your newsletters and email campaigns guides the content and strategy effectively.

8. **Content Accessibility**: Ensuring content is concise and mobile-friendly caters to the diverse preferences of your audience.

9. **Strategic Call to Action**: Clear and compelling CTAs in emails direct subscribers toward desired actions, enhancing conversion rates.

10. **Continuous Improvement**: Regular testing, analysis, and adaptation of email strategies based on performance metrics and feedback are essential for ongoing success.

Action Items:

1. **Identify and Research Target Audience:** Conduct thorough research to understand your audience's interests and behaviors.

2. **Develop Incentives:** Create and offer compelling incentives like free eBooks or exclusive content for email sign-ups.

3. **Create and Integrate Opt-In Forms:** Design user-friendly opt-in forms on your website and social media platforms.

4. **Promote Email List:** Actively promote your email list across various digital platforms to increase visibility and subscribers.

5. **Craft Regular Newsletters:** Develop a schedule for sending out informative and engaging newsletters consistently.

6. **Personalize Email Content:** Tailor email content to align with individual subscriber preferences and interests.

7. **Engage with Subscribers:** Respond promptly to subscriber feedback and encourage interactive discussions.

8. **Segment Email List:** Organize your email list into different segments for more targeted and relevant communication.

9. **Design Engaging Book Trailers:** Create captivating book trailers with strong narratives and visuals.

10. **Establish Clear Email Campaign Objectives:** Set specific goals for each newsletter or email campaign.
11. **Optimize for Mobile Devices:** Ensure that all email content is optimized for a seamless mobile experience.
12. **Test and Refine Email Strategies:** Regularly experiment with and refine email strategies based on performance analytics and subscriber feedback.
13. **Monitor and Analyze Results:** Use analytics tools to track the success of your email campaigns and make data-driven improvements.

In our next Section...

In our next section, we'll dive deeper into the art of successful collaborations in the writing world. We'll explore the nuances of building and nurturing relationships with influencers and fellow authors, and how these connections can dramatically amplify your reach and impact. We'll discuss the importance of identifying the right partners, understanding their audience, and creating content that resonates with both your followers and theirs. This section is important for authors looking to broaden their horizons and make a significant mark in their genre or field.

Additionally, we'll provide practical tips on how to craft effective pitches for collaborative projects, the best practices for engaging with your new audience, and strategies for measuring the success of these partnerships. The focus will be on creating mutually beneficial relationships that not only enhance your visibility but also contribute positively to the writing community. By the end of this section, you'll have a clear roadmap for leveraging collaborations to expand your authorial presence and forge lasting connections in the literary world.

SECTION NINE: NETWORKING AND COLLABORATION

LEVERAGING AUTHOR NETWORKS AND COMMUNITIES:

LEVERAGING author networks and communities can be a powerful way to enhance your writing journey and succeed as an author. By connecting with like-minded writers, you have access to a wealth of knowledge, support, and opportunities that can propel your career forward. Here are ways to make the most of author networks and communities:

Join Writing Groups: Seek local or online writing groups that cater to your genre or writing style. Engage in discussions, share your work, and give constructive feedback to other writers. These groups often offer valuable critiques, advice, and encouragement, helping you improve your writing skills.

Go to Workshops and Conferences: Participate in writing workshops and conferences related to your genre or industry. These events offer opportunities to learn from established authors, literary agents, and publishers. Networking with fellow attendees can open doors to collaboration, mentoring, and future partnerships.

Build an Online Presence: Utilize social media platforms, such as Twitter, Instagram, and Facebook, to connect with fellow authors. Share your experiences, showcase your writing, and engage in conversations with readers and other professionals in the industry. Join writing-centric communities like Goodreads, Wattpad, or Medium to reach a wider audience and gain valuable feedback.

Collaborate on Anthologies or Writing Projects: Collaborative writing projects, such as anthologies or joint author ventures, let you tap into the networks and readerships of other authors. By pooling your talents and connections, you can reach a larger audience, increase exposure, and learn from your fellow writers.

Support and Promote Fellow Authors: Building strong relationships with other authors is a two-way street. Support fellow authors by reading and reviewing their work, promoting their books on your social media platforms or blog, and attending their book signings or online events. By reciprocating this support, you strengthen your network and create a community of authors who help each other succeed.

Join Online Writing Communities: Connect with authors through online forums, writing websites, or specialized platforms like Patreon or Ko-fi. Engage in conversations, seek advice, and offer your expertise to others. These communities often organize workshops, contests, and mentoring programs that can further boost your writing skills and visibility.

Seek Beta Readers and Critique Partners: Find beta readers or critique partners within your author network to provide fair feedback on your work. Exchanging manuscripts and critiques can help you polish your writing, identify areas for improvement, and create a stronger final product.

Seek Publishing and Marketing Advice: Engage in conversation with authors who have achieved success in the publishing world. Learn from their experiences, ask for advice on querying agents, self-publishing, or marketing strategies. Their insights can save you time, help you avoid common pitfalls, and guide you toward making informed decisions.

Remember, building and leveraging author networks and communities is not just about benefiting from existing connections; it's about contributing to the community and supporting others as well. By fostering genuine relationships, you can create a strong support system that propels you toward success as an author.

∿

COLLABORATING WITH INFLUENCERS AND FELLOW AUTHORS FOR CROSS-PROMOTION:

COLLABORATING with influencers and fellow authors for cross-promotion can be a powerful strategy to expand your audience reach and boost your visibility as an author. By teaming up with others with a similar target audience, you can tap into their existing followers and vice versa. Here are tips on how to effectively collaborate for cross-promotion:

Identify target influencers: Look for influencers in your niche or genre who may have an interest in your work. Research their audience size, engagement levels, and relevance to ensure they align with your goals and target readers. Social media platforms like Instagram, YouTube, and TikTok are great places to start searching.

Build genuine relationships: Engage with influencers and fellow authors by following them, commenting on their posts, and sharing their content. Building a sincere connection with them will make it easier to approach them later on for collaborative opportunities.

Reach out with a personalized pitch: When you're ready to propose a cross-promotion collaboration, craft a personalized pitch that explains how the partnership can help both parties. Be specific about what you're offering and what you hope to gain. Highlight any unique angles or ideas that make the collaboration appealing.

Create mutually beneficial content: Collaborate on creating content that will engage and interest both audiences. This can include joint blog posts, videos, giveaways, or even a shared podcast episode. Make sure the content is valuable to both sets of followers and showcases the unique parts of your work.

Leverage each other's platforms: During the collaboration, make sure to cross-promote each other's work by sharing the collaborative content on your respective platforms. This will help expose your audience to your partner's work while also expanding your reach to their followers.

Monitor and engage with the collaboration: Keep an eye on the comments, messages, and engagement generated from the collaboration. Respond to comments, thank followers for their support, and engage with the new audience you have gained. Building relationships with this new audience will help you cultivate a loyal following.

Track and measure results: After the collaborative campaign, analyze the results to determine its effectiveness. Look at metrics such as increased followers, engagement rates, website traffic, or book sales. This will help you assess the success of the collaboration and identify areas for improvement in future partnerships.

Remember, collaboration is a two-way street. Be open to supporting your partners' work and reciprocating their efforts. By working together, you can leverage each other's strengths and expand your reach, ultimately driving more readers to your books.

SECTION NINE KEY TAKEAWAYS AND ACTION ITEMS

1. **Join Writing Groups:** Join local or online groups to share your work, get feedback, and connect with writers in your genre.
2. **Go to Workshops and Conferences:** Learn from professionals, network, and open doors to collaborations and partnerships.
3. **Build an Online Presence:** Use social media and writing communities like Goodreads, Wattpad, or Medium to share your work and connect with readers and writers.
4. **Collaborate on Projects:** Team up for anthologies or joint ventures to tap into other authors' networks and increase your exposure.
5. **Support Fellow Authors:** Read, review, and promote their work to strengthen your network and build a supportive community.
6. **Join Online Writing Communities:** Engage in forums and websites for advice, participation in workshops, and mentoring opportunities.

7. **Seek Beta Readers and Critique Partners:** Exchange feedback to improve your work and create a stronger final product.
8. **Seek Publishing and Marketing Advice:** Learn from successful authors to navigate the publishing world more effectively.
9. **Collaborate for Cross-Promotion:** Partner with influencers and authors to reach new audiences and boost visibility.
10. **Build Genuine Relationships:** Engage sincerely with influencers and authors for more effective collaborations.
11. **Create Mutually Beneficial Content:** Develop content like blog posts or videos that appeal to both audiences.
12. **Leverage Each Other's Platforms:** Share each other's work to expand your reach.
13. **Monitor and Engage with Collaboration:** Interact with the audience from the collaboration to build a loyal following.
14. **Track and Measure Results:** Analyze the effectiveness of the collaboration and identify areas for improvement.

Action Items:

1. **Find and Join Groups:** Research and join writing groups that align with your interests.
2. **Register for Events:** Look for upcoming workshops or conferences and plan to attend.
3. **Establish Social Media Profiles:** Set up profiles on relevant platforms and start engaging.
4. **Explore Collaboration Opportunities:** Reach out to authors for potential collaborative projects.
5. **Actively Support Others:** Regularly read, review, and share fellow authors' works.
6. **Participate in Online Communities:** Engage actively in online writing communities.

7. **Seek Out Partners:** Find beta readers or critique partners for your work.
8. **Connect with Experienced Authors:** Network with successful authors for advice.
9. **Identify Potential Collaborators:** Research influencers and authors for cross-promotion.
10. **Develop a Relationship-building Strategy:** Plan how to build connections with potential collaborators.
11. **Create a Content Plan:** Develop ideas for collaborative content that benefits both parties.
12. **Share and Promote Collaborations:** Use your platforms to promote collaborative content.
13. **Engage with New Audiences:** Actively interact with audiences gained from collaborations.
14. **Analyze Collaboration Outcomes:** Review the success of collaborations and plan for future improvements.

In our next Section...

In our next section, we'll focus on the advanced strategies for maximizing the impact of book reviews and testimonials. This will delve into innovative ways authors can use these powerful tools not just for immediate gains, but for establishing a long-lasting presence in the literary world. We'll explore cutting-edge techniques for attracting top-tier reviews, engaging with influential book bloggers and critics, and turning every piece of feedback, whether positive or negative, into a stepping stone for success. This section is a must-read for authors looking to elevate their writing career to new heights through the strategic use of reviews and testimonials.

We'll be discussing the art of cultivating and nurturing superfans. These are the passionate readers who become the backbone of an author's support system. We'll guide you through identifying these superfans, building meaningful relationships with them, and leveraging their enthusiasm in a way that benefits both the author and the fan. This includes creating exclusive experiences, using user-generated content effectively, and fostering a vibrant community around your work. This section promises to equip authors with the knowledge and skills necessary to create a loyal and engaged readership, turning casual readers into lifelong fans.

~

SECTION TEN: GETTING REVIEWS AND TESTIMONIALS

HARNESSING THE POWER OF BOOK REVIEWS AND TESTIMONIALS - OVERVIEW:

BOOK REVIEWS and testimonials wield the power to significantly affect the success and popularity of an author's work. These feedback and endorsement mechanisms provide valuable insights, enhance credibility, and connect authors with their target audience. Harnessing the power of book reviews and testimonials can bolster sales, build a loyal fan base, and contribute to long-term success in the publishing industry.

Importance of Book Reviews:

Book reviews serve as the lifeblood of a book's promotion. They not only influence potential readers but also play an important role in marketing strategies. Positive book reviews can attract new readers, generate buzz, and help establish an author's reputation. But negative reviews offer constructive criticism and opportunities for improvement. Harnessing the power of book reviews helps authors understand their strengths and weaknesses, refine their writing, and connect with their audience effectively.

Leveraging Testimonials:

Testimonials are personal statements or endorsements from readers, critics, or notable personalities who have experienced an author's work firsthand. Unlike traditional reviews, testimonials focus on personal experiences and emotions, further enhancing an author's connection with readers. Harnessing this power helps authors strengthen their community, build trust, and expand their reach to new audiences.

Building Credibility:

Positive reviews and testimonials contribute to an author's credibility and enhance their professional reputation. Many potential readers rely on the opinions of others before making a purchase or investing their time in a book. By showcasing positive reviews and testimonials, authors gain credibility and trust, making it more likely for readers to take a chance on their work.

Increasing Book Sales:

Positive reviews and testimonials can significantly affect sales. According to various studies, books with higher ratings and positive testimonials have a greater chance of being purchased by potential readers. Leveraging these endorsements can lead to increased exposure, increased sales, and a broader audience base.

Connecting with the Audience:

Reviews and testimonials not only provide feedback but also help authors foster a connection with their readership. Authors can engage with their audience by responding to reviews, acknowledging testimonials, and addressing feedback. This personalized interaction humanizes the author and strengthens the bond between the creator and their readers.

Long-term Success:

Harnessing the power of book reviews and testimonials is not just a short-term marketing strategy. Positive feedback and endorsements contribute to an author's long-term success. By constantly improving their craft based on reviews, testimonials, and reader feedback, authors can adapt their writing style, strengthen their storytelling abilities, and create books that resonate with their audience well into the future.

Book reviews and testimonials hold immense power in the publishing industry. By leveraging their influence, authors can enhance credibility, increase sales, and connect with their audience on a deeper level. Harnessing the power of book reviews and testimonials paves the way for long-term success in the competitive world of publishing.

IDENTIFYING AND CONNECTING WITH YOUR SUPERFANS:

RESEARCH AND IDENTIFY YOUR SUPERFANS:

Start by analyzing your audience and collecting data on your most engaged and loyal followers. Look for individuals who consistently interact with your brand, share your content, and show genuine enthusiasm for your products or services. Consider using social media analytics tools to gather information about their demographics and preferences.

Engage and Interact with Them:

Superfans appreciate businesses that actively engage with them. Respond to their comments, messages, and mentions on social media platforms promptly and authentically. Show gratitude for their support and build a personal connection by mentioning them or featuring their content in your posts. This interaction will make them feel valued and strengthen their loyalty toward your brand.

Offer Exclusive Perks and Experiences:

To nurture your relationship with superfans, consider creating exclusive perks or experiences that make them feel like VIPs. This could include early access to new products, exclusive discounts, or invitations to special events or webinars. By providing these extra benefits, you reinforce their dedication to your brand and make them feel appreciated and recognized.

Leverage User-generated Content:

Develop a strategy to encourage superfans to create and share their own content related to your brand. User-generated content (UGC) not only adds authenticity to your marketing efforts but also enhances the bond between your superfans and the broader community. Create branded hashtags and run UGC contests to incentivize them to contribute and share their experiences with your products or services.

Cultivate a Sense of Community:

Build a community where superfans can connect with each other and share their experiences. This could be a private Facebook group, an online forum, or a dedicated hashtag on social media. By fostering interactions among superfans, you create a sense of belonging and provide an opportunity for them to expand their network and dive deeper into their shared passion for your brand.

Seek Their Feedback and Input:

Superfans are often highly knowledgeable about your products or services and can provide valuable insights. Don't hesitate to seek their feedback or involve them in product development processes. Their input will not only help improve your offerings but also strengthen their connection to your brand as they see their ideas and opinions being valued.

Show Appreciation Regularly:

Never shy away from expressing gratitude toward your superfans. Highlight them in special content features, send personalized thank-you messages, or surprise them with small tokens of appreciation. Regularly show that their support means a lot to your brand, as this will continue to foster a strong and lasting relationship.

Remember, superfans are your brand advocates who can help promote your business and attract new customers. By identifying and connecting with them, you can create a loyal and engaged community that will contribute to your long-term success.

STRATEGIES FOR ACQUIRING BOOK REVIEWS AND RECOMMENDATIONS:

BUILD AN AUTHOR PLATFORM: Establishing a strong online presence through a website, blog, or social media profiles can help attract readers who may be interested in reviewing and recommending your book. Engage with your audience by sharing excerpts, behind-the-scenes details, and updates about your writing process to build a loyal following.

Leverage your network: Reach out to friends, family members, and colleagues who may read and review your book. Word-of-mouth recommendations can be powerful in generating buzz and attracting new readers. Ask them to share their thoughts on their social media platforms or on websites such as Goodreads or Amazon.

Join author communities: Participate in online communities or forums specifically created for authors and readers. Connect with fellow authors and offer to swap reviews or recommend each other's books. These communities often have dedicated sections for authors to promote their works and find reviewers.

Engage with book bloggers and reviewers: Research and identify influential book bloggers or reviewers who specialize in your book's genre. Contact them by sending a personalized email introducing yourself and your book. Offer to provide a complimentary copy in exchange for an honest review. Make sure their preferred method of contact is stated on their blog or website.

Use promotional services: Consider using online platforms like NetGalley or BookSirens to offer your book to a wider audience of book bloggers and reviewers. These platforms let authors offer advanced copies of their books in exchange for honest reviews, thus increasing exposure and reaching potential readers.

Offer personalized author interviews: Approach podcasters, radio hosts, or bloggers who conduct author interviews. Offer to be a guest on their show or contribute a guest post to their blog. This lets you share your writing journey, your book's unique parts, and engage with their audience effectively.

Create a launch team: Assemble a group of dedicated readers interested in your work and offer them an advanced copy of your book. Ask them to leave honest reviews on platforms such as Amazon, Goodreads, or on their personal blogs. Reward their efforts by acknowledging them in the book's acknowledgments section or offering them exclusive content or discounts.

Participate in book contests and awards: Submit your book to reputable book contests or awards in your genre. Winning or even being shortlisted can bring attention to your work and provide credibility. Many contests have a review part as part of their judging process, which can result in valuable reviews.

Go to book events and festivals: Participate in local book events, author panels, or book festivals in your area. Network with fellow authors, publishers, and readers who may be interested in reviewing and recommending your book. Consider offering signed copies or giveaways at these events to create excitement and generate word-of-mouth buzz.

Seek feedback: Reach out directly to readers who have bought and read your book via email or social media. Ask them to leave a review if they enjoyed the book or offer them a chance to provide private feed-back. Taking the time to engage with readers personally can lead to positive reviews and recommendations, as well as valuable insights for future books.

ENGAGING WITH READERS AND BUILDING A COMMUNITY AROUND YOUR BRAND:

IN THE CURRENT era where digital connections are important, building a community around your brand is important for success. Engaging with readers and creating a sense of community not only helps to establish brand loyalty but also creates opportunities for growth and expansion. Here are tips for engaging with readers and building a community around your brand:

Know your audience: To effectively engage with readers, you need to understand who they are and what they are looking for. Conduct market research to identify your target audience and gain insights into their interests, preferences, and needs.

Create valuable content: The cornerstone of building a community around your brand is creating content that is informative, entertaining, and valuable to your readers. Give them valuable information, tips, and advice related to your brand or industry. Regularly publish blog posts, articles, videos, or podcasts that resonate with your audience.

Encourage reader interaction: Invite your readers to actively participate in discussions and share their own experiences. Encourage them to leave comments, ask questions, and share their thoughts on your content. Respond to their comments promptly and foster a sense of connection. Thank them for their engagement and make them feel valued.

Use social media effectively: Social media platforms are excellent tools for engaging with readers and building a community. Create profiles on platforms that align with your target audience's interests and engage with them regularly. Post content, respond to comments, share user-generated content, and run contests or giveaways to encourage participation.

Establish a forum or community platform: Consider setting up a forum or community platform on your website where readers can interact with each other and discuss topics related to your brand or industry. This provides a dedicated space for your community to connect and share their thoughts and experiences.

Collaborate with influencers: Partnering with influencers who align with your brand can help you reach a wider audience and build credibility. Engage with influencers on social media, collaborate on content creation, or feature them as guest contributors on your blog or podcast. Their involvement can bring new perspectives and fresh insights to your community.

Host events or webinars: Organize events or webinars where you can share your knowledge or insights with your readers directly. This creates an opportunity for real-time interaction, engagement, and networking. Encourage attendees to ask questions and provide feedback during these events.

Reward community members: Show appreciation for your community members by rewarding their loyalty. Offer exclusive discounts, early access to new products or services, or special perks. Recognize their contributions by featuring their testimonials, guest articles, or user-generated content on your website or social media platforms.

Be consistent and authentic: Consistency is key when building a community. Regularly publish new content, respond to comments and messages promptly, and maintain a consistent tone and branding across all platforms. Stay true to your brand values and be authentic in your interactions.

Monitor and analyze: Keep track of your community's engagement levels and analyze which strategies are proving most successful. Monitor metrics such as website traffic, social media engagement, and community activity to identify areas for improvement and tailor your efforts.

Remember, building a community takes time and effort. Stay consistent, be patient, and always focus on delivering value to your readers. By engaging with your audience and fostering a sense of community, you can create a loyal following that not only supports your brand but becomes advocates for it as well.

SECTION TEN KEY TAKEAWAYS AND ACTION ITEMS

Key Takeaways:

1. **Book Reviews and Testimonials are important:** They significantly affect an author's success by providing insights, enhancing credibility, and connecting with audiences.
2. **Importance of Book Reviews:** They influence potential readers, contribute to marketing, and help authors understand their strengths and weaknesses.
3. **Leveraging Testimonials:** These personal endorsements focus on experiences and emotions, enhancing the author-reader connection.
4. **Building Credibility:** Positive reviews and testimonials establish credibility and trust, encouraging readers to explore an author's work.
5. **Increasing Book Sales:** Higher ratings and positive testimonials directly influence sales and audience expansion.
6. **Connecting with the Audience:** Reviews and testimonials enable authors to engage with readers, humanizing the author and strengthening relationships.

7. **Long-term Success:** Constant improvement based on feedback contributes to an author's longevity and relevance in the industry.
8. **Identifying Superfans:** Analyze and engage with your most loyal followers, offering them exclusive experiences and using their user-generated content.
9. **Building a Community:** Create a platform for superfans to connect and share experiences, fostering a sense of belonging.
10. **Acquiring Reviews and Recommendations:** Establish a strong author platform, leverage your network, and engage with book bloggers and reviewers.
11. **Strategies for Book Reviews:** Utilize promotional services, offer author interviews, and create a launch team for your book.
12. **Engaging with Readers:** Understand your audience, create valuable content, and use social media effectively to build a community around your brand.
13. **Rewarding Community Members:** Show appreciation with exclusive offers and recognize their contributions.
14. **Monitoring and Analyzing Engagement:** Track community engagement and adjust strategies for maximum impact.

Action Items:

1. **Gather and Showcase Reviews/Testimonials:** Actively seek and display reviews and testimonials on your author platform and marketing materials.
2. **Respond to Reviews:** Engage with reviewers, both positive and negative, to build rapport and improve based on feedback.
3. **Identify and Connect with Superfans:** Use social media analytics to find your most engaged followers and create personalized interactions with them.
4. **Create Exclusive Offers:** Develop special perks for superfans to foster loyalty and encourage word-of-mouth promotion.

5. **Collaborate with Influencers:** Reach out to influencers for cross-promotion and content collaboration.
6. **Host Events/Webinars:** Organize events to directly engage with your audience and provide value.
7. **Engage on Social Media:** Regularly post and interact with followers on social media platforms.
8. **Create a Community Platform:** Develop a space for your audience to interact, such as a forum or social media group.
9. **Use Promotional Services:** Explore platforms like NetGalley or BookSirens for wider exposure and reviews.
10. **Offer Personalized Author Interviews:** Approach podcasters or bloggers for interviews to reach new audiences.
11. **Form a Launch Team:** Assemble a team of readers to provide early reviews and promote your book.
12. **Submit to Book Contests/Awards:** Enter contests for recognition and potential reviews.
13. **Go to Book Events/Festivals:** Network and promote your book in person at relevant events.
14. **Seek Direct Reader Feedback:** Reach out to readers for reviews and constructive criticism.
15. **Analyze Community Engagement:** Regularly review the effectiveness of your engagement strategies and adapt as needed.

In our next Section...

In our upcoming section, we'll delve into the post-launch phase, a critical period that often determines the long-term success of your book. Here, we'll explore effective strategies for sustaining the momentum generated by your book launch. This includes techniques for keeping your audience engaged, methods to continuously promote your book through various channels, and tactics for leveraging the initial surge of interest to secure more reviews and recommendations. We'll discuss the importance of adapting your marketing strategies based on the feedback and data gathered during the launch, ensuring your book remains visible and appealing to new readers.

Additionally, this section will focus on expanding your reach beyond the initial launch. We'll cover advanced strategies for tapping into new markets, exploring more platforms for promotion, and potentially branching into other formats like audiobooks or translated editions. This phase is all about growth and adaptation, learning from the launch experience, and applying those insights to extend the life cycle of your book. Whether you're a first-time author or a seasoned writer, this section will provide valuable insights into keeping your book relevant and successful in the ever-evolving world of publishing.

SECTION ELEVEN: BOOK LAUNCH STRATEGIES

PLANNING AND EXECUTING A SUCCESSFUL BOOK LAUNCH:

PLANNING AND EXECUTING a successful book launch requires careful planning, attention to detail, and effective execution. Here are steps to help you plan and execute a book launch that will create buzz and generate book sales:

Set clear goals: Start by identifying the specific goals you want to achieve with your book launch. This could generate sales, building buzz, reaching a specific target audience, or proving yourself to be an authority in your niche.

Create a timeline: Develop a timeline that outlines all the tasks and milestones leading to your book launch. This includes setting a launch date and working backward to determine when to start your marketing efforts, book cover design, editing, and printing. Give yourself enough time to complete each task and adjust the timeline if necessary.

Build a launch team: Recruit a launch team of friends, family, colleagues, and enthusiastic readers who can help spread the word about your book. Give them advance copies of the book and ask for their support in leaving reviews, sharing on social media, and recommending your book to others.

Develop a marketing plan: Craft a comprehensive marketing plan that includes online and offline strategies. This can involve creating a dedicated website or landing page for your book, engaging with influencers and bloggers in your genre, hosting a virtual launch event, planning book signings, and using social media platforms to increase exposure.

Generate buzz pre-launch: Start generating buzz about your book before the launch through social media posts, blog posts, guest articles, podcast interviews, or online events. Tease the content of your book, share snippets or quotes, and give your audience a taste of what to expect.

Plan a launch event: Whether it's a physical or virtual event, plan a launch party that creates excitement and draws attention to your book. This could include a book reading, Q&A session, giveaways, or special promotions. Invite influential people in your industry or community who can help spread the word.

Leverage media opportunities: Seek media opportunities to amplify your book launch. This can include pitching to podcasts, radio shows, or local newspapers for interviews or features about your book. Prepare a press release and send it out to relevant media outlets.

Engage your audience: Engage your audience throughout the launch process by posting updates, behind-the-scenes content, or hosting contests and giveaways. Encourage your readers to share their thoughts and reviews and respond to all comments and messages to build a strong connection with your audience.

Monitor and adjust: Monitor the progress of your book launch and adjust your strategies. Track your sales, engagement metrics, and feedback from readers to determine what is working and what needs improvement. Be flexible and open to making changes to maximize the impact of your book launch.

Remember, a successful book launch is the beginning of your book's journey. Continue to promote and market your book even after the launch to maintain momentum and reach new readers.

PRE-LAUNCH AND LAUNCH DAY TACTICS:

Build anticipation: Create a buzz around your upcoming launch by teasing your audience with sneak peeks, behind-the-scenes content, and countdowns. Use social media, email marketing, and your website to generate excitement.

Start a pre-launch campaign: Offer exclusive discounts, early access, or giveaways for those who sign up or pre-order before the launch. This strategy can help you drive pre-orders and build a loyal customer base.

Reach out to influencers and bloggers: Identify influential individuals or popular bloggers in your niche and offer them early access to your product or service. Encourage them to review or share their experiences with their audience, which can help generate buzz and increase brand awareness.

Use paid advertising: Consider investing in paid advertising, such as Facebook ads or Google AdWords, to promote your upcoming launch. Target ads toward your target audience and use compelling visuals and messaging to capture their attention.

Leverage email marketing: Send out regular updates to your subscriber list, sharing important milestones, sneak peeks, and reminders about the upcoming launch. Offer special exclusive deals for email subscribers to drive engagement and conversions.

LAUNCH DAY TACTICS:

HOST A LAUNCH EVENT: Create a physical or virtual event to celebrate your launch. This could include a live-streamed presentation, product demos, guest speakers, or interactive Q&A sessions. Promote the event on your website, social media platforms, and through your email list.

Offer limited-time promotions: Drive immediate sales and create a sense of urgency by offering limited-time promotions, such as introductory discounts, free shipping, or bundled deals. Highlight these offers prominently on your website and through email marketing.

Engage with your audience: Be active on social media platforms throughout the launch day. Respond to comments, address any concerns or questions, and share customer testimonials or user-generated content. This will help build trust, foster engagement, and create a positive launch day experience.

Collaborate with influencers: Tap into the power of influencers by partnering with them for your launch day. They can promote your product or service through their channels, create content related to your launch, or host giveaways on their platforms to generate maximum exposure.

Monitor and analyze performance: Track key metrics such as website traffic, conversion rates, and social media engagement during the launch day. Use analytics tools to gain insights into customer behavior and identify areas of improvement. Adjust your tactics if necessary to maximize success.

Remember that both pre-launch and launch day tactics are important parts of your overall marketing strategy. By planning and executing these tactics effectively, you can build momentum, generate excitement, and achieve a successful launch.

SECTION ELEVEN KEY TAKEAWAYS AND ACTION ITEMS

KEY TAKEAWAYS:

1. **Set Clear Goals:** Define specific goals for your book launch, like sales targets or audience reach.
2. **Create a Timeline:** Develop a detailed timeline for all pre-launch activities including marketing, cover design, and printing.
3. **Build a Launch Team:** Recruit enthusiastic supporters to help promote your book.
4. **Develop a Marketing Plan:** Craft a strategy that encompasses both online and offline channels.
5. **Generate Pre-Launch Buzz:** Use social media, blog posts, and other platforms to create excitement before the book launch.
6. **Plan a Launch Event:** Organize a memorable event, either in-person or virtual, to mark the release of your book.
7. **Leverage Media Opportunities:** Seek interviews and features in various media outlets.
8. **Engage Your Audience:** Keep your audience involved through updates, contests, and direct interactions.

9. **Monitor and Adjust Strategies:** Track the effectiveness of your launch strategies and be ready to make changes as needed.
10. **Continue Promotion Post-Launch:** Maintain marketing efforts even after the book launch to keep the momentum going.
11. **Pre-Launch Campaign:** Run a campaign offering perks for early orders or sign-ups.
12. **Influencer Outreach:** Collaborate with influencers and bloggers for wider exposure.
13. **Paid Advertising:** Invest in targeted ads to promote the launch.
14. **Email Marketing:** Use email blasts to keep your audience informed and engaged.
15. **Launch Day Promotions:** Offer special deals and promotions on the day of the launch.
16. **Active Social Media Engagement:** Interact with your audience on social media throughout the launch day.
17. **Influencer Collaboration on Launch Day:** Partner with influencers for more promotion.
18. **Performance Monitoring:** Track key metrics and adjust tactics for better results.

Action Items:

1. **Identify Your Launch Goals:** Write down specific goals for your book launch.
2. **Prepare a Detailed Timeline:** Map out each task leading to the launch date.
3. **Assemble Your Launch Team:** Reach out to potential team members and organize their roles.
4. **Craft Your Marketing Plan:** Develop a comprehensive marketing strategy for your book.
5. **Start Creating Buzz:** Begin your pre-launch marketing activities on social media and other platforms.

RAE A. STONEHOUSE

6. **Organize Your Launch Event:** Plan the details of your launch event, including location, format, and activities.
7. **Pitch to Media Outlets:** Create and send out a press release to relevant media channels.
8. **Engage with Your Audience:** Regularly post updates and interact with followers online.
9. **Evaluate Launch Progress:** Continuously track the effectiveness of your launch strategy.
10. **Plan Post-Launch Marketing:** Develop a strategy to keep promoting your book after the launch.
11. **Start Pre-Launch Campaign:** Start your campaign for early sign-ups or orders.
12. **Reach Out to Influencers:** Identify and contact influencers who can help promote your book.
13. **Set Up Paid Advertisements:** Create and launch targeted advertising campaigns.
14. **Leverage Email Marketing:** Send out regular updates and exclusive offers to your email list.
15. **Prepare Launch Day Offers:** Plan special deals for the day of the book launch.
16. **Engage on Social Media on Launch Day:** Actively post and respond to feedback on social media.
17. **Coordinate with Influencers for Launch Day:** Finalize collaboration details with influencers.
18. **Analyze Launch Day Results:** Review the performance and adjust your ongoing marketing strategy.

In our next Section...

In our next section, we'll delve into the important phase of analyzing and refining your paid advertising strategies. This stage is all about understanding the data behind your campaigns and using those insights to fine-tune your approach. We'll explore how to interpret key metrics like click-through rates, conversion rates, and return on ad spend to gauge the effectiveness of your ads. Additionally, this section will guide you through the process of A/B testing, a critical technique for optimizing your advertising efforts. By comparing different versions of your ads, you can identify which elements resonate most with your audience and adjust your campaigns. This analytical approach makes sure your advertising budget is being used efficiently, maximizing your book's visibility and sales potential.

We'll focus on advanced tactics for scaling up your successful ad campaigns while maintaining a budget-friendly approach. This includes exploring more sophisticated advertising platforms and techniques, such as retargeting campaigns and advanced audience segmentation, to further increase your reach to potential readers. We'll also discuss the importance of staying updated with the latest trends in digital advertising and how to adapt these trends to your unique book marketing needs. Whether you're a new author experimenting with your first paid campaign or a seasoned writer looking to expand your reach, this section will provide valuable insights into making your paid advertising efforts more impactful and cost-effective.

SECTION TWELVE: PAID ADVERTISING FOR AUTHORS

AN OVERVIEW OF PAID ADVERTISING CHANNELS:

PAID advertising channels refer to the platforms and methods through which businesses can promote their products or services by paying for placement or exposure. These channels let businesses reach a wider audience, attract new customers, and increase their brand visibility and sales. Here is an overview of some popular paid advertising channels:

Search Advertising: One of the most common forms of paid advertising, search advertising involves placing ads on search engine results pages (SERPs). Businesses bid on keywords relevant to their offerings, and their ads seem when users search for those keywords. Google Ads and Bing Ads are the primary platforms for search advertising.

Display Advertising: Display advertising encompasses banner ads, rich media ads, and video ads that appear on websites, apps, or social media platforms. These ads are typically visually appealing and can be highly customizable. Google Display Network, Facebook Ads, and programmatic advertising platforms (such as DoubleClick) are popular options for display advertising.

Social Media Advertising: With billions of active users, social media platforms offer an excellent opportunity for businesses to advertise their products and services. Platforms like Facebook, Instagram, Twitter, LinkedIn, and Pinterest provide highly targeted advertising options to reach specific demographics or interests.

Video Advertising: Video advertising involves placing ads within online videos, such as YouTube or other video-sharing platforms. These ads can be skippable or non-skippable and can appear before, during, or after a video. Video advertising is effective for storytelling and capturing users' attention.

Native Advertising: Native advertising refers to ads that seamlessly blend with the content of a website or app, providing a non-disruptive user experience. These ads are designed to match the look, feel, and format of the platform they appear on. Advertisers can use platforms like Outbrain or Taboola for native advertising.

Affiliate Marketing: This form of paid advertising is a partnership between the advertiser and affiliates who earn a commission for driving traffic and generating sales. Affiliate marketing is commonly practiced through affiliate networks like Amazon Associates, Commission Junction, or ShareASale.

Influencer Marketing: Influencer marketing focuses on leveraging the influence of well-known individuals in a particular niche to promote a product or service. Brands collaborate with influencers, with a dedicated following, to showcase their offerings. This form of advertising is common on social media platforms like Instagram, YouTube, and TikTok.

Paid Search on Ecommerce Platforms: For businesses operating in the ecommerce space, platforms like Amazon, eBay, and Shopify offer paid search advertising options. These channels let businesses advertise their products within specific search results on the platform.

When planning a paid advertising campaign, businesses should consider factors such as their target audience, budget, goals, and the nature of their offerings to choose the most suitable advertising channels. Tracking and analytics tools can help measure the effectiveness and return on investment of these channels, letting businesses refine their strategies for ideal results.

CREATING EFFECTIVE AD CAMPAIGNS ON A BUDGET:

ADVERTISING IS an essential part of promoting your business and reaching your target audience. However, it can often be costly, especially for small businesses with limited budgets. The good news is, with strategic planning and creativity, you can create effective ad campaigns on a budget. Here are tips to help you get started:

Define your target audience: Before you start creating your ad campaign, it's important to clearly understand who your target audience is. Knowing their demographics, interests, and behaviors will help you craft a more focused and effective campaign that resonates with them.

Set clear goals: Determine what you want to achieve with your ad campaign. Is it to generate brand awareness, drive website traffic, or increase sales? Having measurable goals will help you stay focused and evaluate the success of your campaign.

Use digital advertising: Digital advertising is often more cost-effective than traditional media channels like TV or print ads. Use platforms like Google AdWords, social media advertising (Facebook, Instagram, Twitter, etc.), or targeted email marketing to get your message across effectively.

Harness the power of social media: With billions of active users, social media platforms offer great opportunities for cost-effective advertising. Create engaging and shareable content that aligns with your target audience's interests. Use relevant hashtags, run contests or giveaways, and collaborate with influencers to amplify your reach.

Focus on native advertising: Native advertising blends seamlessly into the natural content of a platform, making it less intrusive and more appealing to the audience. Collaborate with publishers or content creators to create native ads that provide value or entertainment to the viewers.

Optimize your website for search engines: SEO is essential to increase your organic online visibility. By optimizing your website's content and structure, you can drive more organic traffic to your site without spending money on ads. This can be achieved by incorporating relevant keywords, creating quality content, and improving website loading speed.

Leverage user-generated content: Encourage your customers to generate content related to your brand or products. User-generated content is not only cost-effective but also increases authenticity and engagement. Run contests or ask for reviews and testimonials to gather user-generated content to use in your ads.

Collaborate with complementary businesses: Identify businesses or influencers in your niche with a similar target audience but are not direct competitors. Collaborate with them on joint advertising efforts or cross-promotions. This way, you can reach a wider audience without stretching your budget too thin.

A/B test your ad campaigns: Testing different elements of your ad campaigns, such as headlines, images, or CTAs, can help you identify what works best for your audience. Split your budget and test multiple variations simultaneously to find the most effective combination.

Measure and optimize: Set up tracking mechanisms to measure the performance of your ad campaigns. Monitor key metrics like click-through rates, conversions, and return on ad spend. Analyze the data, identify the strengths and weaknesses of your campaigns, and adjust continuously to improve your results.

Creating effective ad campaigns on a budget requires careful planning, creativity, and a deep understanding of your audience. By leveraging digital advertising, embracing social media, and optimizing your online presence, you can effectively promote your business without breaking the bank.

~

SECTION TWELVE KEY TAKEAWAYS AND ACTION ITEMS

Key Takeaways:

1. **Diverse Paid Advertising Channels:** Utilize various platforms like search advertising, display advertising, social media advertising, video advertising, native advertising, affiliate marketing, influencer marketing, and paid search on ecommerce platforms.
2. **Target Audience Understanding:** Know your audience's demographics, interests, and behaviors for effective ad targeting.
3. **Clear Objectives Setting:** Define specific goals for your advertising campaign, such as brand awareness or sales going up.
4. **Digital Advertising Utilization:** Leverage digital platforms for cost-effective advertising.
5. **Social Media Power:** Use social media's extensive reach for engaging and shareable content.
6. **Native Advertising Focus:** use native advertising for a less intrusive and more natural ad experience.

7. **SEO for Organic Traffic:** Optimize your website for search engines to increase organic visibility.
8. **User-Generated Content Leveraging:** Encourage and use customer-generated content for authenticity.
9. **Collaboration with Complementary Businesses:** Partner with similar businesses or influencers for joint advertising efforts.
10. **Ad Campaigns A/B Testing:** Test different elements of your ads to find the most effective strategy.
11. **Performance Measurement and Optimization:** Track key metrics and adjust strategies based on performance data.

Action Items:

1. **Choose Suitable Advertising Channels:** Select the most appropriate channels for your book based on your audience and goals.
2. **Define Your Target Audience:** Research and clearly define who your target readers are.
3. **Set Campaign Goals:** Write down specific goals for your advertising campaign.
4. **Plan Your Digital Advertising Strategy:** Develop a plan for using digital platforms effectively.
5. **Create Engaging Social Media Content:** Design content for social media that resonates with your audience.
6. **Develop Native Ads:** Create ads that fit naturally within the content of chosen platforms.
7. **Implement SEO Techniques:** Apply SEO strategies to improve your website's organic search ranking.
8. **Encourage User-Generated Content:** Create campaigns or contests that encourage readers to create content related to your book.
9. **Seek Collaborative Opportunities:** Identify potential partners for joint marketing efforts.

10. **Conduct A/B Tests on Ads:** Experiment with different ad variations to see which performs best.
11. **Track Ad Performance:** Set up tools to track the effectiveness of your ads and make data-driven decisions for optimization.

In our next Section...

In our next section, we'll delve into advanced techniques for enhancing public speaking and presentation skills, focusing on the nuances of engaging storytelling and persuasive communication. This part of the guide will offer authors strategies to weave compelling narratives into their presentations, making sure each speech or reading captivates and resonates deeply with their audience. We'll explore how to use story-telling elements like tension, character development, and emotional connection to enrich public speaking engagements. Additionally, this section will provide insights into persuasive communication techniques, including the use of rhetorical devices, effective argument structure, and the art of persuasion to influence and inspire audiences. These skills are invaluable not only in promoting written work but also in various parts of an author's career, such as pitching to publishers, engaging in literary discussions, and building a personal brand.

We'll address the challenges and opportunities presented by the evolving landscape of digital communication and virtual events. This includes mastering the art of engaging audiences in a virtual setting, using digital platforms to extend reach, and leveraging multimedia tools to enhance presentations. We'll provide practical tips for creating dynamic and interactive virtual presentations, maintaining audience engagement in an online environment, and effectively using social media and other digital platforms to maximize the impact of virtual speaking engagements. This section is designed to equip authors with the skills needed to thrive in both traditional and digital speaking forums, enhancing their ability to share their stories, connect with readers, and succeed in the digital age of literature.

SECTION THIRTEEN: THE ART OF PUBLIC SPEAKING AND PRESENTATIONS FOR AUTHORS

As AN AUTHOR, expanding your reach and connecting with your audience is important to the success of your writing career. While the written word may be your forte, the ability to effectively communicate your ideas and engage your readers is equally important. This guide aims to help authors develop their skills in public speaking and presentations, enabling them to connect with their readers, promote their books, and establish a powerful presence in the literary world.

OVERCOMING THE FEAR OF PUBLIC SPEAKING:

UNDERSTANDING THE IMPORTANCE OF PUBLIC SPEAKING FOR AUTHORS:

PUBLIC SPEAKING IS an important skill for authors. While writing may be the primary medium through which authors communicate their ideas, the ability to speak confidently in public enhances their reach, impact, and credibility.

First, public speaking lets authors connect with their readers on a personal level. When authors deliver speeches, readings, or presentations, they have an opportunity to engage directly with their audience, enabling a deeper connection and understanding of their work. This interaction can help authors receive immediate feedback, answer questions, and gain valuable insight into how their writing is resonating with their readers.

Second, public speaking gives authors a platform to promote their work. By delivering speeches at book events, literary festivals, or even on radio or television interviews, authors can raise awareness about their books and attract a wider audience. Public speaking lets authors effectively communicate their key messages, share their story, and generate interest in their writing, leading to increased book sales and visibility for their work.

Additionally, public speaking can enhance an author's credibility and professional reputation. When authors confidently present their ideas before an audience, it showcases their expertise and knowledge on the topic. This leads to increased trust and respect from both readers and the literary community. The ability to speak articulately and convincingly about their work can also attract opportunities such as speaking engagements, collaborations, and media appearances, further boosting an author's standing in the industry.

Public speaking is also a valuable skill for authors when networking and building relationships. By attending conferences, workshops, and events related to their genre or field of interest, authors can meet fellow writers, editors, agents, and publishers. These interactions not only provide opportunities for collaboration and mentorship but also open doors to new publishing deals, book deals, and other professional connections that can advance their writing career.

Public speaking can aid authors in honing their craft. Presenting to an audience forces authors to clarify and refine their ideas, making sure their message is understood effectively. It can also help authors become better communicators overall, teaching them how to engage an audience, structure their presentations, and use rhetorical techniques to captivate their listeners. These skills translate into stronger writing, as authors learn to convey their ideas more coherently and persuasively on the page.

Public speaking is important for authors as it enables them to connect with readers, promote their work, establish credibility, build relationships, and improve their writing skills. By embracing public speaking opportunities, authors can amplify their impact, expand their audience, and elevate their career as successful and influential writers.

IDENTIFYING AND ADDRESSING FEARS AND ANXIETY:

Identifying and addressing fears and anxiety is an important process that can help individuals overcome their obstacles and live a more fulfilling life. Here are steps to effectively identify and address fears and anxiety:

Recognize the fear or anxiety: The first step is to acknowledge and identify the specific fear or anxiety you are experiencing. Reflect on your thoughts and emotions and try to pinpoint the root cause of your fear or anxiety.

Explore the source: Delve deeper into the source of your fear or anxiety. It could be triggered by a past trauma, a specific event, or even a general feeling of unease. Understanding the underlying reasons behind your fears can help you address them more effectively.

Seek professional help: If your fears and anxiety are significantly affecting your daily life, it is advisable to seek professional help. A therapist or counselor can provide guidance and support in dealing with your fears, helping you develop coping mechanisms, and providing valuable insights.

Challenge negative thoughts: Our fears and anxieties often stem from negative or irrational thoughts. Challenge these thoughts by questioning their validity and replacing them with positive and realistic ones. This process, known as cognitive restructuring, can help shift your mindset and decrease anxiety levels.

Practice relaxation techniques: Engage in relaxation techniques such as deep breathing exercises, meditation, or yoga. These practices can help calm your mind, reduce anxiety symptoms, and foster a sense of inner peace. Regularly incorporating these techniques into your routine can be beneficial in managing and overcoming fears and anxiety.

Gradual exposure: Gradual exposure, also known as systematic desensitization, involves gradually confronting your fears or anxiety-inducing situations in a controlled way. Start by exposing yourself to less intense situations that evoke mild anxiety and progressively work your way up to more challenging situations. This technique helps build resilience and confidence while gradually reducing fear or anxiety responses.

Build a support system: Sharing your fears and anxieties with trusted friends or family members can provide relief and support. Surrounding yourself with a positive and understanding support system can provide encouragement and guidance as you work through your fears.

Practice self-care: Prioritize self-care by engaging in activities that promote overall well-being. Regular exercise, enough sleep, maintaining a balanced diet, and engaging in hobbies and activities that bring joy can significantly reduce stress and anxiety levels.

Remember, addressing fears and anxiety takes time and effort. Be patient with yourself and celebrate your progress along the way.

Building Confidence Through Practice and Preparation:

Building confidence through practice and preparation is a crucial part of personal and professional growth. It involves consistently engaging in activities or tasks that challenge you and push you outside of your comfort zone. Through deliberate practice and thorough preparation, you can develop the skills, knowledge, and mindset necessary to foster a strong sense of confidence.

One way to build confidence is through practice. Whether it is giving presentations, playing a musical instrument, or improving your athletic abilities, regular practice lets you become proficient in a particular skill or activity. Each time you practice, you enhance your knowledge and ability, which boosts your confidence.

Practicing also helps you become familiar with the task or challenge at hand, reducing anxiety and uncertainty. The more you practice, the more comfortable and confident you become in your abilities. This increased confidence lets you tackle more difficult challenges, take risks, and handle unexpected situations with ease.

In addition to practice, thorough preparation is necessary to bolster confidence. Proper preparation involves gathering information, developing a plan, and setting realistic goals. By doing your homework and understanding the task or situation ahead of time, you can expect potential hurdles and make contingency plans. This level of preparation instills a sense of control and preparedness, leading to increased confidence.

Preparation also includes mental and emotional readiness. Visualizing success, affirming positive beliefs, and managing stress or anxiety contribute to building confidence. By mentally rehearsing scenarios and focusing on positive outcomes, you condition yourself to approach challenges with a mindset geared toward success. When faced with obstacles, you can draw on your preparations and affirmations to maintain confidence and overcome hurdles.

It is essential to embrace failure and view it as a steppingstone to growth rather than a negative reflection of your abilities. Confidence is not built only on success but on the resilience and perseverance showed when faced with setbacks. By understanding that failures are opportunities for learning and improvement, you can bounce back stronger and more confident.

The combination of practice and preparation empowers you to face challenges head-on, develop self-assurance, and build a strong foundation of confidence. Remember that confidence is not a fixed trait but a skill that can be cultivated and strengthened. By consistently engaging thorough preparation, and maintaining a positive mindset, you can continuously build and reinforce your confidence in various areas of your life.

USING POSITIVE BODY LANGUAGE AND VOCAL TECHNIQUES:

Using positive body language and vocal techniques is essential in effectively communicating and expressing oneself. These techniques can help convey confidence, credibility, and establish a positive connection with others. Here are tips for using positive body language and vocal techniques:

Maintain good posture: Stand or sit up straight, with your shoulders relaxed and your head held high. Good posture not only makes you seem more confident but also helps you project your voice effectively.

Smile: A genuine smile can instantly create a positive and welcoming atmosphere. It shows you are approachable and friendly, making others more receptive to your message.

Eye contact: Maintain eye contact with the person or audience you are speaking to. This shows attentiveness and interest in the conversation, and it helps establish trust and rapport.

Use open gestures: Avoid crossing your arms or hunching your shoulders, as these closed-off gestures can make you seem less approachable. Instead, use open and welcoming gestures, such as keeping your arms relaxed at your sides or using hand movements to emphasize your points.

Be mindful of your tone and pacing: Your voice is a powerful tool for conveying emotions and engaging others. Speak with a clear and confident tone, avoiding monotony. Vary your pitch and volume to add emphasis and interest to your words. Maintain a steady pace, neither too fast nor too slow, allowing others to follow your message easily.

Practice active listening: Show you are actively engaged in the conversation by nodding your head, using facial expressions to indicate understanding or agreement, and providing verbal cues like "yes" or "mm-hmm". This encourages the other person to continue speaking and feel valued.

Mirror body language: When appropriate, mirror the body language of the person you are speaking with. This can create a sense of rapport and connection. However, be subtle and natural in your mirroring, as being too obvious or exaggerated can come across as insincere.

Use gestures purposefully: Use gestures to enhance your message and make it more engaging. For example, point to important information, use hand movements to illustrate ideas, or open your arms wide to show inclusiveness.

Stay calm and composed: Control any nervous movements or fidgeting that may distract from your message. Take deep breaths and focus on speaking confidently.

Practice and seek feedback: Continually practice and refine your body language and vocal techniques. Record yourself speaking or seek feedback from trusted friends or mentors to identify areas for improvement. Regular practice will help you become more comfortable and polished in your communication skills.

Using positive body language and vocal techniques, you can effectively convey your message, build strong connections, and enhance your overall communication skills.

CRAFTING COMPELLING PRESENTATIONS:

IDENTIFYING YOUR PURPOSE AND DESIRED OUTCOME.

BEFORE STARTING ANY JOURNEY, it is important to clearly understand your purpose and desired outcome. This applies to both personal and professional endeavors. By identifying your purpose, you gain direction and motivation, while a desired outcome sets a specific target to work toward. Here are steps to help you identify your purpose and desired outcome:

Reflect on your values and passions: Consider what matters to you and what brings you joy. Reflect on your interests, hobbies, and the activities that make you feel fulfilled. This introspection will help you understand what aligns with your values and passions.

Set goals: Think about what you want to achieve in the short-term and long-term. Setting specific goals lets you focus your energy and efforts. These goals can be related to various parts of your life, such as career, relationships, personal development, or health.

Consider your strengths and skills: Reflect on your strengths and the skills you excel at. Identifying these attributes enables you to align your purpose with activities that use your strengths and skill sets.

Visualize your ideal outcome: Imagine a future where you have met your goals and are living in alignment with your purpose. Picture the details of this ideal outcome and how it would make you feel. Visualization helps clarify your desires and provides a clear picture of what you are working toward.

Seek inspiration: Learn from others who have achieved similar outcomes or are living a life that aligns with your purpose. Read books, listen to podcasts, or go to seminars to gain inspiration and learn from their experiences. This will also help you refine your purpose and gain insight into potential outcomes.

Focus on and make changes: Review your purpose and desired outcome and focus on them based on importance and feasibility. Make any necessary changes or refinements to ensure they align with your values and capabilities.

Create action plans: Break down your purpose and desired outcome into actionable steps. Develop a plan that outlines what actions you need to take to meet your goals and desired outcomes. Assign deadlines and track your progress to stay focused and motivated.

Remember that purpose and desired outcomes may evolve. Allow yourself to adapt and make changes as you gain new insights and experiences. Identifying your purpose and desired outcome is an ongoing journey that requires self-reflection, introspection, and a commitment to personal growth.

STRUCTURING YOUR PRESENTATION FOR MAXIMUM IMPACT.

Structuring your presentation effectively is important for maximizing its impact on your audience. Here are key tips to structure your presentation for maximum impact:

Start with a compelling opening: Capture your audience's attention right from the start with a strong opening. This can be done through a thought-provoking question, an interesting fact or statistic, a powerful quote, or a personal story that relates to the topic.

Outline the purpose and main points: Clearly state the purpose of your presentation and summarize what you will cover. This will help your audience understand the flow and structure of your presentation, making it easier for them to follow along.

Use a logical flow: Organize your presentation in a logical and sequential order. Each main point or idea should naturally transition to the next, creating a flow easy for your audience to follow. Consider using signposting phrases, such as "Next, I will discuss...", "Moving on to...", or "Now, let's explore...".

Support main points with evidence: Back up your main points with relevant and credible evidence, such as research findings, statistics, case studies, or expert quotes. This will help strengthen your arguments and make your presentation more persuasive.

Include engaging visuals: Incorporate visuals like slides, diagrams, images, or videos to complement your main points and make your presentation more visually appealing. Visuals can help convey information more effectively and keep your audience engaged throughout.

Break up content with stories or anecdotes: Humanize your presentation by including stories or anecdotes that relate to the topic. Personal experiences or real-life examples can make your content more relatable and memorable for your audience.

Use transitions effectively: Smooth transitions between different sections or points in your presentation help maintain the flow and prevent your audience from getting lost. Use transitional phrases or words, such as "Furthermore", "In addition", or "On the other hand", to indicate shifts in content.

Summarize and reinforce key points: At the end of each section or your overall presentation, summarize your main points to reinforce them in the minds of your audience. This will help them remember the key takeaways and make sure your message is effectively conveyed.

Conclude with a strong ending: End your presentation on a high note by summarizing your main points and providing a strong closing statement or CTA. Leave your audience with a clear message or a thought-provoking question that will linger in their minds.

Remember, structuring your presentation effectively is not just about delivering information but also about creating an engaging and memorable experience for your audience. By following these tips, you can structure your presentation in a way that leaves a lasting impact on your audience.

UNDERSTANDING YOUR TARGET AUDIENCE

Understanding your target audience is important for any successful business or marketing campaign. It involves gaining insight into the preferences, needs, desires, and behaviors of the group of people you aim to reach and engage with. By understanding your target audience, you can tailor your products, services, and marketing messages to effectively meet their needs, increasing the likelihood of success.

Here are key steps to help you understand your target audience better:

Define your audience: Start by identifying the specific group of people you want to target. Consider their demographics such as age, gender, location, income level, occupation, and education. Additionally, think about their psychographics, including their values, attitudes, interests, and lifestyle choices.

Conduct market research: Conduct thorough market research to gather data and insights about your target audience. This can be done through surveys, interviews, focus groups, or by analyzing existing data and trends. The research will help you understand the behavior, preferences, and buying patterns of your audience.

Create buyer personas: Develop fictional representations of your target audience called buyer personas. These personas should encompass the key features, motivations, and needs of your target audience. Give each persona a name, age, job title, and personal background to make them more relatable.

Analyze competitors: Study your competitors and see who they are targeting. Analyzing their strategies and the audience they appeal to can help identify gaps or opportunities you can tap into within your target market.

Engage with your audience: Engage with your target audience directly through social media, surveys, or feedback forms. This will not only help you gain valuable insights but also create a connection with your audience, making them feel valued and heard.

Monitor analytics: Utilize web analytics tools to track the behavior and engagement patterns of your website visitors or social media followers. This data will help you understand what content or products resonate the most with your target audience.

Stay updated: Markets and consumer preferences evolve. Stay up to date with industry trends, technological advancements, and changes in customer behavior. Being aware of these changes will help you maintain a strong understanding of your target audience and make necessary changes to your strategies.

Understanding your target audience is an ongoing process that requires continuous research and adaptation. By investing time and effort into understanding your audience's needs and desires, you can make informed decisions that effectively cater to them, ultimately leading to increased customer satisfaction and business success.

LEVERAGING STORYTELLING TECHNIQUES TO CAPTIVATE YOUR LISTENERS

Leveraging storytelling techniques is a powerful way to captivate your listeners and make your message resonate with them. Whether you're giving a presentation, pitching an idea, or trying to engage an audience, storytelling can help you connect on a deeper level. Here are techniques to consider:

Start with a compelling opening: Begin your story with an attention-grabbing hook. This could be a surprising fact, an anecdote, or a thought-provoking question. Your goal is to immediately capture your listeners' interest and make them want to hear more.

Create relatable characters: Introduce characters that your listeners can connect with. Develop their personalities, motivations, and challenges. By making your characters relatable, you evoke empathy and draw your listeners into the story.

Develop a clear narrative arc: Every story has a beginning, middle, and end. Make sure your narrative has a clear structure and progression. Establish the setting and conflict, build tension, and resolve the conflict in a satisfying way. This will keep your listeners engaged and eager to hear what happens next.

Use vivid imagery and descriptive language: Paint a vivid picture with your words. Use sensory details to bring your story to life. Engage your listeners' senses by describing how things look, sound, smell, taste, and feel. This helps create a rich and immersive experience for your audience.

Incorporate emotions: Emotions are the key to making a story impactful. Tap into your listeners' emotions by evoking empathy, joy, sadness, excitement, or surprise. Share personal experiences, anecdotes, or testimonials to make your message more relatable and resonant.

Show, don't tell: Instead of simply stating facts or information, show your listeners through storytelling. Use anecdotes, examples, and experiences to illustrate your point. This lets your audience connect with your message on a deeper level and makes it more memorable.

Use pacing and timing: Pay attention to your storytelling rhythm. Vary your pace and tone to create suspense, emphasize key moments, or add humor. Pauses can also be effective, letting your listeners reflect or expect what comes next.

Craft a memorable ending: End your story with a powerful closing that leaves a lasting impact. This could be a surprising twist, a memorable quote, or a CTA. Make sure your ending ties back to your main message and leaves your listeners thinking.

Remember, storytelling is a skill that can be honed with practice. By incorporating these techniques into your presentations, pitches, or speeches, you can captivate your listeners and make a lasting impression.

$\sim$

EFFECTIVE PRESENTATION DELIVERY:

CAPTURING ATTENTION WITH A STRONG OPENING

HERE IS AN EXAMPLE...

"Attention, ladies and gentlemen! I stand before you today to share a revelation that will challenge your beliefs, ignite your curiosity, and leave you pondering the secrets of the universe. Are you ready to embark on a journey of the mind, exploring the realms of untapped potential? Brace yourselves, for we are about to unravel the essence of human existence and reveal the hidden mysteries that lie within the depths of our subconscious minds."

ENGAGING YOUR AUDIENCE THROUGH DYNAMIC DELIVERY

Engaging your audience through dynamic delivery is an important skill for any speaker or presenter. It is not enough to simply present information; you must connect with and captivate your audience to ensure they are listening and participating in your presentation. To achieve this, you need to use strategies that create a dynamic and inter-active experience for your audience. Here are ways to engage your audience through dynamic delivery:

Use visual aids: Incorporate visually appealing slides, images, or videos that complement your presentation. Visual aids can help simplify complex ideas, grab attention, and make your content more memorable.

Tell stories: Storytelling is a powerful way to engage your audience. Share relatable anecdotes, personal experiences, or case studies that illustrate your main points. It helps create an emotional connection with your audience and makes your content more relatable and memorable.

Use humor: Humor is a great way to break the ice, grab attention, and create a positive atmosphere. Inject relevant humor throughout your presentation to keep your audience engaged and entertained.

Encourage audience participation: Make your presentation interactive by asking questions, conducting polls, or inviting volunteers to participate. Engaging your audience through participation not only creates a more dynamic experience but also helps reinforce key concepts.

Vary your delivery style: Adopt a dynamic delivery style to keep your audience engaged. Use a mixture of different tones, pacing, and body language to emphasize important points, create suspense, or infuse energy into your presentation. Avoid a monotone delivery that can bore your audience and make it difficult for them to stay engaged.

Incorporate technology: Use technology such as live polls, interactive presentations, or virtual reality to enhance audience engagement. Leveraging technology can make your presentation memorable and provide a unique and immersive experience for your audience.

Engage with eye contact: Maintain eye contact with your audience throughout your presentation. Eye contact creates a personal connection and makes your audience feel involved and acknowledged.

Encourage questions and feedback: Allocate time for questions and feedback from your audience. Encouraging audience participation and addressing their queries helps create a two-way communication flow and keeps them engaged.

Use storytelling techniques: Use narrative elements like suspense, conflict, or resolution to create an engaging flow in your presentation. Building a compelling story around your content helps your audience connect with your message on a deeper level.

Practice dynamic vocal delivery: Use voice modulation, emphasize key points, and vary your volume and pace to avoid a monotone delivery style. Captivate your audience with your speech patterns and keep them attentive throughout your presentation.

Remember, engaging your audience through dynamic delivery involves keeping their attention, stimulating their interest, and encouraging them to actively participate in the presentation. By incorporating these strategies, you can create a memorable and impactful experience that will leave a lasting impression on your audience.

USING VISUAL AIDS FOR ENHANCED COMMUNICATION

Using visual aids is a powerful way to enhance communication and create a lasting impact on your audience. Whether you are presenting at a business meeting, delivering a lecture, or simply explaining a concept to someone, incorporating visual aids can make your message more engaging, memorable, and easily understood. Here are tips on using visual aids effectively to enhance communication:

Choose the right visual aid: Depending on your topic and audience, you can choose from a variety of visual aids such as slideshows, charts, graphs, diagrams, images, videos, props, or even interactive tools. Consider what type of visual aid will best support your message and help your audience visualize and comprehend the information you are sharing.

Keep it simple: Avoid clutter and overwhelming visuals. Stick to clear, concise, and easy-to-understand content. Use a simple color scheme and font size that can be easily seen and read from a distance. Use visuals that complement your verbal message rather than distract or confuse your audience.

Visualize data and statistics: Instead of presenting raw, complex data, transform it into easily readable charts, graphs, or infographics. These visual representations can make data more digestible and relatable. Your audience will appreciate and understand numerical information better when it is visually displayed.

Use visual aids to tell a story: Humans are naturally drawn to stories. Use visual aids to tell a narrative that captures your audience's attention and helps them connect emotionally with your message. For example, you can use images, videos, or props to illustrate a real-life scenario and make your content more relatable and impactful.

Use visuals for comparisons and illustrations: When explaining complex concepts, use visuals to simplify and illustrate your ideas. Use diagrams, flowcharts, or animations to show relationships between different elements, processes, or ideas. Visuals can help your audience grasp abstract concepts or intricate details more easily.

Use humor and creativity: Adding humor or creativity to your visual aids can make your message more enjoyable and memorable. Using funny images, humorous anecdotes, or quirky illustrations can create a lighthearted atmosphere and leave a lasting impression on your audience.

Practice and rehearse: Visual aids should enhance your communication, not hinder it. Practice your presentation with the visual aids to make sure they are integrated smoothly, flow logically, and are timed appropriately. Be familiar with your visual aids so you can confidently navigate through them during your communication.

Using visual aids can significantly enhance your communication and help your audience better understand and remember your message. When used effectively, visual aids can engage your audience, simplify complex information, illustrate concepts, and create an enjoyable and memorable experience for everyone involved.

HANDLING QUESTIONS AND FEEDBACK PROFESSIONALLY

Handling questions and feedback professionally is an essential skill in any professional setting. Here are tips to effectively handle questions and feedback:

Actively listen: When someone asks a question or provides feedback, listen attentively. Give the person your full attention and avoid interrupting them. This will show you value their input and will consider their perspective.

Stay calm and composed: Even if the question or feedback is unexpected or challenging, it is important to remain composed and professional. Avoid becoming defensive or reactive. Instead, take a deep breath and respond in a calm and respectful manner.

Repeat and clarify: Before responding to a question or feedback, repeat or paraphrase what the person has said to ensure your understanding. This not only shows your active listening skills but also helps you address their concerns accurately.

Provide accurate and helpful information: When responding to a question, provide accurate and relevant information. If you don't know the answer, it is better to admit it rather than providing incorrect information. In such cases, offer to find the information or direct them to someone who can help them further.

Show appreciation: Appreciate the person for sharing their question or feedback. Express gratitude for their input and let them know that their opinion is valued. This will encourage open communication and build a positive rapport with your stakeholders.

Avoid personal attacks or defensiveness: If the feedback is critical, it is important not to take it personally. Instead, focus on the content of their feedback and address it constructively. Respond respectfully, even if you disagree, and provide a rational explanation or alternative viewpoint.

Take ownership of mistakes: If the question or feedback highlights a mistake or oversight, take responsibility for it. Apologize if necessary and assure the person that you will rectify the issue or try to prevent it from happening again.

Seek clarification if needed: If you are unsure about the intent or content of a question or feedback, seek clarification from the person. This shows you are committed to understanding their concern and providing a proper response.

Offer solutions or alternatives: When responding to feedback, consider providing possible solutions or alternatives. This proactive approach shows your commitment to resolving any issues and shows you value the person's input.

Follow up when necessary: If the question or feedback requires further action, follow up promptly. Inform the person about the steps taken to address their concern and keep them updated on any progress made.

Remember, handling questions and feedback professionally is not just about providing answers but also about fostering open communication and building trust. By using these tips, you can effectively address questions and feedback in a constructive and professional manner.

PUBLIC SPEAKING FOR BOOK READINGS AND LITERARY EVENTS:

PREPARING FOR BOOK READINGS AND SIGNINGS

PREPARING for book readings and signings is essential for authors looking to engage with their readers and promote their work. Whether you're a seasoned author or a debut novelist, these tips will help you make the most of your book events.

Choose the right location: Select a venue that aligns with your target audience and has the capacity to accommodate the expected turnout. Bookstores, libraries, community centers, and literary festivals are popular choices. Book the venue well in advance to secure your preferred date.

Promotion and marketing: Create a buzz around your event through various channels. Use social media to announce the details, create event pages, and share regular updates. Contact local newspapers, radio stations, and bloggers for coverage. Leverage your network of friends, family, and followers to spread the word. Consider creating flyers or posters to display in relevant locations.

Prepare your presentation: Plan a captivating reading that showcases the best parts of your book. Pick sections engaging, intriguing, or emotionally charged. Practice reading aloud to perfect your delivery and timing. Consider using visual aids, props, or multimedia elements, if applicable. Remember to keep your presentation concise to leave ample time for questions and interaction with your audience.

Stock up on books and merchandise: Ensure you have enough copies of your book to sell at the event. Coordinate with the venue to handle sales or consider bringing your own portable point-of-sale (POS) system. Consider bundling books with other merchandise, such as bookmarks, posters, or tote bags, to incentivize purchases and provide more options for fans.

Create a signing routine: Prepare a short and personalized message to write in each book. Practice your signature to make it legible and consistent. Consider using colorful markers or pens that stand out. Engage with readers during the signing by striking up conversations, asking questions, and showing genuine interest in their feedback or thoughts.

Build a mailing list: Set up a sign-up sheet or digital form for attendees who want to stay informed about future events or book releases. Offer an incentive, such as a free short story or exclusive content, to encourage sign-ups. Having a mailing list lets you maintain contact with your readers and tell them about future opportunities to engage with your work.

Bring support materials: Carry business cards, bookmarks, or postcards with your book cover, website, and social media handles. These materials serve as effective reminders for readers, even if they don't buy a book immediately. Make these materials visually appealing and easy to understand.

Dress appropriately and be professional: Dress in a way that reflects your writing style or the theme of your book. Consider what will make you feel confident and comfortable, while also presenting a professional image. Remember to be punctual, polite, and courteous to everyone you encounter, including event organizers, fellow authors, and attendees.

Practice author etiquette: Engage with your readers, answer their questions, and express gratitude for their support. Be open to constructive feedback and take the time to connect with each person who attends. Encourage them to leave reviews on online platforms, share their experience on social media, or recommend your book to others.

Enjoy the experience: last, remember to have fun and enjoy the opportunity to connect with readers who appreciate your work. Interact with fellow authors, learn from their experiences, and build relationships within the writing community. Make the most out of this chance to showcase your talent and share your passion for literature with others.

ENGAGING THE AUDIENCE DURING BOOK READINGS

Engaging the audience during book readings is important as it helps to create a memorable and interactive experience for both the author and the listeners. Here are ways to engage your audience and make the most out of your book reading:

Set the tone: Begin by creating a warm and friendly atmosphere. Greet your audience with a smile and build a connection by sharing a personal story or anecdote related to your book. This will help to establish a rapport with the listeners and grab their attention from the start.

Choose interesting passages: Select captivating excerpts from your book that showcase the best of your writing style, intriguing plot, or compelling characters. Look for sections that have suspense, humor, emotion, or any other elements that will captivate the audience. By choosing these passages, you can make sure you keep the audience engaged throughout the reading.

Use expressive reading: Bring your words to life by using expressive reading techniques. Vary your tone, pace, and volume to match the mood of the story or dialogue. Emphasize important phrases or sentences, add pauses for effect, and use different voices for different characters. This will make the reading more engaging and help the audience to visualize the scenes in their minds.

Encourage audience participation: Involve your audience by asking questions, seeking their opinions, or encouraging them to share their own experiences related to the themes of your book. This interactivity not only engages the audience but also creates a sense of community and connection. It also provides an opportunity for you to learn more about your readers and their perspectives.

Incorporate visuals: Provide visuals that complement your story. This could include showing relevant images, illustrations, or videos to enhance the audience's understanding and engagement. Visual aids can help bring the world of your book to life and leave a lasting impression on your audience.

Share behind-the-scenes insights: Offer insights into your writing process, the inspiration behind your book, or any interesting experiences you encountered while writing. This not only gives the audience a peek behind the curtain but also adds an extra layer of interest and excitement to the reading.

Interact with the audience after the reading: Encourage the audience to ask questions, share their thoughts, or even participate in a discussion about the book. Take the time to listen attentively, provide thoughtful responses, and engage in meaningful conversations. This will make the event more interactive and leave a lasting impression on your audience.

Provide opportunities for book signings or Q&A sessions: A book reading event is a fantastic opportunity for you to connect with your readers on a personal level. Set aside time for book signings, letting your audience have a one-on-one experience with you and potentially ask questions or have a brief chat. Engaging with your audience individually will make them feel valued and appreciated.

Remember, engaging the audience during book readings is all about creating an enjoyable and immersive experience. By implementing these strategies, you can leave a lasting impact on your audience, increase their interest in your book, and build a stronger connection as an author.

CRAFTING IMPACTFUL INTRODUCTIONS AND ACKNOWLEDGMENTS

The power of a well-crafted introduction cannot be overstated. It sets the tone for the rest of your writing and determines whether your readers will be engaged and continue reading. Crafting impactful introductions requires careful thought and consideration. In this guide, we will explore key strategies and techniques to help you grab your readers' attention from the beginning and set the stage for a compelling piece of writing.

Start With a Hook:

One of the most effective ways to engage your readers is by starting with a strong hook. This can be a thought-provoking question, a surprising fact or statistic, a compelling anecdote, or even a bold statement. The goal is to pique your readers' curiosity and make them eager to find out more.

Provide Context:

After hooking your readers, it is important to give them some context. This can include an overview of the topic, a historical background, or an explanation of why the subject is relevant and important. By doing so, you set the stage for the rest of your piece and help your readers understand the significance of what you are about to discuss.

State Your Thesis:

In an introduction, it is important to clearly state your thesis or main argument. This sets the roadmap for your writing and lets your readers know what to expect. Your thesis should be concise, specific, and debatable, giving your readers a reason to continue reading to explore your argument further.

~

ACKNOWLEDGMENTS

Acknowledgments are an opportunity for you to express gratitude and recognize those who have contributed to your work. Whether you are writing a research paper, a book, or a report, showing appreciation to individuals or organizations who have supported you is a common practice.

Identify Key Contributors:

Begin by identifying the people or organizations who have significantly contributed to your work. This may include mentors, advisors, research partners, funding agencies, or anyone else who has assisted you. Acknowledge their specific contributions and how it has made a difference in your work.

Use a Heartfelt and Genuine Tone:

When expressing your acknowledgments, use a tone that is heartfelt and genuine. Avoid generic or superficial statements. Instead, express sincere gratitude and explain the impact their support has had on your work or personal growth. This will not only make your acknowledgments more meaningful but also strengthen your relationships with those you are acknowledging.

Be Concise and Focused:

While it is important to acknowledge the contributions of others, it is equally important to keep your acknowledgments concise and focused. Avoid including unnecessary details or going off on tangents. Stick to the essential individuals and organizations that have played a significant role in your work.

Crafting impactful introductions can captivate your readers' attention and set the stage for a compelling piece of writing. By starting with a hook and providing context, you can grab your readers' attention from the beginning. Additionally, acknowledging the contributions of others through heartfelt and genuine acknowledgments can strengthen your relationships and show appreciation for their support. By following these strategies and techniques, you can make sure your introductions and acknowledgments leave a lasting impact on your readers.

LEVERAGING SOCIAL MEDIA AND DIGITAL PLATFORMS TO PROMOTE EVENTS

Today, social media and digital platforms have become powerful tools for promoting events. Leveraging these platforms can enhance event visibility, attract a wider audience, and generate buzz around your event. Here are strategies to effectively use social media and digital platforms to promote your next event:

Identify your target audience: Before diving into social media promotion, identify your target audience. Who are you trying to reach with your event? Understanding their demographics, interests, and online behaviors will help tailor your social media strategy to effectively engage with them.

Create a strong social media presence: Build a strong presence on popular social media platforms such as Facebook, Instagram, and Twitter. Develop visually appealing profiles, use consistent branding, and ensure your profile information is up to date. This will make it easier for people to find and engage with your event.

Create event-specific content: Develop content tailored specifically for your event. This could include teasers, behind-the-scenes footage, interviews with speakers or performers, or sneak peeks of what attendees can expect. Creating engaging, unique, and shareable content will generate interest in your event and encourage people to spread the word.

Use event hashtags: Create a unique hashtag for your event and encourage attendees, sponsors, and speakers to use it when posting about the event. This will help create a buzz around your event on social media and make it easier for people to find related content.

Collaborate with influencers and partners: Identify relevant influencers in your industry or community with a significant following on social media. Collaborating with them to promote your event can significantly extend your reach. Additionally, partner with other organizations or businesses with similar target audiences. Cross-promotion on their social media platforms will expose your event to a wider audience.

Engage with your audience: Social media is a two-way street, so always remember to engage with your audience. Respond to comments, questions, and inquiries promptly to create a positive impression. Encourage attendees to share their excitement about the event and engage in discussions related to it.

Use paid advertising: Consider investing in paid advertising on social media platforms to reach a wider audience. Platforms like Facebook and Instagram offer various targeting options that let you reach people likely to be interested in your event. This can be a cost-effective way to increase event visibility.

Leverage live video: Live video streaming on platforms like Facebook or Instagram can be an excellent way to promote your event. Stream interviews with speakers, behind-the-scenes preparations, or live performances. This will create a sense of excitement and urgency among viewers, encouraging them to go to the event in person.

Run giveaways and contests: Organize social media giveaways or contests where participants have to like, share, or comment on your event-related posts to enter. This will increase engagement and generate more visibility for your event.

Monitor and analyze results: Track the performance of your social media efforts by monitoring metrics such as reach, engagement, and conversions. Analyzing this data will help you understand what strategies worked best for promoting your event and let you make necessary adjustments for future events.

By leveraging social media and digital platforms effectively, you can amplify the promotion of your event and achieve greater success in attracting attendees and creating a buzz around your event.

NAVIGATING PANEL DISCUSSIONS AND CONFERENCES:

PREPARING FOR PANEL DISCUSSIONS AND CONFERENCE PRESENTATIONS

PANEL DISCUSSIONS and conference presentations offer great opportunities for professionals to share their expertise and engage with peers in their field. However, it is important to be well-prepared to make a lasting impact on the audience. Here are tips to help you prepare for panel discussions and conference presentations:

Understand the purpose and goals: Start by understanding the purpose and goals of the panel discussion or conference presentation. Familiarize yourself with the topic, theme, and goals to focus your preparation.

Research and gather information: Conduct thorough research on the topic you will discuss. Read relevant articles, books, and publications to gain in-depth knowledge. Stay updated with the latest trends and advancements in your field.

Organize your thoughts: Define the key messages you want to convey and align them with the theme of the discussion or presentation.

Create an outline or structure that will guide your presentation and ensure a logical flow of ideas.

Practice your delivery: Practice is essential to feel comfortable and confident during your panel discussion or presentation. Rehearse your speech or responses to potential questions. Pay attention to your body language, tone of voice, and timing.

Engage with the audience: Consider the interests, needs, and expectations of the audience. Aim to engage them through interactive elements such as asking open-ended questions or incorporating multimedia. Encourage participation and create opportunities for dialogue during panel discussions.

Prepare visual aids: If allowed, create visuals aids such as slides, charts, or graphs to support your presentation. Make sure they are clear, concise, and visually appealing. Limit the amount of text on each slide to prevent overwhelming the audience with information.

Anticipate questions and prepare responses: Anticipate potential questions that might arise during the panel discussion or Q&A session. Prepare concise and well-thought-out responses to ensure you deliver a confident and knowledgeable impression.

Time management: Respect the allocated time for your panel discussion or presentation. Practice timing your speech to ensure it fits within the assigned time frame. Be ready to adapt and adjust your content if necessary.

Dress professionally: Present yourself in a way that is appropriate for the event. Dress professionally and consider the overall image you want to project to the audience.

Network and build connections: Take advantage of panel discussions and conference presentations to network and build connections within your field. Engage with the audience and fellow panelists or presenters, exchange contact information, and follow-up after the event.

Repeat and refine: After the panel discussion or conference presentation, evaluate your performance and identify areas for improvement.

Seek feedback from colleagues, attendees, or mentors to refine your skills and enhance future presentations.

By following these tips and preparing thoroughly, you will be well-equipped to deliver a successful panel discussion or conference presentation that leaves a lasting impact on the audience.

COLLABORATING WITH FELLOW AUTHORS AND PANELISTS

Collaborating with fellow authors and panelists can be an enriching and rewarding experience. It lets you harness the collective knowledge and creativity of a group, leading to a more comprehensive and engaging outcome. Here are tips to make collaboration with fellow authors and panelists a success:

Establish clear communication: Communication is essential when working with others. Make sure everyone understands the goals, expectations, and timeline for the collaboration. Regularly check in with your team to discuss progress, address any issues, and share updates.

Divide tasks and responsibilities: Divide the workload among team members based on their strengths and interests. This makes sure everyone has a sense of ownership and contributes meaningfully to the collaboration. Create a shared document or task management tool to keep track of assigned tasks and deadlines.

Respect diverse perspectives: Collaboration is an opportunity to benefit from different perspectives and approaches. Embrace the diversity of ideas and opinions, actively listen to your team members, and encourage open and respectful discussions. This will result in a richer end product that incorporates various viewpoints.

Foster a supportive and inclusive environment: Create an atmosphere where everyone feels comfortable sharing their ideas and opinions. Encourage constructive feedback and make sure everyone's contributions are valued and acknowledged. Celebrate the achievements and milestones reached as a team.

Set up regular meetings and brainstorming sessions: Schedule regular meetings with your fellow authors and panelists to discuss progress, exchange ideas, and brainstorm creative solutions. These sessions can foster collaboration and inspire new concepts and perspectives.

Be open to compromise: Collaboration involves finding common ground and making compromises. Be willing to adapt your ideas and solutions to align with those of your team members. Collaboration is about finding the best outcome for the collective, not just individual aspirations.

Use technology and collaboration tools: Take advantage of various digital tools that help with collaborative work. Platforms like Google Docs, Trello, Slack, or Zoom can streamline communication, document sharing, and project management, making collaboration more efficient and organized.

Celebrate successes and learn from challenges: Celebrate the achievements and milestones reached as a team. Recognize and appreciate the efforts and contributions of your fellow authors and panelists. Similarly, learn from challenges and setbacks, using them as opportunities for growth and improvement.

Remember, collaborating with fellow authors and panelists is an ongoing process, and effective communication and teamwork are key. By embracing collaboration, you can harness the collective power of a group and create something remarkable together.

MODERATING AND PARTICIPATING EFFECTIVELY IN PANEL DISCUSSIONS

Moderating and participating effectively in panel discussions requires careful preparation and thoughtful execution. Here are tips to help you excel in this role:

As a Moderator:

Familiarize yourself with the topic: Study the topic thoroughly to understand the nuances and potential viewpoints. This will help you guide the discussion effectively.

Coordinate with panelists beforehand: Contact each panelist before the discussion to brief them on the format, time limits, and overall goals. Make sure they understand their roles and specific questions or topics they need to address.

Tailor questions to each panelist: Craft questions that allow each panelist to showcase their knowledge and contribute unique perspectives. Avoid generic or closed-ended questions and instead focus on stimulating thoughtful discussions.

Manage time effectively: Be mindful of the given time for the panel discussion. Start and end on time to maintain the schedule. Politely intervene if any panelist goes off-topic or exceeds the time limit, ensuring fairness to all participants.

Encourage audience interaction: Allocate time for audience questions or comments. Actively engage with the audience, moderating their queries or sharing relevant anecdotes. This involvement helps create an inclusive and interactive atmosphere.

As a Panelist:

Research the topic: Thoroughly prepare by understanding the intricacies and trends related to the area. Back your opinions with facts, data, or personal experience to strengthen your arguments.

Listen actively: Pay attention to fellow panelists' remarks to build on their ideas rather than only focusing on your own perspective. Listening demonstrates respect and helps foster a collaborative atmosphere.

Present concise points: As a panelist, share your insights and opinions concisely and clearly. Avoid long monologues and instead strive for succinct and coherent contributions that add value to the discussion.

Engage with fellow panelists: Address the other panelists by their names and refer to their points to establish a connection. Build on their ideas or politely question their viewpoints, encouraging healthy debates and meaningful exchanges.

Embrace diversity of thought: Be open to different perspectives even if you disagree. Respectfully challenge ideas or provide alternative viewpoints based on your knowledge or experiences. Remember, panel discussions thrive on diverse opinions and respectful disagreement.

By following these guidelines, both moderators and panelists can ensure an informative, engaging, and fruitful panel discussion that leaves a lasting impact on participants and audience members.

NETWORKING STRATEGIES FOR AUTHORS IN CONFERENCE SETTINGS

Plan ahead and research the conference: Before attending a conference, do some research on the speakers, attendees, and the agenda. Identify the sessions, workshops, or networking events where you can connect with other authors, literary agents, publishers, or industry professionals. This will help you make the most of your time and focus your networking efforts.

Be prepared with promotional materials: Bring business cards, brochures, and any other promotional materials that showcase your work. Make sure they are visually appealing and include your contact information, social media handles, and website link. These materials will help you leave a lasting impression and make it easy for others to contact you later.

Go to relevant sessions and engage in discussions: Participate actively in the conference sessions and ask thoughtful questions during the Q&A sessions. Engaging in discussions will not only help you prove yourself to be an informed author but also provide opportunities to connect with other like-minded individuals. Exchange contact information with anyone you meaningfully converse with.

Use social media: Use social media platforms like Twitter, LinkedIn, or Facebook to connect with conference attendees before, during, and after the event. Follow the conference hashtag and interact with posts and discussions related to the conference. Engage with other authors, industry professionals, and speakers by sharing their content or responding to their posts. This will help you establish a digital presence and create networking opportunities even if you couldn't meet someone in person during the conference.

Go to networking events and socialize: Take advantage of any networking events organized as part of the conference, such as cocktail receptions, book signings, or author meetups. Mingle with fellow authors and strike up conversations by sharing your interests, experiences, and challenges. Additionally, be attentive and curious about others' work; this will build rapport and make your interactions more meaningful. Don't forget to exchange business cards or connect on social media after you've met someone interesting.

Follow up after the conference: Once the conference is over, don't miss the opportunity to follow up with people you met. Send personalized emails to continue the conversation, express your gratitude for the interaction, or explore potential collaborations. Keep in touch regularly by sharing updates on your writing progress, new projects, or relevant industry news.

Remember, networking is not just about promoting your work but also about building genuine relationships and learning from others. Approach it with a mindset of mutual support and collaboration, and you'll build a strong network within the author community.

VIRTUAL SPEAKING ENGAGEMENTS:

ADAPTING TO VIRTUAL SPEAKING ENVIRONMENTS

ADAPTING to virtual speaking environments has become increasingly important as technology continues to advance and communication platforms like Zoom, Microsoft Teams, and Google Meet become more common. Here are tips and strategies for adapting to virtual speaking environments:

Familiarize yourself with the platform: Take the time to learn about the features and settings offered by the virtual speaking platform you are using. Practice using the platform before your actual speaking engagement to ensure a smooth and error-free experience. Familiarity with the platform will help you feel more confident and comfortable during your presentation.

Test your equipment: Ensure that your microphone, webcam, and internet connection are all working properly before your speaking engagement. Test the audio and video quality to make sure that your audience can hear and see you clearly. Having reliable equipment is essential for effective virtual speaking.

Create a suitable environment: Choose a quiet and well-lit room for your virtual speaking session. Remove any distractions and make sure the background is professional and not cluttered. Consider using a virtual background or a physical backdrop relevant to your topic.

Engage with your audience: Virtual speaking can feel impersonal, so actively engage with your audience to maintain their attention and involvement. Encourage audience participation through polls, Q&A sessions, or chat discussions. Use eye contact by looking into the camera rather than at your screen to create a more engaging experience.

Take advantage of visual aids: Utilize visual aids such as slides, videos, or images to enhance your presentation. Make sure the visual aids are clear and easily viewable, as the audience may view them on smaller screens. Use bullet points and concise information to make your message easily digestible.

Be mindful of your body language: Although virtual speaking eliminates the need for physical movement, your body language still plays a significant role in conveying your message effectively. Sit up straight, maintain good posture, and use hand gestures to emphasize important points. Smile and use facial expressions to convey enthusiasm and build rapport with your audience.

Practice, practice, practice: like with in-person speaking engagements, practice is key to delivering a successful virtual presentation. Rehearse your speech, timing, and transitions to ensure a smooth delivery. Consider recording yourself and reviewing the playback to identify areas for improvement.

Adapting to virtual speaking environments requires a combination of technical know-how, preparation, and engagement. By following these tips and strategies, you can deliver impactful and engaging presentations in virtual settings.

UTILIZING DIGITAL TOOLS FOR ENGAGING PRESENTATIONS

Today, using digital tools for engaging presentations can significantly enhance communication and capture the attention of your audience. Here are effective ways to leverage digital tools in your presentations:

Visuals and Multimedia: Incorporate visuals, such as images, videos, and infographics, into your presentation to make it more visually appealing and dynamic. Tools like PowerPoint, Prezi, and Canva offer various templates and features to help you create engaging visual content.

Interactive Elements: Engage your audience by adding interactive elements to your presentation. Tools like Mentimeter, Poll Everywhere, and Slido let you include live polls, quizzes, and audience feedback to encourage participation and make your presentation more interactive.

Augmented and Virtual Reality: Take your presentation to the next level by incorporating augmented reality (AR) or virtual reality (VR) elements. These emerging technologies can provide an immersive and interactive experience for your audience. Platforms like Aurasma, Google VR, or Unity can help you create AR or VR content.

Storytelling: Digital storytelling tools such as Adobe Spark and Microsoft Sway enable you to present your content in a compelling and narrative way. Incorporate multimedia elements and create a storyline that captivates your audience's attention throughout the presentation.

Collaboration and Sharing: Use collaborative tools like Google Slides, Microsoft Teams, or Zoom to involve your audience in the presentation process. These platforms allow real-time collaboration, shared editing, and interactive features that enable your audience to actively participate and contribute to the presentation.

Data Visualization: Present complex data or statistics in an easily understandable format using digital tools like Tableau, Microsoft Excel charts, or Google Data Studio. These tools can help you create visually appealing and interactive data visualizations, making it easier for your audience to grasp the information.

Remember, when using digital tools in your presentation, it's important to keep your audience's needs and preferences in mind. Avoid overwhelming them with too many effects or distractions. Use digital tools selectively and purposefully, making sure they enhance your message rather than overpower it.

MASTERING WEBCAM PRESENCE AND VIRTUAL BODY LANGUAGE

Mastering webcam presence and virtual body language has become increasingly important in today's digital world, where remote communication and virtual meetings have become the norm. Effectively conveying your message and establish a professional presence through a webcam requires a conscious effort to understand and adapt to the nuances of virtual body language. Here are tips to help you enhance your webcam presence:

Dress appropriately: like in a physical meeting, it's essential to dress professionally during virtual meetings. Choose clothing appropriate for the occasion and reflects your professionalism. Dressing well not only establishes your credibility but also helps maintain focus during the meeting.

Maintain good posture: Sit up straight and maintain an upright posture while interacting through the webcam. Slouching or leaning back can give off a laid-back or uninterested impression. Good posture exudes confidence and engagement, making you seem more attentive and present.

Establish eye contact: Look directly into the webcam to create the illusion of eye contact with the participants. Avoid constantly looking at yourself on-screen or other distractions. By maintaining eye contact through the webcam, you seem more engaged and attentive to the conversation.

Gesture naturally: Use hand gestures to enhance your communication, just as you would in face-to-face conversations. However, be mindful of keeping your gestures within the frame of the camera and avoid excessive movements that may distract or create noise.

Mind your facial expressions: Since participants on the other side of the webcam cannot see your full body, facial expressions play a pivotal role in conveying your emotions. Be mindful of your facial expressions and ensure they align with your intended message. Smiling, nodding, and maintaining an open and friendly expression can help create a positive and approachable impression.

Pay attention to audio and vocal tone: Speak and maintain a proper volume to ensure your voice is heard by everyone in the meeting. Be mindful of your vocal tone, as it can convey your attitude and emotions. Speak in a confident and pleasant manner to establish a positive presence.

Reduce distractions: As much as possible, eliminate background distractions to maintain focus. Ensure your surroundings are well-lit, and the background is neat and professional. Close unnecessary applications on your computer and mute your mobile phone notifications to avoid interruptions during the meeting.

Engage actively: Demonstrate active participation in the meeting by listening attentively, taking notes, and asking relevant questions. Show genuine interest and engagement in the discussion to prove yourself to be an active and valuable participant.

Practice and seek feedback: Regularly practice virtual communication skills, record yourself, and review your performance. Solicit feedback from colleagues or trusted individuals to identify areas for improvement and refine your webcam presence.

To master webcam presence and virtual body language, it's important to be aware of how your actions translate through the webcam. With time, practice, and continuous refinement, you can effectively communicate and establish a professional presence in the virtual realm.

LEVERAGING SOCIAL MEDIA AND ONLINE PLATFORMS TO REACH WIDER AUDIENCES

Social media and online platforms have become powerful tools for businesses to reach wider audiences. With billions of people using platforms such as Facebook, Instagram, Twitter, and LinkedIn, leveraging these platforms effectively can significantly increase brand visibility, engagement, and customer acquisition.

To make the most of social media and online platforms, businesses should follow strategies:

Identify the target audience: Before creating social media and online campaigns, it's important to identify the target audience. This lets businesses create content and messaging that resonates with their intended demographic.

Develop a content strategy: A well-defined content strategy ensures a consistent and engaging presence on social media. It includes identifying the content (text, images, videos, etc.), frequency of posting, and key messaging guidelines.

Produce high-quality content: The quality of content plays an important role in attracting and retaining audiences. Content should be informative, entertaining, and visually appealing. Infographics, videos, and user-generated content often perform well on social media.

Engage with the audience: Social media is not just about sharing content; it's also about building relationships with the audience. Businesses should actively engage with followers by responding to comments, asking questions, and starting conversations. This helps foster a sense of community and loyalty.

Use paid advertising: Most social media platforms provide advertising options that let businesses reach a wider audience. Paid advertising can be highly targeted, ensuring content is seen by the right people at the right time. Continuously monitor and analyze ad performance to make data-driven changes.

Collaborate with influencers: Influencer marketing has become increasingly popular as it helps businesses tap into an influencer's large following. Collaborating with influencers relevant to the brand results in increased brand visibility and credibility.

Analyze and optimize: To maximize the impact of social media and online platforms, businesses should regularly analyze performance metrics such as engagement rates, reach, and conversions. This data provides insights into what works and what needs improvement, allowing for effective optimization strategies.

By leveraging social media and online platforms, businesses can extend their reach and connect with a wider audience. With the right strategies in place, these platforms present a significant opportunity to generate brand awareness, drive customer engagement, and ultimately, increase sales.

∼

DEALING WITH UNEXPECTED CHALLENGES AND TECHNICAL ISSUES:

OVERCOMING UNEXPECTED EVENTS OR SETBACKS

LIFE IS full of unexpected events and setbacks that can throw us off track. Whether it's a sudden illness, a job loss, a breakup, or a natural disaster, these unexpected events can leave us feeling overwhelmed and uncertain about the future. However, it is essential to remember that setbacks are a natural part of life, and with the right mindset and approach, we can overcome them.

Here are strategies for overcoming unexpected events or setbacks:

Accept your emotions: It's normal to feel shocked, disappointed, or upset when faced with unexpected events. Instead of suppressing your emotions, allow yourself to acknowledge and experience them. This will help you process your feelings and move toward acceptance.

Assess the situation: Take a step back and objectively evaluate the situation. What are the facts? What are the potential impacts? This will help you gain clarity and develop a plan of action.

Adaptability and flexibility: One key to overcoming unexpected events is being adaptable and flexible. Things may not go as planned, but being open to new possibilities and adjusting your goals can help you navigate through challenging circumstances.

Seek support: Don't be afraid to contact family, friends, or professionals for support. Share your experience and seek advice from those who have faced similar setbacks. Sometimes, a fresh perspective or a listening ear can make all the difference in finding a way forward.

Focus on the controllables: In any situation, there are factors beyond our control. Rather than dwelling on what you can't change, shift your focus to what you can control. This may include your attitude, actions, and the steps you can take toward recovery.

Learn from the experience: Every setback comes with valuable lessons. Reflect on the situation and identify what you can learn from it. This will not only help you grow as an individual but also empower you to better handle future challenges.

Take small, achievable steps: Break down your recovery process into small, manageable steps. By setting realistic goals and acting, no matter how small, you will gradually regain control over your life.

Practice self-care: During difficult times, it is important to focus on self-care. Ensure you are taking care of your physical, emotional, and mental well-being. Engage in activities that bring you joy, practice mindfulness, eat well, exercise, and get enough rest.

Maintain a positive mindset: It's easy to get stuck in negative thoughts during setbacks. However, cultivating a positive mindset can help shift your perspective and let you maintain hope and optimism. Surround yourself with positive influences, practice gratitude, and visualize a successful outcome.

Embrace the journey: Remember that setbacks are a part of the journey toward personal growth and success. Embrace the challenges as opportunities for learning and development. Trust in your ability to overcome obstacles and remain resilient in the face of adversity.

Unexpected events and setbacks can be challenging, but they can also provide an opportunity for personal growth and development. By accepting your emotions, seeking support, staying adaptable, and focusing on what you can control, you can overcome any setback and emerge stronger and wiser on the other side.

ADDRESSING TECHNICAL ISSUES PROFESSIONALLY

When addressing technical issues professionally, it is important to approach the situation with a calm and logical mindset. Here are steps to take to effectively address technical issues:

Gather all relevant information: Before contacting a technician or support team, make sure you have all the details about the issue. This includes error messages, screenshots, or any other information that can help the technician understand the problem.

Clearly describe the issue: When communicating with a technician, provide a clear and concise description of the problem. Avoid technical jargon and use layman's terms to make sure the issue is easily understood. Include any relevant steps or actions that led to the problem.

Patience and respect: remember that the technician you are dealing with is there to help you. Maintain a respectful and patient demeanor throughout the interaction. Avoid becoming confrontational or accusatory as it can hinder the troubleshooting process.

Follow instructions: Technicians may provide troubleshooting steps or ask questions to better understand the issue. Follow these instructions and give any necessary information to the best of your ability. Be open and responsive to their requests for clarification or further help.

Document the process: Keep track of the troubleshooting steps taken, any changes made to settings, and any other relevant information. This will be helpful if the same issue occurs or if you need to escalate the problem.

Test proposed solutions: If the technician suggests a solution, take the time to test it. Provide feedback on whether it worked or not, and if any additional issues arise from the proposed solution. This will help the technician further refine their approach.

Follow up and show appreciation: Once the issue has been resolved, follow up with the technician or support team to express your gratitude for their help. This shows professionalism and helps have a positive working relationship.

By adhering to these guidelines, you can effectively address technical issues in a professional and efficient manner, making sure your concerns are properly resolved.

THE POWER OF IMPROVISATION AND FLEXIBILITY

In today's fast-paced and ever-changing world, the ability to think on your feet and adapt to unexpected situations has become an important skill. Improvisation and flexibility are not just important for comedians and musicians; they are important for success in all areas of life.

One of the greatest benefits of improvisation is its ability to unlock creative thinking. When forced to come up with solutions on the spot, we tap into a different part of our brain. We become more open to new ideas and can think outside the box. This can lead to innovative and unexpected solutions to problems that seemed unsolvable at first.

Flexibility lets us adapt to changing circumstances. The ability to adjust our plans and goals when faced with unexpected challenges is what separates those who succeed from those who struggle. People who are rigid and resistant to change often find themselves left behind, while those who embrace flexibility can pivot and find new opportunities.

Improvisation and flexibility also go hand in hand with resilience. When we encounter setbacks or failures, the ability to adapt and bounce back is important. Thinking on our feet and coming up with alternative strategies helps us navigate through difficult times and come out stronger on the other side.

Improvisation and flexibility can enhance our relationships with others. Adapting to different personalities and communication styles lets us connect more effectively with others. It helps us break down barriers and find common ground, leading to better collaboration and understanding.

In a professional setting, the power of improvisation and flexibility can be especially valuable. As industries evolve and technology advances, job roles and requirements often change rapidly. Those who can quickly adapt to new technologies and learn new skills thrive in the modern workplace.

Ultimately, the power of improvisation and flexibility lies in their ability to help us navigate the unpredictable nature of life. They equip us with the tools to face challenges head-on, embrace change, and find creative solutions to problems. By cultivating these skills, we become more resilient, adaptable, and successful in all parts of our lives.

LEARNING FROM CHALLENGING EXPERIENCES TO IMPROVE FUTURE PRESENTATIONS

When giving presentations, challenging experiences can often provide valuable opportunities for growth and improvement. Instead of shying away from these difficult moments, it is important to embrace them as learning opportunities to enhance your future presentations. Here are strategies for leveraging challenging experiences to improve your future presentations:

Reflect on the experience: Take the time to reflect on the challenging presentation experience and identify areas that didn't go as planned or areas that could have been improved. Consider what factors contributed to the difficulties, such as lack of preparation, technical issues, or nervousness. This reflection will help you pinpoint specific areas to work on.

Seek feedback: Ask for feedback from trusted colleagues, friends, or mentors present during the presentation. They can provide valuable insights about your strengths and areas for improvement. Be open to constructive criticism and use their feedback as a guide for your future presentations.

Identify key takeaways: Identify the key lessons you have learned from the challenging experience. Perhaps you realized the importance of thorough preparation or the need to engage your audience more effectively. Write down these takeaways to serve as reminders for your future presentations.

Practice, practice, practice: Use the challenging experience as motivation to improve your presentation skills. Regularly practice delivering your presentation, paying special attention to the areas of weakness identified during your reflection. The more you practice, the more confident and polished you will become.

Go to workshops or seek training: Look for workshops, training sessions, or public speaking courses that can help you develop the specific skills you need to improve your presentations. These resources can give you valuable tips, techniques, and guidance to enhance your future presentations.

Embrace experimentation: Use the challenging experience as an opportunity to explore new presentation styles, techniques, or tools. Trying out different approaches can help you discover what works best for you and your audience. Don't be afraid to step out of your comfort zone and try new things.

Learn from successful presenters: Study successful presenters and note their techniques, storytelling abilities, and engagement strategies. Watch TED talks or go to conferences to learn from expert speakers. Observing and learning from others can provide valuable insights to enhance your own presentations.

Remember, challenging experiences are not meant to discourage or discourage you – they are opportunities to learn, grow, and improve. Embrace these experiences, reflect on them, and use them as stepping-stones for future success in your presentations. With persistence and dedication to growth, you will become a more confident and effective presenter.

Section Conclusion:

Mastering the art of public speaking and presentations as an author can significantly boost your writing career, letting you connect with readers, promote your books, and establish a strong presence in the literary world. By conquering the fear of public speaking, crafting compelling presentations, and embracing new digital platforms, authors can confidently showcase their work and engage their audience on various platforms. With practice and dedication, authors can transform from great writers into exceptional communicators, captivating audiences and leaving a lasting impact with each presentation.

SECTION THIRTEEN KEY TAKEAWAYS AND ACTION ITEMS

1. **Importance of Public Speaking for Authors:** Enhances reach, impact, and credibility; connects personally with readers; promotes work effectively.
2. **Addressing Fears and Anxiety:** Recognize and explore the source of fears, seek professional help, challenge negative thoughts, and practice relaxation techniques.
3. **Building Confidence Through Practice:** Regular practice and preparation help in honing presentation skills and building confidence.
4. **Using Positive Body Language and Vocal Techniques:** Maintain good posture, smile, use eye contact, and engage in active listening.
5. **Crafting Compelling Presentations:** Identify purpose, structure presentation logically, use engaging visuals, and summarize key points.
6. **Understanding Your Target Audience:** Tailor presentations to audience's interests and preferences.

7. **Leveraging Storytelling Techniques:** Create a narrative arc, use descriptive language, and incorporate emotions.

8. **Effective Presentation Delivery:** Capture attention with a strong opening and engage the audience through dynamic delivery.

9. **Using Visual Aids Effectively:** Enhance communication with clear, concise, and visually appealing aids.

10. **Handling Questions and Feedback Professionally:** Actively listen, stay calm, clarify queries, and provide helpful information.

11. **Preparing for Book Readings and Literary Events:** Choose appropriate venues, promote events, and prepare engaging presentations.

12. **Engaging the Audience During Book Readings:** Choose interesting passages and use expressive reading.

13. **Crafting Impactful Introductions and Acknowledgments:** Start with a hook and provide context; show appreciation in acknowledgments.

14. **Leveraging Social Media for Event Promotion:** Utilize social media to create buzz and engage with the audience.

15. **Navigating Panel Discussions and Conferences:** Prepare thoroughly, engage with the audience, and manage time effectively.

16. **Networking Strategies at Conferences:** Research events, bring promotional materials, and follow up post-conference.

17. **Adapting to Virtual Speaking Environments:** Test equipment, create a suitable environment, and practice delivery.

18. **Using Digital Tools for Engaging Presentations:** Incorporate visuals, interactive elements, and storytelling techniques.

19. **Mastering Webcam Presence and Virtual Body Language:** Dress appropriately, maintain eye contact, and gesture naturally.

20. **Overcoming Unexpected Challenges:** Embrace setbacks as learning opportunities and adapt strategies for future presentations.

. . .

Action Items:

1. **Practice Public Speaking:** Regularly practice and seek opportunities to speak publicly.
2. **Seek Feedback and Coaching:** Get feedback on speaking skills and consider professional coaching.
3. **Research and Prepare Content:** Thoroughly research and prepare content for presentations.
4. **Engage in Workshops:** Participate in workshops for public speaking and presentation skills.
5. **Use Technology Effectively:** Familiarize with and use digital tools for presentations.
6. **Develop a Strong Online Presence:** Use social media and online platforms to promote work and engage with audiences.
7. **Participate in Literary Events:** Regularly attend and participate in book readings, signings, and literary festivals.
8. **Network Effectively:** Build and maintain professional networks in the literary community.
9. **Handle Technical Issues:** Prepare for and adeptly manage technical issues during virtual events.
10. **Reflect on Experiences:** Regularly reflect on speaking experiences to identify areas for improvement.

In our next Section...

In our next section, we will focus on advanced strategies for maximizing your book's reach post-launch and maintaining momentum in the long term. We'll dig into innovative marketing techniques and continuous engagement tactics that can help keep your book in the spotlight. This includes exploring the potential of digital marketing campaigns, leveraging email marketing for sustained reader engagement, and using analytics to refine your promotional strategies. We will also discuss how to maintain an active and engaging presence on social media platforms, making sure your author's brand remains relevant and appealing to your audience.

Additionally, this upcoming section will guide authors on expanding their reach beyond their current audience. We'll explore opportunities in different markets, including international audiences, and discuss strategies for adapting your book and promotional content to resonate with diverse cultural contexts. Emphasis will be placed on building partnerships with other authors, industry professionals, and influencers to create new promotional avenues and collaborative projects. This section is designed to equip authors with the tools and insights needed to sustain their book's success, grow their reader base, and establish a lasting impact in the literary world.

SECTION FOURTEEN: PUBLIC RELATIONS AND MEDIA EXPOSURE

GAINING MEDIA EXPOSURE AS AN INDEPENDENT AUTHOR:

GAINING media exposure as an independent author can be a challenging task, but it is not impossible. With the right strategies and perseverance, you can effectively promote yourself and your work to reach a wider audience. Here are tips to help you gain media exposure as an independent author:

Create a professional online presence: Begin by establishing a professional website and blog dedicated to your writing. Make sure your website showcases your author bio, book summaries, sample chapters, and links to buy your work. Regularly update your blog with engaging content related to your writing process, author experiences, and industry insights.

Engage with social media: Utilize social media platforms like Twitter, Instagram, Facebook, and LinkedIn to connect with your readers, fellow authors, and media professionals. Share sneak peeks of your work, writing progress updates, book recommendations, and behind-the-scenes content. Engaging with your audience and building a strong online community will draw attention and generate interest in your books.

Network with other authors: Collaborate with other authors in your genre or niche to cross-promote each other's work. Consider participating in author panels, podcasts, or interviews to expand your network and increase exposure.

Leverage book reviews: Seek respected book review platforms, such as literary blogs, online communities, or booktubers, and offer them complimentary copies of your work in exchange for honest reviews. Positive reviews can encourage readers to buy your books and attract media attention.

Write guest posts or articles: Pitch your writing to relevant publications or online magazines to secure guest blogging opportunities. Offer to write articles or opinion pieces on topics related to your writing genre, self-publishing, or the writing process. This will position you as an expert in your field and expose your writing to new audiences.

Contact local media outlets: Reach out to local newspapers, radio stations, or TV channels to pitch yourself as a local author with an interesting story. Provide them with a press release that highlights your accomplishments, unique writing style, and the themes in your book. If you can offer a captivating angle or a connection to a local event or issue, it will increase your chances of being featured.

Use book promotions and giveaways: Running limited-time promotions or giveaways can attract attention and generate buzz about your books. Use social media, email newsletters, and book promotion websites to promote these offers and encourage readers to spread the word to increase visibility.

Participate in literary events: Attend book fairs, writer conferences, and local literary events to connect with potential readers, media representatives, and industry professionals. Seek opportunities to speak on panels, conduct workshops, or host book signings to increase your visibility and prove yourself to be an author worth paying attention to.

Remember, gaining media exposure takes time and effort, so be patient and consistent in your promotional activities. By leveraging multiple channels and staying connected with your audience, you can increase your visibility as an independent author and boost your chances of success in the competitive publishing world.

CRAFTING PRESS RELEASES AND MEDIA PITCHES:

CRAFTING press releases and media pitches is an essential skill for any organization or individual seeking to generate media coverage and spread their message effectively. These documents serve to capture journalists' attention and interest in covering a story or topic. Here is a step-by-step guide on how to create compelling press releases and media pitches:

Understand your audience: Before starting, identify the journalists and media outlets relevant to your subject matter. Research their past work and preferred writing styles to better tailor your press release or pitch to their interests. This will increase the likelihood of grabbing their attention.

Write a catchy headline: Your headline should be attention-grabbing, concise, and reflect the most newsworthy part of your story. It should encourage the journalist to read further.

Craft a compelling opening paragraph: The first paragraph of your press release or media pitch should summarize the most important information in a clear and engaging manner. Journalists often receive many pitches, so it's important to make a strong first impression to capture their interest.

Provide all relevant details: In the subsequent paragraphs, provide more context, facts, and quotes to support the overall story. Include relevant statistics, research, or case studies to add credibility and give depth to your pitch.

Use concise language: Keep your press release or pitch concise and to the point. Avoid jargon or technical terms that make it difficult to understand. Use clear and straightforward language that any reader can comprehend.

Highlight news value: Emphasize the uniqueness, relevance, or timeliness of the story you are pitching. Journalists are more likely to cover a story if they perceive it as newsworthy.

Include multimedia elements: If applicable, include images, videos, or infographics that can enhance the story. Providing visuals to go along with your pitch can make it more appealing to journalists and increase the chances of media coverage.

Make it easy to follow up: Include your contact information and availability for follow-up interviews or more inquiries. Responding promptly to journalists' queries will foster strong relationships and increase the chances they will engage with your story.

Personalize your pitches: Take the time to personalize your media pitches to individual journalists and their specific interests. Referencing their work and showing a genuine understanding of their beat can make your pitch more compelling and show that you've done your research.

Proofread and edit: Before sending out your press release or media pitch, proofread it for any grammatical errors or typos. Ask a colleague or supervisor to review it as well to ensure accuracy and clarity.

Remember, journalists receive countless pitches, so stand out. Crafting a well-written, tailored, and engaging press release or media pitch is critical to capturing the attention of journalists and maximizing your chances of media coverage for your story or organization.

∿

MASTERING BOOK LAUNCHES AND AUTHOR EVENTS:

LAUNCHING a book and organizing author events is an important step in the success of any author or their work. A well-executed book launch and author event can generate buzz, build an audience, and boost book sales. However, planning and executing these events requires careful attention to detail and effective strategies. This guide aims to provide authors with a step-by-step approach to mastering book launches and author events, ensuring they create a memorable and impactful experience.

∼

PREPARING FOR THE LAUNCH:

SETTING YOUR GOALS:

- Assess your goals and determine what you hope to achieve with your book launch and author event.
- Establish clear and realistic goals that align with your target audience and book's theme.

CREATING A TIMELINE:

- Develop a timeline that outlines key activities and deadlines leading to the launch and author event.
- Identify tasks such as securing a venue, designing promotional materials, and organizing event logistics.

BUDGETING:

- Estimate your expenses and create a budget that covers all parts of the book launch and author event.

- Allocate funds for marketing, venue rental, catering, and other necessary expenses.

BUILDING BUZZ AND CREATING A MARKETING PLAN:

IDENTIFYING YOUR TARGET AUDIENCE:

- Conduct market research to understand your ideal readers and target demographic.
- Tailor your marketing efforts to reach and engage this specific audience.

DEVELOPING A PROMOTIONAL STRATEGY:

- Utilize various marketing channels, such as social media, email marketing, and online advertising, to promote your book launch and author event.
- Craft compelling content that highlights the unique features of your book and event.

COLLABORATING WITH INFLUENCERS AND PARTNERS:

- Identify potential influencers, bloggers, book reviewers, or organizations that can help generate buzz and reach a broader audience.
- Build partnerships and leverage their networks to amplify promotion efforts.

PLANNING THE BOOK LAUNCH:

SELECTING THE RIGHT VENUE:

- Research and select a suitable location that aligns with the theme and target audience of your book.
- Consider factors such as capacity, accessibility, and atmosphere.

ORGANIZING EVENT LOGISTICS:

- Secure necessary permits, licenses, and insurance.
- Arrange seating, sound systems, decorations, and any other specific requirements for the event.

INVITING GUESTS AND INFLUENCERS:

- Compile a guest list of industry professionals, potential readers, and influential figures.
- Personalize invitations and follow up to ensure a good turnout.

CREATING A MEMORABLE AUTHOR EVENT:

CRAFTING A COMPELLING PRESENTATION:

- Structure your talk or presentation in a way that engages and captivates the audience.
- Incorporate elements like storytelling, interactive activities, or multimedia to enhance the presentation.

ENCOURAGING AUDIENCE PARTICIPATION:

- Design opportunities for attendees to ask questions, share their experiences, or interact with you as the author.
- Create a welcoming and inclusive space for different voices and perspectives.

OFFERING AUTHOR SIGNINGS AND MERCHANDISING:

- Plan a book signing session where attendees can meet you and get a signed copy of your book.

- Use merchandising opportunities to sell more merchandise related to your book or author brand.

MAXIMIZING POST-EVENT OPPORTUNITIES:

COLLECTING ATTENDEE FEEDBACK:

- Implement feedback forms or surveys to gather insights and opinions from attendees.
- Use this feedback to improve future book launches and author events.

LEVERAGING MEDIA AND PRESS COVERAGE:

- Identify local media outlets, bloggers, or podcasters to generate post-event coverage.
- Prepare press releases, interviews, or articles to maintain momentum and extend the reach of your book launch.

MAINTAINING RELATIONSHIPS WITH ATTENDEES:

- Encourage attendees to join your mailing list or follow you on social media to stay connected.

- Nurture these relationships by providing exclusive content, updates, or future event announcements.

Section Conclusion:

Mastering book launches and author events involves careful planning, effective marketing strategies, and engaging events. By following the step-by-step approach outlined in this guide, authors can create memorable experiences that generate buzz, build an audience, and enhance their book's success. By investing time and effort into the planning and execution of book launches and author events, authors can establish their presence in the industry and connect with their target audience on a deeper level.

SECTION FOURTEEN KEY TAKEAWAYS AND ACTION ITEMS

Key Takeaways:

1. Establish a comprehensive online presence showcasing your author bio, book details, and buying information.
2. Actively use social media to connect with readers, other authors, and media professionals.
3. Network and collaborate with other authors for increased exposure and cross-promotion.
4. Seek book reviews from respected platforms to attract attention from readers and the media.
5. Write guest posts for publications related to your genre or writing to gain visibility.
6. Engage with local media by pitching your story with unique angles or local relevance.
7. Use promotions and giveaways to create excitement and increase visibility for your books.
8. Attend and participate in literary events for networking and promotional opportunities.
9. Create engaging press releases with compelling headlines and informative content.

10. Personalize media pitches to match the interests and styles of targeted journalists.
11. Enhance media pitches and releases with relevant multimedia elements.
12. Include clear contact information and respond promptly to media inquiries.
13. Tailor each media pitch to individual journalists for a more effective outreach.
14. Ensure all press materials are professionally written and free from errors.
15. Define the goals for your book launch and author events.
16. Develop a detailed timeline and budget for all launch-related activities.
17. Identify and target your ideal reader demographic in your marketing efforts.
18. Choose event venues that complement your book's theme and target audience.
19. Invite influencers and industry professionals to your events for wider reach.
20. Plan interactive elements for your events to actively engage attendees.
21. Offer book signings and merchandise as part of your event experience.
22. Gather post-event feedback for continuous improvement and sustained momentum.
23. Maintain ongoing engagement with event attendees through social media and newsletters.

Action Items:

1. Build and maintain a professional author website and blog.
2. Regularly post and engage on various social media platforms.
3. Collaborate with fellow authors in your genre for mutual promotion.

4. Actively seek and encourage book reviews on various platforms.

5. Contribute articles or blog posts to relevant online publications.

6. Develop and pitch stories with unique angles to local media outlets.

7. Organize promotional events like giveaways to attract and retain readers.

8. Go to book fairs and literary events for networking and exposure.

9. Write and distribute compelling press releases for significant milestones.

10. Research and customize pitches for different journalists and media outlets.

11. Incorporate images or videos in your press releases to enhance appeal.

12. Make it easy for journalists to contact you and be responsive.

13. Personalize pitches according to each journalist's specific interests and coverage.

14. Proofread all press and media materials to maintain professionalism.

15. Set specific, measurable goals for your book launch and related events.

16. Plan a timeline for your book launch, including marketing and logistics.

17. Budget for all parts of the book launch, including venue and marketing costs.

18. Analyze and understand your target audience for focused marketing.

19. Select and book an appropriate venue for your book launch.

20. Invite industry influencers and professionals to your book launch for greater reach.

21. Design engaging and interactive activities for your book launch.

22. Arrange for book signing sessions and merchandise sales at your events.

23. Collect and analyze feedback from event attendees for future improvements.
24. Continue engaging with your audience post-event via social media and email updates.

In our next Section...

In our next section, we will delve into advanced strategies for authors looking to elevate their book's success. We'll explore the dynamic world of digital marketing, uncovering the latest trends and how to harness them for your book promotion. This includes leveraging new social media platforms, using AI and VR technologies, and understanding the importance of a strong author brand. We'll talk about brand consistency, connecting with your audience, and making your author's voice heard in a crowded market. We'll also touch on advanced email marketing techniques, focusing on list growth, segmentation, and the use of automation to engage readers effectively.

Additionally, we'll dive into using analytics for targeted marketing strategies, offering insights on how to understand and cater to your audience better. Strategic collaborations and networking will be a key focus, helping you to forge beneficial partnerships and engage in collaborative projects. We'll also cover breaking into international markets, adapting your book for a global audience, and the intricacies of translating and localizing your work. The section will include tips on maximizing paid advertising, exploring audio and visual media like audiobooks and podcasts, and adapting your book for different media formats. Finally, we'll discuss sophisticated social media strategies, the power of influencer marketing, and the importance of ethical and sustainable marketing practices, making sure your approach not only boosts your book's success but also contributes positively to the community and environment.

SECTION FIFTEEN: SELLING MORE BOOKS

OPTIMIZING YOUR BOOK'S AMAZON PAGE:

OPTIMIZING your book's Amazon page is important for increasing its visibility, attracting potential readers, and ultimately boosting sales. Here are tips to help you optimize your book's Amazon page for maximum impact:

Engaging Book Title and Subtitle: Ensure your book's title and subtitle are clear, compelling, and relevant to your target audience. Research popular keywords and incorporate them naturally to help improve search rankings.

Eye-Catching Book Cover: Invest in a professional book cover design visually appealing and aligns with your book's genre. Remember, readers often judge a book by its cover, so make sure it stands out and grabs attention.

Compelling Book Description: Craft a persuasive book description that highlights the unique selling points, key themes, and benefits of your book. Use concise and powerful language, incorporating keywords to improve your search rankings.

Engage With Reviews: Actively encourage readers to leave reviews by including a CTA at the end of your book. Positive reviews not only increase trust but also influence potential readers to make a purchase.

Use Categories and Keywords: Select relevant categories for your book and use high-demand keywords in your Amazon backend dashboard. This will aid Amazon's algorithm in recommending your book to interested readers.

Leverage Amazon Author Central: Create a compelling author bio on Amazon Author Central and link it to your book's page. This helps establish your credibility and build a connection with potential readers.

Implement Amazon Advertising: Use Amazon Advertising to increase the visibility of your book by running targeted advertisements. Experiment with different ad formats to find the most effective strategy for your book.

Use Enhanced Content: Take advantage of Amazon's Enhanced Brand Content (EBC) or Kindle Edition Normalized Pages (KENP) for your eBook. These features let you add extra content, such as author interviews, more images, or bonus material, which can help attract readers.

Optimize Pricing Strategy: Analyze the market and set a competitive price for your book. Consider temporary price promotions, discounted bundle offers, or Kindle Countdown Deals to attract readers and stimulate sales.

Promote Your Book: Leverage various promotional tools and strategies, including social media marketing, email marketing, book review sites, and author interviews. Expand your online presence to generate buzz and drive more traffic to your Amazon page.

By optimizing your book's Amazon page using these strategies, you'll increase the chances of attracting potential readers and turning them into loyal fans. Remember to regularly test and analyze the effectiveness of your optimization efforts to continually refine and improve your book's performance on Amazon.

ADVERTISING AND PROMOTION FOR VISIBILITY & SALES: PRICING, SALES PAGES, AND CALLS TO ACTION:

Businesses seeking effective strategies to enhance visibility and boost sales can find valuable insights here. The outlined advertising and promotion techniques aim to help businesses reach their target audience, create engaging sales pages, and utilize strong CTAs for higher conversions. Discover more about pricing, sales pages, and CTAs that can give any business a competitive edge.

Pricing: Selecting the appropriate pricing strategy for products or services is crucial for attracting customers. This approach involves analyzing market trends, considering production costs, and setting competitive prices that appeal to the target audience.

Sales Pages: An effective sales page is key to persuading potential customers to buy. Expert copywriters craft persuasive sales pages that showcase the unique features and benefits of products or services. With compelling headlines, detailed product descriptions, and testimonials from satisfied customers, these sales pages are designed to engage and motivate the audience.

Calls to Action: A compelling CTA is vital for encouraging visitors to make a purchase. The process involves creating CTAs that guide users toward buying, using phrases like "Buy Now," "Add to Cart," or "Subscribe," and creating a sense of urgency with terms like "Limited-Time Offer" or "Exclusive Discount."

Advertising and Promotion: To boost business visibility, a comprehensive advertising and promotion plan is essential. This may include online tactics like pay-per-click campaigns, social media advertising, and email marketing, as well as offline methods like print ads and radio spots. The approach involves analyzing the target audience, selecting effective channels, and creating ads that capture attention and drive traffic.

Measurement and Optimization: The journey doesn't end with the launch of campaigns. Continual measurement and optimization of strategies are crucial. Advanced analytics are used to monitor key metrics and refine approaches, aiming for better visibility, sales, and overall business growth.

For businesses ready to elevate their market presence, this comprehensive guide on advertising and promotion offers the tools and insights needed to increase visibility, optimize sales pages, and create effective CTAs. This is a chance to stand out in the market and boost sales, beginning the advertising and promotion journey for lasting success and revenue growth.

RUNNING EFFECTIVE BOOK PROMOTIONS:

BOOK PROMOTION IS an essential part of marketing and selling your book. Effective promotions can create buzz, attract readers, and increase sales. Here are tips on how to run effective book promotions:

Define your target audience: Before promoting your book, identify who your target readers are. Understanding their preferences, interests, and demographics will help you tailor your promotions to reach the right audience.

Plan ahead: Develop a promotional timeline that includes a range of activities leading to and following the book's launch. This could include creating a buzz on social media, organizing author events or book signings, obtaining book reviews, and running giveaways.

Leverage social media: Social media platforms such as Facebook, Twitter, Instagram, and LinkedIn are powerful tools for book promotion. Create engaging content related to your book, such as quotes, teasers, behind-the-scenes photos, and author insights. Engage with your followers, respond to comments, and use relevant hashtags to expand your reach.

Connect with influencers: Identify influencers in your genre or niche and connect with them. Share your book with them and ask for their support in promoting it. This could be through guest blog posts, endorsements, or mentions on their social media platforms. Their endorsement can help to boost your book's credibility and increase visibility among their audience.

Use book review sites and bloggers: Research and reach out to book review sites, book bloggers, or bookstagrammers who specialize in your genre. Offer them a free copy of your book in exchange for an honest review. Positive reviews can generate interest and encourage new readers to give your book a chance.

Offer giveaways and contests: Organize giveaways on social media or your website where readers can win a signed copy or a limited edition of your book. Offer incentives for readers to share the giveaway with their friends, increasing your book's visibility and reaching new readers.

Collaborate with other authors: Partner with other authors in your genre or niche to cross-promote each other's books. This can involve hosting joint events, featuring each other on your websites or social media, or even bundling your books together for special promotions.

Engage with your readers: Create opportunities for readers to engage with you directly. This could be through live Q&A sessions on social media, author interviews, or virtual book club discussions. Building a relationship with your readers helps foster loyalty and word-of-mouth promotion.

Attend book fairs and conferences: Participate in book fairs or literary conferences to showcase your book to a wider audience. Network with other authors, publishing professionals, and potential readers. Offer book signings or readings to attract attention and make your book memorable.

Monitor and adjust your promotions: Regularly track the effectiveness of your promotions to see what works best for your book. Monitor sales figures, website traffic, social media engagement, and other metrics to identify which promotional activities are generating the best results. Adjust your strategy to optimize your future promotions.

Remember, effective book promotions require time, effort, and consistency. Continuously explore new opportunities, learn from your experiences, and adapt your promotional strategy to reach a wider audience and maximize your book's success.

GETTING ON SUGGESTED READING LISTS AND ALSO-BOUGHTS:

In the vast sea of books available today, authors often struggle to gain visibility and reach their target readership. However, suggested reading lists have emerged as powerful tools to enhance a book's discoverability. This guide aims to explore the importance of suggested reading lists and how they can effectively affect an author's book promotion strategy.

The Importance of Suggested Reading Lists:

Suggested reading lists are curated collections of books recommended by experts, influencers, or popular platforms. These lists serve as trusted references for readers seeking quality reads. By having your book featured on a suggested reading list, you gain valuable exposure, credibility, and an increased chance of reaching your target audience.

Types of Suggested Reading Lists:

a. Genre-based Lists: These lists categorize books based on genres, such as romance, fantasy, mystery, or science fiction. They can be found on blogs, websites, or even as sections within online bookstores. Targeting such lists lets authors connect with readers actively seeking specific genres.

b. Bestseller Lists: These lists highlight books that have achieved high sales figures or received critical acclaim. Securing a place on a bestseller list can significantly boost a book's visibility and increase its appeal. Various platforms, publications, and online retailers offer such lists.

c. Book Club Recommendations: Many book clubs curate their own reading lists to guide their members in selecting their next read. By getting your book recommended by a book club, you tap into a dedicated group of readers who value and trust the club's suggestions.

d. Awards and Prizes Lists: Literary awards and prizes generate increased interest in the recognized books. Winning or being shortlisted for such awards can result in a considerable sales boost and attract broader attention to your book.

3. Targeting Your Audience through Suggested Reading Lists:

a. Research: Identify influential and relevant reading lists that cater to your target audience's reading preferences. Study the list's criteria, submission guidelines, and earlier choices to understand what kind of books they typically feature.

b. Engage with Influencers: Reach out to curators, influencers, and book bloggers who create and share reading lists. Offer them a complimentary copy of your book and kindly request them to consider featuring it in their recommended reads.

c. Leverage Social Media: Utilize social media platforms to engage with authors, readers, and publishers who actively share reading lists. Participate in discussions, share captivating content, and let people know about your book's availability on the suggested reading lists you have been featured on.

d. Collaborate with Bookstores and Libraries: Approach local, independent bookstores and libraries to ask for the inclusion of your book on their curated lists or display shelves. These physical spaces still hold sway with readers who appreciate personalized recommendations.

4. Building Your Own Suggested Reading List:

Consider creating your own suggested reading list to not only promote your book but also help fellow authors and readers discover new titles. Curate a list of books that align with your own book's theme, genre, or writing style. Share this list on your website, social media, and author profiles to prove yourself to be an authority in your niche.

Suggested reading lists offer authors a valuable opportunity to enhance a book's discoverability and connect with their target audience. By effectively targeting different types of reading lists, authors can increase their chances of securing book sales and gaining recognition. Understanding the importance of these lists and incorporating them into your book promotion strategy can significantly affect your book's success.

HARNESSING THE POWER OF ALSO-BOUGHTS:

UNLEASHING the Force Behind Book Purchasing Decisions

Today, bookstores have transformed from physical spaces into online platforms. Readers now rely heavily on algorithms and recommendation systems to guide their purchasing decisions. Among the factors influencing these systems, also-boughts play a significant role. Understanding the significance of also-boughts and putting strategies into practice to appear in this section can greatly enhance your book's visibility and ultimately boost sales. In this guide, we will explore the importance of also-boughts and give you techniques to ensure your book takes its rightful place among other successful titles in your genre.

UNVEILING THE POWER OF ALSO-BOUGHTS

- **What are Also-Boughts?**

Also-Boughts is a term commonly used in ecommerce, specifically in online marketplaces and platforms such as Amazon. Also-Boughts refer to a set of products that customers usually purchase together or in addition to the item they are viewing or considering.

When a customer is browsing a product on an online marketplace, the platform's algorithm analyzes buy data from other customers to determine patterns and trends. Based on these patterns, the algorithm then generates a list of relevant products that have been often bought by customers who have also bought the item the customer is viewing. This list of related products is known as the Also-Boughts.

The Also-Boughts section can usually be found on a product page or as a recommendation widget on the website. It is designed to provide more information and suggest other products that customers might have an interest in. This feature aims to enhance the customer's shopping experience and increase the chances of making more sales by offering products likely to complement the original item.

Also-Boughts can be beneficial for both customers and sellers. For customers, it provides a convenient way to discover complementary products or alternatives that they may not have considered. For sellers, these recommendations can lead to increased cross-selling opportunities and higher sales volumes.

Additionally, analyzing Also-Bought data can provide valuable insights to businesses. By understanding the purchasing behavior of their customers, sellers can optimize their product listings, marketing strategies, and inventory management decisions. They can identify trends and popular product combinations, letting them tailor their offerings and promotions to better meet customer demands.

Also-Boughts serve as a useful feature in ecommerce platforms, enabling customers to discover relevant products and helping sellers drive more sales.

- **The Influence of Also-Boughts on Purchasing Decisions:**

The influence of Also-Boughts on purchasing decisions cannot be underestimated. Also-Boughts refer to the suggestions made by online retailers based on the purchasing patterns of other customers. These recommendations are often displayed on product pages, showing customers what other items have been purchased by people who bought the same product.

One of the key factors behind the influence of Also-Boughts is social proof. People have a natural tendency to rely on the experiences and choices of others when making decisions. When customers see that others who bought a product have also bought certain other items, they perceive it as a validation of the product's quality or relevance.

Another important part of Also-Boughts is the convenience factor. Online shopping platforms have made it easier for customers to browse through related items and make more purchases. By showcasing Also-Boughts on product pages, retailers eliminate the need for customers to conduct separate searches for related products or accessories. This convenience often leads to impulsive buying behavior, as customers are more likely to make more purchases based on the suggestions provided.

Also-Boughts also serve as a form of personalized marketing. With the help of algorithms and data analysis, online retailers can tailor the Also-Boughts recommendations to individual customers based on their browsing and buying history. By showing customers products that align with their interests and preferences, the likelihood of making a purchase increase significantly.

The influence of Also-Boughts extends beyond the individual product level. Retailers also leverage these recommendations to cross-sell or upsell to customers. When customers see a range of related products or complementary items that can enhance their initial purchase, they are more likely to be tempted and persuaded to add those items to their shopping cart.

The influence of Also-Boughts is not limited to the online retail space. Physical stores have also adopted similar practices by carrying out recommendation systems based on sales patterns. For example, supermarkets often place related items near each other to encourage customers to make more purchases.

Also-Boughts play a significant role in shaping purchasing decisions. They provide social proof, convenience, personalized marketing, and opportunities for cross-selling and upselling. As online retailers continue to improve their recommendation algorithms, the influence of Also-Boughts is only expected to grow, further influencing consumer behavior and driving sales.

- **How Also-Boughts Benefit Authors and Publishers:**

Also-Boughts are a powerful feature on online book retailer platforms that benefit both authors and publishers in several ways.

First, Also-Boughts provide authors and publishers with valuable market insights. By analyzing the books frequently purchased together, authors and publishers can gain a better understanding of their target audience's reading preferences and trends. This information can make informed decisions about marketing strategies, book promotions, and even future book development. It lets authors and publishers identify potential crossover genres or niche markets they may have overlooked, helping them tailor their content and reach a wider reader base.

Second, Also-Boughts serve as a form of social proof for authors and publishers. When potential readers see that other readers who have bought a book have also bought specific related titles, it creates a sense of credibility and trust. This can influence their decision to buy the book, especially if it aligns with their interests or reading habits. By having their books featured in Also-Boughts sections, authors and publishers can increase their visibility and enhance their chances of attracting new readers.

Also-Boughts contribute to increased discoverability for authors and publishers. When a book appears in the Also-Boughts section of a popular or best-selling title, it exposes the book to a wider audience who may not have been aware of it otherwise. This can lead to an increase in sales and exposure, as readers are more likely to explore related books if they enjoyed their initial purchase. Also-Boughts provide authors and publishers with a valuable marketing tool that can help generate organic growth and boost sales.

Last, Also-Boughts let authors and publishers build strategic partnerships. By observing the books that often appear in their Also-Boughts sections, authors and publishers can identify potential collaborators or authors who write in a similar genre. This opens up opportunities for cross-promotion, co-authoring projects, or other collaborative efforts that can help both parties. By leveraging the insights gained from Also-Boughts, authors and publishers can form beneficial relationships and expand their networks within the industry.

Also-Boughts provide authors and publishers with valuable market insights, social proof, increased discoverability, and opportunities for strategic partnerships. Using this feature, authors and publishers can optimize their marketing efforts, connect with readers, and ultimately increase their reach and success within the book industry.

UNDERSTANDING THE ALSO-BOUGHT ALGORITHM

The Algorithmic Process Behind Also-Bought Recommendations:

Also-bought recommendations are an important feature in many ecommerce websites and online platforms. These recommendations are used to suggest related products or services to customers based on their browsing and buy history. The algorithmic process behind also-bought recommendations involves several steps to ensure correct and relevant suggestions for the users.

Data collection: The first step in the algorithmic process is to gather relevant data from the users. This data includes their browsing history, buy history, and interactions such as clicks, likes, and reviews. The more data that is collected, the better the recommendations will be.

Pre-processing: Once the data is collected, it needs to be pre-processed to make it usable for the algorithm. This involves cleaning the data, removing any irrelevant or duplicate entries, and organizing it in a meaningful way. For example, grouping similar products together or categorizing them based on their attributes.

User profiling: Next, the algorithm creates user profiles based on the collected data. These profiles have information about the user's preferences, behaviors, and interests. This profiling is done using various techniques such as collaborative filtering, which looks at the similarities between users, or content-based filtering, which analyzes the attributes of the products.

Similarity calculation: In this step, the algorithm compares the user profiles to find similar users or similar products. Similarity can be measured using different algorithms such as cosine similarity, Jaccard similarity, or Euclidean distance. The goal is to find users with similar preferences or products similar in terms of attributes, categories, or characteristics.

Recommendation generation: Once the similarities are calculated, the algorithm generates the actual recommendations. This can be done using techniques like item-based filtering, where the algorithm identifies products frequently bought together or user-based filtering, where it recommends products that similar users have bought.

Filtering and ranking: The generated recommendations are then filtered and ranked based on relevance and other parameters. These parameters can include popularity, product ratings, recency of purchase, or any other personalized factors. The goal is to present the most relevant and useful recommendations to the user.

Displaying recommendations: Finally, the recommendations are displayed to the user as personalized suggestions on the website or app. This can be done using a recommendation widget or section that showcases the recommended products alongside the user's current browsing or shopping experience.

The algorithmic process behind also-bought recommendations is iterative and continuously learns and improves. As more data is collected and new interactions occur, the algorithm refines its recommendations to better match the user's preferences and needs. Additionally, optimization techniques like A/B testing can evaluate the performance of the algorithm and make further improvements if necessary.

THE ROLE OF READER BEHAVIOR IN SHAPING ALSO-BOUGHTS

The "also-boughts" section on online retail websites plays an important role in influencing consumer behavior. It recommends products often purchased with the item the reader is viewing. This section is not randomly generated; rather, it is shaped by the behavior of the readers themselves.

Reader behavior in terms of clicks, purchases, and browsing history is tracked and analyzed to create a personalized shopping experience. By tracking these actions, the retailer can better understand the preferences and interests of its customers. This information is then used to curate the also-boughts section.

When a reader purchases a product, their behavior provides valuable insights into their preferences. If someone buys a book on photography, for example, the also-boughts might include other photography books or related equipment such as tripods and camera bags. By suggesting products that are complementary or of interest to the reader, the retailer aims to enhance the customer's shopping experience and increase the likelihood of making more purchases.

Similarly, if a reader often clicks or browses certain categories or authors, their behavior is considered when generating the also-boughts. This enables the retailer to offer recommendations more likely to align with the reader's preferences.

Reader behavior can also influence the ranking of products within the also-boughts section. If a certain product consistently receives high click-through rates, purchases, and positive feedback from readers, it is more likely to appear prominently in the also-boughts of related items.

Reader behavior also plays a role in shaping the overall selection and diversity of the also-boughts section. Retailers aim to provide a range of recommendations to cater to different tastes and preferences. By analyzing the behavior of various types of readers, retailers can make sure the also-boughts section appeals to a wide audience.

Reader behavior plays a significant role in shaping the also-boughts section on online retail websites. By tracking and analyzing clicks, purchases, and browsing history, retailers can provide personalized recommendations to enhance the shopping experience. This not only benefits the retailer by increasing sales, but also benefits the reader by offering relevant and interesting product suggestions.

HOW AMAZON AND OTHER PLATFORMS UTILIZE ALSO-BOUGHTS:

Amazon and other platforms use the concept of "also-boughts" in various ways to enhance their ecommerce experience. Also-boughts refer to the products frequently purchased with a particular item. These recommendations are generated based on the purchasing patterns and browsing history of other users.

Personalized Recommendations: The primary way platforms use also-boughts is by displaying personalized recommendations to individual users. When a customer views a product, the platform suggests other items commonly bought by customers who bought the same item. This helps users discover related products or accessories they may find useful or interesting.

Cross-Selling: Also-boughts effectively help with cross-selling opportunities for platforms. By analyzing the purchasing behavior of customers, the platform can identify items often bought together and promote them on relevant product pages. For example, if a customer is browsing for a smartphone, the platform may display recommended accessories like cases or screen protectors.

Bundling: Another way platforms use also-boughts is through bundling products together. They may create product bundles by combining items frequently purchased together. This strategy encourages customers to buy multiple items at once, leading to increased sales and a higher average order value.

Upselling: Platforms can use also-boughts to upsell customers by suggesting higher-priced alternatives or premium versions of products. If a customer is considering a certain item, the platform may display similar products with superior features or better quality, aiming to convince the customer to upgrade their purchase.

Enhanced Product Discovery: Also-boughts play a significant role in improving product discovery on platforms. When customers browse a specific product, the platform showcases a section featuring other often bought items. This helps shoppers find related products they may not have considered, thus expanding their options and helping with a more personalized shopping experience.

Data Analysis: Platforms use the data generated from also-boughts to understand customer behavior and preferences better. By analyzing patterns and trends, they can make informed decisions about inventory management, marketing strategies, and product recommendations. This data-driven approach helps platforms optimize their operations and provide a more tailored shopping experience.

Amazon and other platforms extensively use also-boughts to provide personalized recommendations, cross-sell related products, bundle items, upsell customers, enhance product discovery, and analyze customer data. By doing so, they aim to improve customer satisfaction, increase sales, and create a strong and engaging ecommerce ecosystem.

TECHNIQUES TO GET FEATURED IN ALSO-BOUGHTS:

IDENTIFYING THE RIGHT TITLES AND AUTHORS TO TARGET

IDENTIFYING the right titles and authors to target is important regarding effective book promotion and marketing. By strategically selecting the proper titles and authors, you can reach your target audience, maximize exposure, and increase the chances of connecting with readers. Here are tips to help you in this process:

Understand your genre: Start by understanding the genre of your book. What category does it fall into - fiction, nonfiction, romance, mystery, science fiction, self-help, etc.? Knowing your genre will help you determine which titles and authors have a similar style or topic that may resonate with your potential readers.

Research bestseller lists: Look into bestseller lists for your genre or category. These lists can be found on websites like Amazon, Goodreads, The New York Times, and Publishers Weekly. Analyze the books that consistently rank high on these lists and note their authors. These authors hold credibility and have established a reader base you can target.

Study book reviews: Pay attention to book reviews on platforms such as Amazon, Goodreads, and book blogs. Reviews provide insights into readers' preferences and help you identify authors and titles that are well-received within your target audience. Look for books that have received positive reviews and align with the themes or style of your own work.

Connect through social media: Social media platforms like Twitter, Instagram, and Facebook can be great tools for connecting with authors and readers in your genre. Follow authors who write similar books to yours and engage with their posts. Engaging in conversations and building relationships with authors and readers can lead to potential collaborations, joint promotions, or endorsements.

Attend book fairs and conferences: Attend book fairs, conferences, and literary events related to your genre. These events provide an opportunity to meet authors, industry professionals, and like-minded individuals. Engage in conversations, ask questions during panels, and connect with authors and readers who share similar interests.

Collaborate with book clubs: Book clubs are a fantastic resource for finding readers passionate about a specific genre or type of book. Contact local book clubs or join online communities focused on your genre to discuss books and connect with potential readers. By engaging in these discussions, you can gain insights into popular authors and titles that resonate with your target audience.

Stay updated with industry news: Keep up with industry news through blogs, online publications, and newsletters that focus on books and publishing. Stay informed about new releases, trends, and popular authors in your genre. This knowledge will help you tailor your marketing efforts to the right audience and target authors relevant at the moment.

Remember, targeting the right titles and authors requires research, understanding your target audience, and engaging with the book community. By identifying and connecting with the right authors, you can foster meaningful relationships and improve your chances of success in the competitive world of publishing.

OPTIMIZING YOUR BOOK'S METADATA:

Optimizing your book's metadata is an important step in ensuring its discoverability and increasing its chances of being found by potential readers. Metadata refers to the descriptive information about your book that helps search engines and online retailers categorize and index it correctly. Here are tips to help you optimize your book's metadata:

Title: Choose a clear and catchy title that accurately reflects the content of your book. Avoid using vague or misleading titles that may confuse readers or hinder SEO.

Subtitle: Including a subtitle provides an opportunity to further describe your book and incorporate relevant keywords. Use it to highlight the key themes or unique selling points of your book.

Author Name: Ensure your author's name is consistent across all platforms and formats. This helps maintain your author brand and enables readers to easily find other books written by you.

Description: Write a compelling and concise book description that captures the essence of your story or nonfiction content. Use relevant keywords naturally throughout the description to aid in SEO.

Categories and Genres: Choose the most accurate and specific categories and genres for your book. This is important for placement on online retailer platforms and can greatly affect visibility to target readers.

Keywords and Tags: Research and select relevant keywords and tags that reflect the themes, sub-genres, and key concepts in your book. Incorporate these keywords into your metadata to improve search engine rankings.

Reviews and Awards: Include positive reviews, endorsements, and any awards your book has received in your metadata. These endorsements can influence potential readers and help establish credibility.

ISBN and Other Identifiers: Ensure that your book's ISBN and other identifiers are correctly listed and consistent across different platforms. This helps avoid potential confusion and ensures accurate indexing.

Author Bio and Profile: Craft an engaging author biography that highlights your credentials, writing experience, and any notable achievements. This helps build trust with readers and increases your author credibility.

Regular Review and Update: Review and update your book's metadata periodically to keep it relevant and optimizing its visibility. Stay up to date with industry trends and adjust your metadata.

By optimizing your book's metadata, you can improve its visibility, attract more readers, and increase its chances of success. Take the time to refine your metadata and make sure it accurately reflects your book's content to maximize its discoverability.

UTILIZING EFFECTIVE KEYWORD STRATEGIES:

Keywords play an important role in SEO and online marketing strategies. Using effective keyword strategies can help increase organic traffic to a website and improve its visibility in search engine results. Here are tips to effectively use keyword strategies:

Conduct Keyword Research: Start by conducting thorough keyword research to identify relevant and high-ranking keywords. Use tools like Google Keyword Planner, SEMrush, or Moz Keyword Explorer to discover popular search terms related to your niche. Consider factors such as search volume, competition, and relevance to choose the most effective keywords.

Focus on Long-Tail Keywords: Long-tail keywords are longer, more specific phrases that target a niche audience. These keywords may have lower search volume but generally have higher conversion rates. Incorporate long-tail keywords into your content to attract more targeted traffic and increase the chances of conversion.

Target Both Head and Long-Tail Keywords: While long-tail keywords are valuable, it's important to strike a balance and target head keywords. Head keywords are shorter, more general terms with higher search volume but greater competition. Using a mix of head and long-tail keywords can help reach a wider audience while also targeting specific niche segments.

Optimize On-Page Elements: Once you have identified your target keywords, optimize your website's on-page elements to improve its visibility. Include the primary keyword in the meta title, meta description, heading tags (H1, H2, etc.), and the URL. Sprinkle relevant keywords naturally throughout the content to enhance keyword density without compromising readability.

Create High-Quality, Relevant Content: Keyword strategy should be integrated with a strong content strategy. Create high-quality, relevant content around your target keywords to provide value to your audience. Aim to answer their questions, solve their problems, or fulfill their needs. When your content addresses the users' intent and offers valuable information, it has a higher chance of ranking well in search results.

Optimize Images and Multimedia: Don't forget to optimize images and multimedia elements on your website. Use descriptive filenames and ALT tags that incorporate relevant keywords. This helps search engines understand the content of your media files and improves their visibility in image search results.

Track and Refine: SEO is a continuous process, and keyword strategies should be tracked and refined regularly. Keep track of keyword rankings, website traffic, and user engagement metrics to identify areas for improvement. Analyze the performance of different keywords and adjust your strategy.

Effective keyword strategies are essential for improving website visibility and attracting targeted organic traffic. Conduct thorough keyword research, target both head and long-tail keywords, optimize on-page elements, create high-quality content, optimize images, and regularly track and refine your keyword strategy. By applying these tactics, you can enhance your online presence and drive more qualified traffic to your website.

BUILDING A NETWORK OF AUTHOR CO-PROMOTION:

In today's competitive publishing world, building a network of author co-promotion can significantly boost book sales and increase the visibility of your work. By collaborating with fellow authors, you can tap into a wider audience and benefit from shared resources and promotional efforts. Here are steps to help you build a strong network of author co-promotion.

Identify Complementary Authors: Start by identifying authors whose writing style or genre aligns with yours. Look for authors whose target audience might overlap with yours, but who aren't direct competitors. For example, if you write historical romance novels, consider connecting with authors who write historical fiction or romance in different sub-genres.

Connect on Social Media: Once you have identified potential author partners, connect with them on social media platforms. Follow their profiles, engage with their posts, and build a genuine connection by commenting and sharing their content. This will help establish a relationship before moving forward with a collaborative effort.

Create a Co-promotion Strategy: Collaborate with fellow authors to create a co-promotion strategy that benefits all parties involved. This strategy could include cross-promotion on social media, joint giveaways, guest blogging on each other's websites, or even co-authoring an anthology. The key is to brainstorm ways in which you can leverage each other's audience and promotional platforms.

Organize Dedicated Promotional Events: Plan dedicated promotional events that highlight the works of multiple authors. This could be a virtual book tour, a joint virtual book launch party, or even a panel discussion where authors share insights and promote each other's work. By pooling your resources and organizing these events together, you can attract a bigger audience and create a buzz around your books.

Share Marketing Materials: Share marketing materials with your author network. This could involve swapping book cover images, bookmarks, or even book excerpts to include in your newsletters or social media posts. Sharing these materials helps introduce your work to new readers through your co-promotion partners' platforms.

Collaborate on Cross-Promotion: Collaborate with your author network to cross-promote each other's books. This can be done through dedicated social media posts, blog tours, newsletters, or even joint advertising campaigns. By amplifying each other's book releases or promotions, you can reach a wider audience and increase the chances of attracting new readers.

Maintain Regular Communication: Keep the lines of communication open with your author network. Regularly check in with each other, share updates on your writing or promotional efforts, and offer support and encouragement. This will foster a sense of camaraderie and encourage long-term collaboration within the network.

Building a network of author co-promotion takes time and effort, but the benefits are well worth it. By leveraging the strengths of multiple authors and working together toward common goals, you can expand your reach, increase book sales, and establish a supportive community of fellow writers.

ENGAGING WITH READERS AND ENCOURAGING REVIEWS:

Engaging with readers and encouraging reviews is a crucial part of building a strong online presence as a writer. By actively interacting with your readers and encouraging their feedback, you not only strengthen your relationship with them but also boost the visibility of your work and attract new readers. Here's how you can engage with your readers and encourage reviews effectively:

Be responsive: Respond promptly to comments, messages, and emails from your readers. This shows you value their input and appreciate their time. Take the time to address their questions, concerns, or simply engage in a conversation. By being approachable, you create a welcoming atmosphere for your readers.

Incentivize reviews: Offer incentives to motivate your readers to leave reviews. For example, you could hold a giveaway or a contest where participants have to leave a review to enter. This not only encourages reviews but also generates buzz about your work.

Engage on social media: Use social media platforms to engage with your readers on a more personal level. Share updates about your writing process, ask for their opinions or feedback, and create polls or quizzes related to your work. This helps build a loyal fan base and sparks discussions among readers.

Create a newsletter: Start a newsletter to keep your readers informed about new releases, upcoming projects, and other exciting updates. Include a section dedicated to reader reviews, where you can showcase their feedback and express your gratitude. This helps create a sense of community and encourages others to contribute their own reviews.

Provide easy review options: Make it simple for readers to leave reviews by including direct links or buttons on your website, blog, or social media platforms. Make sure the process is straightforward and doesn't require multiple steps or logins. The easier it is for readers to review your work, the more likely they are to do so.

Share positive reviews: Highlight positive reviews or testimonials from readers on your website, social media channels, or book covers. This not only shows potential readers that your work is well-received but also encourages others to leave their own reviews.

Host Q&A sessions: Periodically host Q&A sessions where readers can ask you questions directly. This can be done through social media live sessions, online forums, or even dedicated discussion threads on platforms like Reddit. Engaging in direct conversation with your readers deepens the connection and may result in more reviews as well.

Give thanks: Express your gratitude to readers who take the time to leave reviews. Respond to each review individually, thank them for their feedback, and let them know how much you appreciate their support. This personal touch encourages a strong reader-writer relationship and motivates them to continue supporting your work.

Remember, the key to engaging with readers and encouraging reviews is to build a genuine connection. Show your readers that you value their opinions, make it easy for them to share their thoughts, and always express your appreciation. This will not only foster a supportive community around your writing but also help you improve as a writer based on their valuable feedback.

LEVERAGING ALSO-BOUGHTS FOR LONG-TERM SUCCESS:

MONITORING AND ANALYZING ALSO-BOUGHT TRENDS:

Monitoring and analyzing also-bought trends is essential for any retail business looking to optimize their product offerings and increase sales. Also-bought trends refer to the products that customers often buy together, providing valuable insight into customer behavior and preferences. Here are four steps to effectively track and analyze also-bought trends:

Collect Data: Start by gathering data on customer purchases. This data can be obtained from your sales records and can include information such as the products bought, the time of purchase, and the customer demographics. It's important to collect enough data over a reasonable period to ensure accurate analysis.

Identify Relationships: Once you have collected the data, analyze it to identify patterns and relationships between products. Identify the products frequently purchased together and list also-bought trends. This step can be done manually by reviewing sales records, or you can use data analysis tools and software to help identify patterns and relationships more efficiently.

Analyze Customer Behavior: The next step is to analyze customer behavior based on the also-bought trends. Look for common features among customers who buy specific products together. This analysis can provide insights into customer preferences, needs, and motivations. For example, if customers often buy hiking boots and camping gear together, it suggests they may be outdoor enthusiasts. Understanding customer behavior can help you make informed decisions about product placement, cross-selling opportunities, and marketing strategies.

Optimize Product Offerings: Use the insights gained from tracking also-bought trends to optimize your product offerings. Consider grouping related products together to encourage cross-selling or bundle complementary items as a package deal. This strategy can increase the average order value and enhance the customer experience. Additionally, consider introducing new products based on the customer preferences identified from the analysis. By constantly tracking and analyzing also-bought trends, you can keep your product offerings aligned with customer demand and stay ahead of the competition.

Monitoring and analyzing also-bought trends is important for understanding customer behavior and optimizing product offerings. By collecting data, identifying relationships between products, analyzing customer behavior, and optimizing product offerings, businesses can effectively leverage also-bought trends to increase sales and enhance customer satisfaction.

ADJUSTING YOUR MARKETING AND ADVERTISING STRATEGIES:

Adjusting your marketing and advertising strategies is important to make sure you are effectively reaching your target audience and maximizing your return on investment. Here are steps you can take to make changes:

Analyze your current strategies: Start by evaluating your current marketing and advertising efforts. Analyze data such as sales, website traffic, engagement metrics, and customer feedback to understand what is working and what needs improvement.

Assess your target audience: Take the time to re-evaluate your target audience. Research their demographics, preferences, behaviors, and needs. This will help you better understand their motivations and tailor your marketing messages.

Set clear goals: Clearly define your marketing and advertising goals. Are you looking to increase brand awareness, drive more sales, or improve customer loyalty? Setting specific goals will help you choose the right strategies and tactics.

Stay updated with industry trends: Keep up with the latest industry trends, customer preferences, and emerging technologies. Monitor your competitors' strategies and adapt to changes to maintain a competitive edge.

Experiment with new channels and tactics: Consider exploring new marketing channels and tactics that align with your target audience. This could involve leveraging social media platforms, influencer marketing, SEO, or content marketing. Test and measure the results to determine their effectiveness.

Personalize your messaging: Use the data you've gathered about your target audience to personalize your marketing messages. Tailor your content in a way that speaks directly to their needs, pain points, and aspirations. This will help create a stronger connection and increase engagement.

Optimize your website and landing pages: Ensure that your website and landing pages are user-friendly, visually appealing, and optimized for search engines. This will help improve your visibility and increase the chances of converting visitors into customers.

Use data-driven insights: Track and analyze data from your marketing campaigns to gain insights into your audience's behavior and preferences. Use this information to refine your strategies and make data-driven decisions.

Monitor and measure results: Continuously monitor and measure the results of your marketing and advertising efforts. This will help you identify what's working, what's not, and make necessary changes to improve the overall effectiveness of your campaigns.

Stay adaptable: Remember that marketing and advertising strategies need to be flexible and adaptable. Track the results, be open to change, and make changes as needed to stay relevant and meet the evolving needs of your audience.

By regularly evaluating and adjusting your marketing and advertising strategies, you can make sure you are effectively reaching your target audience and achieving your business goals.

LEVERAGING SOCIAL MEDIA AND INFLUENCER MARKETING:

Social media and influencer marketing have become powerful tools for businesses to reach and engage with their target audience. Leveraging these platforms effectively can increase brand awareness, drive traffic to websites, and boost sales. Here are strategies to maximize the benefits of social media and influencer marketing.

Identify the right social media platforms: It's important to understand which social media platforms your target audience uses the most. For example, if you are targeting younger audiences, platforms like Instagram and TikTok may be more effective. Conduct market research and analyze demographics to select the most relevant platforms for your business.

Create compelling content: To stand out on social media, you need to create content that resonates with your audience. This can be as informative blog posts, entertaining videos, or visually appealing images. Focus on providing value to your audience through educational or entertaining content, rather than promoting your products or services.

Engage with followers: One of the key advantages of social media is the ability to have real-time conversations with your followers. Try to respond to comments and messages promptly and encourage engagement by asking questions or running contests. Building a strong relationship with your audience helps to create brand loyalty and trust.

Collaborate with influencers: Influencer marketing involves partnering with individuals with a significant following on social media. Identify influencers who align with your brand values and target audience. Collaborating with influencers can help you reach a wider audience, gain credibility, and increase product/service visibility. Consider offering influencers exclusive discounts or free products/services in exchange for promoting your brand.

Use social media ads: While organic reach on social media is important, using paid ads can significantly expand your visibility. Platforms like Facebook, Instagram, and LinkedIn offer targeted ad options that let you reach specific demographics, interests, and locations. Set clear goals for your ad campaigns, whether it's increasing brand awareness, driving traffic, or generating leads.

Track and analyze results: Implement social media analytics tools to measure the effectiveness of your social media and influencer marketing efforts. Track metrics such as reach, engagement, click-through rates, and conversions to assess the impact of your campaigns. This data will help you refine your strategies and optimize future marketing initiatives.

Social media and influencer marketing can be powerful tools for businesses when leveraged effectively. By identifying the right platforms, creating compelling content, engaging with followers, collaborating with influencers, using targeted ads, and tracking results, businesses can maximize the benefits of these marketing avenues and meet their goals.

ADAPTING YOUR CONTENT TO ALIGN WITH SUCCESSFUL TITLES

When creating content, one thing that can greatly affect its success is the title. A catchy, intriguing title can capture the attention of readers and entice them to click on your article, blog post, or video. Therefore, adapt your content to align with successful titles to maximize its reach and engagement. Here are tips to help you do that:

Analyze the successful titles in your niche: Take some time to research and analyze the titles of popular content within your niche. Look at the articles, blog posts, and videos that have gained significant attention and try to identify common elements in their titles. Are there certain keywords or phrases that seem to attract more clicks? What makes these titles stand out from the rest? Understanding these patterns will help you adapt your content.

Incorporate relevant keywords: Including relevant keywords in your title is important for improving your content's discoverability. Conduct keyword research to identify key terms and phrases related to your topic commonly searched for. Incorporate these keywords naturally in your title, making sure it accurately represents the content of your piece.

Create intrigue and curiosity: Successful titles often create a sense of intrigue and curiosity, making readers curious enough to click and learn more. Use powerful and attention-grabbing words that evoke curiosity and excitement. Promise value or solve a problem that your target audience might have. By piquing their interest, you increase the likelihood of them engaging with your content.

Embrace variety and creativity: Don't be afraid to think outside the box and experiment with different titles. Try a variety of formats, such as listicles, how-tos, guides, or question-based titles to see what resonates best with your audience. Get creative and use humor, puns, or wordplay in your titles where appropriate. Remember, the goal is to make your content stand out among the sea of information available online.

Test and optimize: Once you have created your title, it's important to track its performance and make changes if necessary. Track the click-through rates and engagement metrics of your content to see how well your titles are resonating with your audience. If you notice that certain titles perform better than others, try to identify the reasons behind their success and apply those elements to future titles.

Aligning your content with successful titles is a powerful way to enhance its reach and engagement. By analyzing popular titles in your niche, incorporating relevant keywords, creating intrigue, embracing variety, and optimizing based on data, you can adapt your content to captivate your audience and increase its chances of success. Remember, a great title is the gateway to your content, so invest time and effort into crafting one that grabs attention and leaves readers wanting more.

CASE STUDIES: AUTHORS WHO EXCELLED WITH ALSO-BOUGHTS:

SUCCESS STORIES OF AUTHORS LEVERAGING ALSO-BOUGHTS:

NOTE: **These are fictional examples for illustrative purposes only.**

Author A self-published their debut science fiction novel and struggled to gain visibility in a saturated market. However, they noticed that their book was consistently being featured in the also-boughts section of popular works by established authors in the same genre. Seeing this as an opportunity, they decided to strategically run targeted advertisements to the readers of those popular books. This strategy helped boost their book's visibility and led to a significant increase in sales, ultimately establishing them as a successful sci-fi writer.

Author B, a nonfiction author, wrote a book about personal development and self-improvement. By studying the also-bought section of similar books in their niche, they discovered that readers of those books were also interested in spirituality and mindfulness. To leverage this information, Author B started collaborating with well-known spiritual influencers and guest posting on relevant blogs, thus exposing their book to a wider audience. This approach resulted in a surge of interest, higher book sales, and speaking engagements, cementing them as a successful author in their field.

Author C had written historical fiction novels set in ancient Rome. They realized that their books often appeared as also-boughts alongside other Roman-themed works by different authors. Taking advantage of this consistent presence, they contacted these authors and formed a strong network of cross-promotion. By recommending each other's books and running joint marketing campaigns, they created a ripple effect that elevated the visibility of all their works. Author C's book sales skyrocketed, leading to multiple book deals and recognition in the historical fiction community.

Author D, a writer of paranormal romance, struggled to expand their readership beyond their initial fanbase. However, they noticed that their books consistently appeared alongside popular urban fantasy novels in the also-bought section. Recognizing this as an opportunity, they approached some authors featured in the also-boughts and organized a joint book bundle promotion. This collaboration introduced their work to a new audience, leading to increased sales and further opportunities to participate in multi-author anthologies. The success of this strategy enabled Author D to make a name for themselves in the paranormal romance genre.

Author E had published a series of crime thrillers with moderate success. After analyzing the also-boughts section, they discovered that their books were often paired with psychological suspense novels by highly regarded authors. Leveraging this information, Author E invested in professional cover design and editing services to ensure their books matched the quality of the highly recommended titles in the also-boughts. Their novels garnered more positive reviews, gained traction among readers of psychological suspense, and earned them a loyal fanbase. This success propelled Author E into becoming a best-selling author and opened doors to traditional publishing opportunities.

In each of these success stories, the authors strategically leveraged the also-boughts section to increase visibility, expand their readership, and ultimately succeed their respective genres. By understanding their target readers' preferences and aligning themselves with established authors in the also-boughts, these authors tapped into existing fan bases and grow their own following.

LESSONS LEARNED FROM CASE STUDIES:

The importance of thorough research: Case studies provide valuable insights into real-world situations, but they are only as good as the research behind them. One key lesson is the need for thorough research to gather accurate and reliable data. This includes gathering multiple sources of information, conducting interviews, and collecting relevant data points.

The power of storytelling: Case studies are often presented as stories, highlighting the experiences and challenges faced by individuals or organizations. This narrative approach helps to engage the reader and create a connection between the reader and the subject of the case study. Apply storytelling techniques effectively to make a case study more compelling and impactful.

Analysis and interpretation: Case studies are not just about presenting factual information; they also require analysis and interpretation of the data. One lesson learned is the importance of critically analyzing the information gathered and interpreting it in the problem or situation being studied. This helps to uncover insights, identify patterns, and draw meaningful conclusions.

Identifying success factors and challenges: Through case studies, we can identify success factors that contributed to positive outcomes as well as challenges that hindered progress. By studying these factors, we can gain valuable insights into what works and what doesn't in a particular context. This can inform future decision-making and help in crafting strategies or solutions more likely to succeed.

The role of context: Case studies emphasize the significance of context in understanding and addressing complex problems. What works in one context may not work in another. Case studies shed light on the impact of various contextual factors such as culture, politics, economics, and technology on the outcomes of a particular situation. This highlights the importance of considering the unique circumstances of each case and tailoring strategies.

APPLYING KEY STRATEGIES FROM SUCCESSFUL AUTHORS:

Successful authors have mastered the art of writing and have developed key strategies that have helped them succeed. By applying these strategies in your own writing, you can improve your skills and increase your chances of becoming a successful author. Here are key strategies you can apply:

Develop a Writing Routine: Successful authors create a consistent writing routine that lets them stay focused and productive. Set aside a specific time each day or week dedicated to writing and stick to it. By making writing a regular habit, you will train your mind to be more creative and productive during those dedicated times.

Set Goals and Deadlines: Successful authors set clear goals and deadlines for their writing projects. Whether it's completing a certain number of words in a day or finishing a draft by a specific date, setting goals and deadlines helps keep you motivated and accountable. Break your writing goals into smaller, manageable tasks, and track your progress to stay on track.

Embrace the Editing Process: Good writing is not just about creating a compelling story, but also about editing and revising it. Successful authors understand the importance of the editing process and are not afraid to significantly change their work. Be open to receiving feedback and criticism and be willing to revise your writing to make it better. Embrace the editing process as an essential part of refining your work.

Read Widely and Analytically: Successful authors are also avid readers. They read widely and analytically, exploring different genres and styles of writing. This helps them expand their knowledge, learn from established authors, and develop their unique voice and writing style. Read books, articles, and essays in different genres and analyze what makes them successful. Note the techniques and writing strategies used by successful authors and try to use them in your own writing.

Find Your Writing Community: Successful authors often surround themselves with like-minded individuals who provide support and encouragement. Connect with other writers, join writing groups or workshops, and share your work with others. Having a writing community will not only provide valuable feedback and advice but also keep you motivated and inspired.

Keep Learning and Improving: Successful authors never stop learning. They continuously seek to improve their writing skills and stay updated on the latest trends and techniques. Take advantage of online writing courses, workshops, and conferences to expand your knowledge and hone your craft. Stay curious, read books on writing, and apply what you learn to your writing practice.

By applying these key strategies from successful authors, you can develop your writing skills, enhance your creativity, and increase your chances of succeeding as an author. Remember, writing is a journey, and practice, persistence, and continuous growth are the keys to becoming a successful author.

Harnessing the power of also-boughts can make a significant difference in your book's success. By understanding the role, they play in influencing readers' buying decisions and putting effective strategies into practice to appear in the also-bought section of successful titles in your genre, you can enhance your book's visibility and increase the likelihood of attracting your target audience. Embrace the power of also-boughts and unlock the full potential of your book's success in the competitive world of online publishing.

~

CRAFTING AN ENGAGING BOOK DESCRIPTION:

WHEN ATTRACTING readers and generating interest in your book, an engaging book description plays an important role. It serves as your book's sales pitch, grabbing readers' attention and convincing them to dive into your story. To help you master this craft, we will explore effective techniques for writing compelling book descriptions that captivate readers from the first sentence.

Begin with a Hook:

Your book description should start with a powerful hook that immediately captivates readers. This can be a thought-provoking question, an intriguing statement, or an enticing teaser that creates a sense of curiosity. The key is to make readers want to know more about your book.

Introduce the Conflict:

Highlighting the central conflict or problem faced by your characters is essential. This helps readers understand what your book is about and what challenges the protagonists must overcome. Write a concise and compelling summary of the conflict, leaving readers eager to discover how it unfolds.

Focus on Emotion:

Appealing to readers' emotions is a powerful way to engage them. Use descriptive language that evokes strong feelings and draws readers into the emotional core of your story. By connecting with readers on an emotional level, you make your book more relatable and enticing.

Use Vivid Imagery and Sensory Details:

Immerse readers in your book's world by incorporating vivid imagery and sensory details. Paint a picture with your words, appealing to readers' senses. This will not only help readers envision the setting but also create a more immersive experience, enticing them to explore the world you've crafted.

Highlight Unique Selling Points:

Identify the unique parts of your book that set it apart from others in its genre. Whether it's an unusual plot twist, an innovative storytelling technique, or a distinct voice, make sure to showcase these selling points. Highlighting what makes your book special will pique readers' interest and compel them to choose your story.

Utilize Keywords:

Keywords play an important role in optimizing your book's chances of being discovered by readers who might enjoy it. Research relevant keywords that align with your book's genre, themes, or target audience. Integrate these keywords naturally into your description, helping search algorithms match your book with potential readers.

Study Also-Boughts:

Analyze the "also-boughts" section on book retail platforms within your genre. These are books frequently purchased alongside others. Studying also-boughts can provide insight into what appeals to your target readers and help you identify more keywords and themes to incorporate into your description.

Keep it Concise and Scannable:

Today, readers usually skim through book descriptions. Therefore, keep your description concise and scannable. Use short paragraphs, bullet points, and bold fonts to make key information stand out. Focus on the most compelling parts of your book, avoiding unnecessary details that might overwhelm or confuse readers.

By implementing these effective techniques, you can craft an engaging book description that grabs readers' attention and compels them to pick up your book. Remember, your book description is a powerful tool in capturing readers' interest, so invest time in honing its quality, appeal, and optimization to maximize your chances of success.

SECURING ENDORSEMENTS AND TESTIMONIALS:

SECURING endorsements and testimonials from established authors, influencers, and experts in your genre is a powerful way to boost your book's credibility and visibility. When someone respected in your field recommends your work, it can significantly enhance your reputation and attract new readers. In this chapter, we will explore proven strategies to approach and secure these valuable recommendations.

First, it's important to do your research and identify potential endorsers who are prominent figures in your genre. Look for authors with a similar target audience and whose work aligns with yours. Influencers and experts with a strong online presence and a large following can also be valuable endorsers. Take the time to get to know their work and understand their reach. This will help you craft a personalized approach when reaching out.

Once you have identified potential endorsers, it's time to make your pitch. Start by sending a polite and professional email or message, introducing yourself and your book. Explain why you think their endorsement would be a valuable asset and how their knowledge or influence aligns with your work. Be clear about what you are asking for and what you hope to achieve.

Providing a sample or preview of your book can help pique their interest and show the quality of your work. If they express interest, offer to send them a complimentary copy or provide them with access to an online version. Be respectful of their time and make it easy for them to review your book.

Once they have read your book, follow up with a thank-you email or message. Express your gratitude for their time and consideration. If they provide a positive review or endorsement, ask for permission to use it in your book's marketing materials, such as on your website, social media, and book cover. Some endorsers may prefer to write a blurb or testimonial themselves, while others may be open to you drafting one for their approval.

Remember that not every approach will result in an endorsement or testimonial, and that's okay. Rejection is a natural part of the process, and it's important to stay positive and persistent. Keep contacting potential endorsers, making connections, and building relationships. Over time, as your book gains traction and visibility, more opportunities for endorsements may arise.

In addition to securing endorsements, it's also important to leverage online retailer algorithms to increase your book's visibility. Algorithms used by popular online retailers, such as Amazon, play a significant role in generating suggested reading lists and also-bought recommendations. By understanding how these algorithms work, you can optimize your book's keywords, categories, and metadata to increase its visibility within these platforms.

Start by conducting keyword research to identify relevant terms that readers in your genre may search for. Incorporate these keywords into your book's title, subtitle, description, and metadata. This will help your book appear in search results when readers are looking for specific topics or themes.

Choosing the right categories for your book is also important. Select categories that accurately reflect the genre and subject matter of your book, as this will help it appear in relevant browsing lists and increase its chances of being discovered by potential readers.

Writing a compelling book description is crucial for enticing readers to click on your book's page. Use your description to highlight the key selling points of your book and communicate its unique value to readers. A well-crafted description that incorporates relevant keywords can significantly improve your book's visibility within retailer algorithms.

Finally, encourage readers to leave reviews and provide feedback on your book's page. Positive reviews not only increase your book's credibility but also signal to the algorithms that readers are engaged with and enjoying your work. Engage with your readers, respond to their comments, and show appreciation for their support.

By securing endorsements and leveraging online retailer algorithms, you can significantly boost your book's credibility and visibility. Take the time to research potential endorsers, craft compelling pitches, and build relationships with influential figures in your genre. Optimize your book's keywords, categories, and metadata to increase its visibility within online retailer algorithms. By implementing these strategies, you can enhance your book's chances of success in the competitive publishing landscape.

BUILDING RELATIONSHIPS WITH INFLUENCERS - EFFECTIVE STRATEGIES TO BOOST YOUR BOOK'S VISIBILITY:

ESTABLISHING strong relationships with influencers is essential for authors and publishers looking to promote their books effectively. Influencers, including bloggers, bookstagrammers, and podcasters, have established loyal audiences and have the power to amplify your book's visibility. This guide will provide insights on how to connect with influencers, nurture these relationships, and use effective outreach strategies to gain mentions, reviews, and features that can help your book earn a spot on recommended reading lists.

UNDERSTANDING THE POWER OF INFLUENCERS:

DEFINING INFLUENCERS IN THE BOOK INDUSTRY:

IN THE MODERN age of social media and online communities, influencers have emerged as powerful figures who can shape consumer behavior and opinions. In the book industry, influencers are individuals or groups who have established credibility and a dedicated following within the literary community. They can influence and shape the opinions and purchasing decisions of their target audiences.

TYPES OF INFLUENCERS:

There are several influencers in the book industry, each with their own unique features and platforms. These include:

Book reviewers: These influencers are avid readers who analyze, critique, and recommend books to their followers through platforms such as Goodreads, book blogs, or YouTube channels. Their in-depth reviews provide insights and opinions that help readers make informed choices.

Booktubers: Booktubers are influencers who create video content focused on book reviews, discussions, hauls, and recommendations. They often display their passion for books through engaging and entertaining videos, attracting a large following of book lovers.

Bookstagrammers: Bookstagrammers are Instagram influencers who showcase their book collections through carefully curated photos. They use eye-catching aesthetics and captions to engage with their audience, creating a visually appealing space for book discussions and recommendations.

Literary podcasters: These influencers host podcasts dedicated to discussing books, interviewing authors, and providing literary insights. Their podcasts cater to a growing audience of book enthusiasts who enjoy the auditory experience and in-depth conversations.

IMPACT ON TARGET AUDIENCES:

Influencers have a significant impact on their target audiences. Readers often trust and rely on influencers' opinions, recommendations, and analyses when discovering new books or deciding on their next read. The authentic and relatable content creators create a sense of community among their followers, fostering engagement and discussion around books and reading.

Influencers have the power to introduce books to a wider audience, giving exposure to lesser-known authors or titles that may have otherwise gone unnoticed. Their influence can result in increased book sales, heightened author visibility, and a boost in the popularity of certain genres or themes. Influencers can also play a role in shaping literary debates, highlighting diverse voices, and promoting social issues through their platforms.

OPPORTUNITIES FOR BOOK PROMOTION:

Collaborating with influencers can provide excellent opportunities for book promotion. Authors, publishers, and literary agents can leverage influencers' reach and impact to increase awareness, engagement, and sales. Some effective strategies include:

Book reviews and recommendations: Sending advanced review copies to influencers in exchange for their opinions can generate buzz and anticipation surrounding a book's release.

Author interviews and features: Engaging influencers to conduct interviews or feature authors on their platforms provides valuable exposure and insight into an author's writing process or backstory.

Giveaways and contests: Collaborating with influencers for book-related giveaways or contests encourages audience participation, boosts engagement, and can lead to increased book sales.

Sponsored content and brand partnerships: Influencers can promote books through sponsored posts or paid partnerships, introducing their followers to new titles and authors.

Influencers in the book industry have become integral to book promotion and discovery. Their opinions carry weight with their target audiences, and partnering with them can provide significant opportunities for authors and publishers to increase visibility, engagement, and sales. Acknowledging and leveraging the influence of these individuals is an important part of successful book marketing and promotion.

RESEARCHING AND SELECTING THE RIGHT INFLUENCERS - MAXIMIZING SUCCESSFUL COLLABORATIONS FOR YOUR BOOK:

Social media influencers now play an important role in promoting books and helping authors connect with their target audience. Collaborating with influencers who align with your book's genre, themes, and target audience can significantly boost its visibility and increase potential readership. This guide will give you valuable insights on how to research and select the right influencers, ultimately increasing the likelihood of a successful collaboration.

UNDERSTANDING YOUR BOOK'S GENRE, THEMES, AND TARGET AUDIENCE:

Before digging into influencer research, it is essential to understand your book's genre, themes, and target audience. Analyze the key aspects of your book, including its genre (e.g., romance, thriller, self-help), underlying themes (e.g., mental health, entrepreneurship, adventure), and the intended demographic (e.g., young adults, parents, professionals). This clarity will serve as a foundation for finding influencers who resonate with your book's content and context.

EXPLORING SOCIAL MEDIA PLATFORMS:

Next, explore various social media platforms to identify which ones align best with your book and target audience. Platforms such as Instagram, YouTube, TikTok, and podcasts have immense reach and are popular among different demographics. Research how each platform can help your book's promotion and engage with readers active on those platforms.

CONDUCTING THOROUGH INFLUENCER RESEARCH:

Once you have identified relevant social media platforms, focus on researching influencers who align with your book's genre, themes, and target audience. There are several ways to discover relevant influencers:

a. Hashtags and Search Functions: Utilize platform-specific search functions and popular hashtags related to your book's genre and themes to find influencers who are discussing or promoting similar content.

b. Influencer Databases: Take advantage of influencer databases such as Influencer Marketing Hub, Grin, or Upfluence, which let you filter influencers based on niche, engagement rate, and follower count.

c. Social Listening and Engaging: Engage in social listening by tracking conversations around your book's genre and themes. Identify influencers who often participate in these discussions, have quality engagement with their audience, and might be suitable for collaborations.

d. Professional Recommendations: Seek recommendations from authors, literary agents, or literary organizations who have collaborated with influencers. They might have insights and recommendations based on their own experiences.

EVALUATING INFLUENCER RELEVANCE AND REACH:

After compiling a list of potential influencers, evaluate their relevance and reach to determine their suitability for collaboration. Consider these factors:

a. Content Alignment: Ensure the influencer's content aligns with your book's genre, themes, and overall messaging. Review their previous collaborations and posts to gauge their consistency and compatibility with your book.

b. Audience Demographics: Scrutinize the influencer's audience demographics, paying attention to age, location, interests, and engagement levels. Compare this data with your target audience to ensure alignment.

c. Engagement Metrics: Analyze an influencer's reach and engagement by examining their follower count, likes, comments, shares, and other relevant metrics. This data shows you how engaged their audience is.

d. Authenticity and Credibility: Evaluate an influencer's authenticity and credibility by considering factors such as their storytelling style, audience trustworthiness, and consistency in delivering genuine content.

BUILDING RELATIONSHIPS AND COLLABORATING:

Once you have identified the most suitable influencers, focus on building meaningful relationships with them. Engage with their content by leaving thoughtful comments, sharing their posts, and supporting their work. Once a relationship is established, contact them directly, introducing your book and proposing a collaboration that benefits both parties. Remember to personalize your approach to show genuine interest in their work.

Researching and selecting the right influencers for your book can significantly affect its success by connecting with the right audience.

By understanding your book's genre, themes, and target audience, exploring relevant social media platforms, conducting thorough influencer research, evaluating relevance and reach, and building relationships, you can maximize the chances of a successful collaboration with influencers who align with your book's values and goals.

~

BUILDING AUTHENTIC RELATIONSHIPS:

ENGAGING WITH INFLUENCERS' CONTENT:

ENGAGING WITH INFLUENCERS' content can be a powerful strategy to build relationships, gain exposure, and increase your own credibility within your niche. Here are effective methods to genuinely engage with influencers:

Participate in discussions: One of the best ways to engage with influencers is by participating in discussions on their social media posts, blog comments, or forums. Share your thoughts, ask questions, or provide valuable insights related to the topic being discussed. This shows your interest and helps prove yourself to be a knowledgeable contributor.

Share their content: Share influencers' content on your social media platforms, blog, or website. Provide proper credit and tag the influencer. By sharing their content, you show your support for their work, which can capture their attention and encourage them to engage with you.

Provide insightful comments: Take the time to craft thoughtful and genuine comments on influencers' posts or articles. Rather than simply leaving generic comments like "Great post!", share your opinion, provide more information, or ask specific questions to spark a conversation. This not only catches the influencer's attention but can also encourage others to engage with your comment.

Tag and mention influencers: Whenever you create relevant content or share something related to an influencer, tag them or mention them in your post. This increases the chances of the influencer noticing and engaging with your content. However, avoid excessive tagging or mentions, as this may come across as spammy or insincere.

Collaborate on content: If you have a genuine interest in working with an influencer, consider reaching out with a proposition for collaboration. This could involve co-creating content, organizing events or webinars together, or even engaging in an interview-style conversation. Collaborating not only lets you engage with the influencer but also exposes you to their audience, thus expanding your reach.

Offer valuable resources: Identify valuable resources, such as articles, studies, or tools, that align with an influencer's interests or content. Share these resources with them and explain why you find them valuable. This shows you've taken the time to understand their niche and can give them useful information, which can lead to further engagement.

Remember, genuine engagement with influencers requires building meaningful relationships and providing value. Avoid spammy tactics or only seeking personal gain from the interaction. Focus on creating quality interactions that show your authentic interest and dedication to the influencer and their content.

CONNECTING ON SOCIAL MEDIA:

To effectively connect and build relationships with influencers on social media platforms, it's important to understand how to use these platforms strategically. Here are tips on leveraging social media to connect with influencers:

Identify the right influencers: Start by identifying influencers in your industry or niche. Look for individuals with a significant following and whose values align with your brand. Tools like BuzzSumo, Ninja-Outreach, or even manual research can help you find relevant influencers.

Follow, like, and share their content: Once you've identified suitable influencers, start by following them on social media. Engage with their content by liking and sharing their posts, while also leaving thoughtful comments. This shows your interest and helps you establish an initial connection.

Engage through direct messages: Direct messages can be a powerful tool to foster relationships. Don't jump straight into a pitch; rather, take the time to engage in meaningful conversations. Share your thoughts on their content, ask questions, or seek advice. This personal interaction can lead to a deeper connection.

Provide value: Influencers appreciate when people bring value to their community. Offer to collaborate on content, co-create a project, or provide support in their initiatives. By being helpful and genuine, you can prove yourself to be a valuable connection.

Attend events and tagging: Keep an eye out for events or conferences where influencers might be present. Go to these events, engage with the influencers in person, and share your experiences on social media by tagging them. This builds familiarity and adds another layer to your relationship.

Maintain consistent engagement: Building relationships takes time and effort. Be consistent in your engagement by regularly interacting with their content, joining discussions, and genuinely showing support. This consistency helps sustain the relationship and keeps you on their radar.

Show appreciation: Influencers often appreciate public recognition and appreciation. Tag them in posts where you promote their content or express your gratitude for their contributions. This not only strengthens the connection but also helps increase your visibility among their followers.

Remember, building relationships with influencers requires patience, empathy, and maintaining genuine connections. Stay focused on creating mutually beneficial relationships and provide value in any way you can.

ESTABLISHING MUTUAL BENEFITS:

Establishing mutual benefits is important when building relationships with influencers. By offering them exclusive content, pre-releases, or opportunities for their audience, you can create win-win collaborations that provide value to both parties. Here's how you can provide value to influencers and foster mutually beneficial partnerships:

Understand their audience: Before approaching an influencer, take the time to understand their audience demographics, interests, and preferences. This information will help you tailor your offerings to provide maximum value to their followers.

Offer exclusive content: Influencers are always looking for fresh and engaging content to share with their audience. Give them exclusive articles, videos, or other relevant materials that align with their niche and captivate their audience's attention. This exclusive content will make the influencer feel special while also offering something valuable to their followers.

Provide pre-releases: If you have upcoming product launches, services, or events, consider offering influencers the opportunity to have an exclusive sneak peek or early access. This gives them the chance to offer their audience unique and exciting content before anyone else, boosting their relevancy and value as an influencer.

Offer promotional opportunities: Collaborate with influencers by arranging promotional opportunities for their audience. This could include special discounts, giveaways, or contests exclusive to their followers. By providing these opportunities, you not only provide value to the influencer but also incentivize their audience to engage with your brand or offerings.

Customize partnerships: Tailor your collaboration offers to match the influencer's goals and interests. This personalization shows you are invested in the partnership and can help establish a stronger connection. For example, if an influencer is passionate about a specific cause or charity, consider partnering with them for a charitable campaign that aligns with both of your values.

Share affiliate programs: Many influencers are open to affiliate partnerships that let them earn a commission for any sales generated from their promotion. By offering influencers an affiliate program, you allow them to monetize their influence while also benefiting from increased brand awareness and sales.

Engage and interact: Building a long-term relationship with influencers requires ongoing engagement and interaction. Regularly like, comment, and share their content to show your support and appreciation. Additionally, consider featuring them on your own platforms or inviting them to collaborate on branded content.

Remember, the key to establishing mutual benefits is to offer value that aligns with the influencer's niche and audience. By providing exclusive content, pre-releases, or opportunities that cater to their audience's interests, you can form collaborations rewarding for both parties involved.

CRAFTING EFFECTIVE OUTREACH STRATEGIES:

PERSONALIZED PITCHES:

HERE IS **an example of a personalized pitch that can be adapted for different purposes.**

Subject: [Name], Let's Connect on Our Shared Passion for [Topic]!

Hi [Name],

I hope this email finds you well! I wanted to reach out as I've been following your work for some time now and I am inspired by your knowledge in the [topic/field]. As an influential figure in this space, we share a common interest and a genuine enthusiasm for [topic/industry].

I recently came across your [blog/article/podcast] on [specific topic] and I was blown away by the depth of your knowledge and the fresh perspective you bring to the table. Your ability to [specific skill] stood out to me and I found myself nodding along as I read/listened to your insights.

Being equally passionate about [topic/industry], I have also been involved in [specific projects/experiences] where I have explored [related topic/field]. Through these experiences, I have realized the importance of connecting with like-minded individuals like yourself who are equally driven to make a positive impact in this sphere.

I genuinely admire the work you do, not only for your knowledge but also for your ability to [specific attribute like inspiring/motivating/educating]. It's clear that your dedication and commitment have made a significant impact on your audience, which is why I believe that collaborating or simply conversing with you could be valuable.

I would love the opportunity to connect with you further to discuss [shared interest or idea], share experiences, and explore potential avenues for collaboration. Perhaps we could have a quick call or exchange emails to bounce off some ideas? I am confident that our shared passion for [topic/industry] would make for an engaging conversation.

Please let me know if you would be available for a call at your convenience or if you have any other preferred mode of communication. I am excited about the prospect of connecting with you and hope to hear from you soon!

Warm regards,

[Your Name]

PROVIDING RELEVANT AND COMPELLING MATERIALS:

Creating targeted press kits, providing advanced reader copies (ARCs), and offering exclusive interviews and guest posts are effective strategies for providing relevant and compelling materials to influencers. These approaches help to gain their attention and cater to their specific needs and preferences. In this section, we will explore each strategy .

Targeted Press Kits:

Press kits are essential tools for sharing information about your product or brand with influencers, journalists, and media outlets. To make your press kit more effective, it is important to tailor it to each influencer's interests and focus on the parts relevant to their audience. Here are tips for creating targeted press kits:

a. Research: Study each influencer's niche, style, and earlier work. This will help you understand their interests and tailor the press kit.

b. Customize: Personalize the press kit by addressing the influencer directly and including relevant information about their previous coverage or reviews.

c. Highlights: Include key points about your product, its unique features, and value proposition. Highlight any statistics, accolades, or awards that might grab their attention.

d. Visuals: Incorporate high-quality images, product shots, or infographics to make your press kit visually appealing and easily shareable.

e. Contact information: Provide clear contact details, including your email and phone number, so influencers can easily reach out with questions or requests.

ADVANCED READER COPIES (ARCS):

Offering ARCs, or pre-publication versions of your book, is an effective way to generate buzz and build anticipation among influencers. Here's how to make your ARCs stand out:

a. Limited availability: Create a sense of exclusivity by offering a few ARCs. This encourages influencers to ask for them promptly, increasing the perceived value of these early copies.

b. Personalized notes: Include a personalized note expressing your appreciation for their interest and explaining why you believe your book aligns with their interests or audience. This personal touch will make them more inclined to read and review the book.

c. Call to action: Encourage influencers to share their thoughts about the book on their platforms or social media channels. Offer to provide more materials, such as author interviews or exclusive content, to go along with their reviews.

d. Follow-up: After a reasonable amount of time, follow up with the influencers to remind them about the book, answer their questions, or offer further help.

EXCLUSIVE INTERVIEWS AND GUEST POSTS:

Offering influencers the opportunity to conduct exclusive interviews or contribute guest posts can give them unique and engaging content for their platforms. Here are tips for making this offer appealing:

a. Customize the pitch: Tailor your pitch to each influencer by referencing their previous work or discussing topics they have shown interest in before.

b. Value proposition: Explain how the interview or guest post will help the influencer's audience, highlighting the unique insights, knowledge, or experiences they will gain.

c. Flexibility: Offer multiple options for the interviews (e.g., email, phone, video call) to accommodate the influencer's preferences and schedule.

d. Collaboration: If it's a guest post, suggest collaborating with the influencer on the topic or offering guidance to make sure it aligns with their audience's interests.

e. Promotion: Promise to promote the interview or guest post on your own platforms to increase the exposure they receive.

By providing these targeted materials, such as press kits, ARCs, interviews, or guest posts, you will show your understanding of influencers' needs and preferences, increasing the likelihood of building strong and mutually beneficial relationships with them.

LEVERAGING EXISTING CONNECTIONS:

Leveraging existing connections can be a powerful strategy to gain the attention of influencers and build meaningful relationships within your industry. Your network of connections includes fellow authors, industry professionals, and earlier contacts, all of whom can offer valuable insights, introductions, and support.

Here are effective ways to use your network to secure influencers' attention and forge relationships:

Leverage author connections: Reach out to fellow authors and establish mutually beneficial relationships by supporting each other's work. Collaborate on joint projects, cross-promote each other's books or articles, or offer to write guest posts for their blogs. By building strong relationships with authors who already have influencer status, you can tap into their networks and increase your visibility.

Engage with industry professionals: Go to conferences, workshops, and industry events to network with professionals in your field. Take the time to connect with influential individuals such as agents, editors, or publishers. Share your work, seek feedback, and express your admiration for their knowledge. Building rapport with professionals who have established relationships with influencers can open doors and provide valuable recommendations.

Leverage previous contacts: Reach out to individuals you've already established relationships with such as former colleagues, mentors, or even friends. Share updates about your work and express your desire to connect with influencers. They may introduce you directly or provide valuable insights on the best approach to engage with specific influencers.

Seek recommendations: Ask for recommendations from your connections with strong relationships with influencers. If they are familiar with your work and belief in your talent, they may vouch for you or provide introductions. Personal recommendations can significantly increase your chances of getting noticed by influencers.

Use social media networks: Engage with influencers on social media platforms where they are active. Share their content, leave meaningful comments, and engage in conversations. By consistently showing your interest and support, you can gradually build a relationship with them. Additionally, consider asking your existing connections to share your work or tag you in relevant conversations to increase your visibility.

Offer value: When approaching influencers, focus on how you can provide value to them and their audience. Consider offering to collaborate on a project, provide content for their blog or podcast, or even act as a speaker or panelist at their event. By offering your knowledge and support, you show your commitment and increase the likelihood of forging a meaningful relationship.

Remember, strong relationships take time to build, so be patient and authentic in your approach. Dedicated efforts to engage with your network and support others will help you secure influencers' attention and open doors to opportunities within your industry.

NURTURING AND MAINTAINING RELATIONSHIPS:

REGULAR COMMUNICATION:

DEVELOPING strategies for consistent and meaningful communication with influencers is important for maintaining rapport, especially when there are no ongoing promotional activities. Here are effective strategies to consider:

Establishing a Communication Plan: Create a well-structured communication plan that outlines the frequency, channels, and goals of your communication with influencers. This plan will help you maintain regular and consistent communication throughout the year.

Personalized Outreach: Treat influencers as valued partners and develop personal relationships with them. Tailor your communication to their interests and preferences, showing genuine interest in their work and lives.

Build a Community: Encourage influencers to become a part of a community where they can interact with each other and with your brand. This can be a private Facebook group, a Slack channel, or even a dedicated forum. This sense of community will foster ongoing communication.

Share Exclusive Content: Keep influencers engaged by providing them exclusive content, such as product sneak peeks, industry insights, or behind-the-scenes information. This makes them feel special and keeps them motivated to communicate with your brand.

Provide Constant Support: Offer influencers assistance beyond promotions. Respond to their queries promptly, provide necessary resources, and actively engage with their content by commenting, sharing, and liking.

Regular Check-ins: Schedule regular check-ins to catch up with influencers about their personal and professional lives. Discuss their current projects, challenges, and plans. These conversations will strengthen the relationship and make it easier to collaborate.

Surprise and Delight: Surprise influencers with unexpected gestures of appreciation, such as sending them personalized gifts, handwritten notes, or featuring them on your brand's social media channels. These small acts go a long way in maintaining rapport.

Collaborate on Non-Promotional Projects: Look for opportunities to collaborate with influencers on non-promotional projects. This could organize joint events, hosting webinars, or even co-creating content. Such collaborations build trust, deepen relationships, and foster ongoing communication.

Use Various Communication Channels: Utilize multiple communication channels to keep the conversation going. These can include email, phone calls, social media direct messages, video calls, and even face-to-face meetings. Adapt your communication style to the influencer's preferences.

Measure and Optimize: Regularly evaluate the effectiveness of your communication strategies. Analyze response rates, engagement levels, and track the impact on your overall influencer marketing goals. Use the insights gained to continuously optimize your communication approach.

Consistent and meaningful communication with influencers is key to maintaining rapport outside of promotional periods. By implementing these strategies, you can nurture a strong and enduring partnership with influencers that extends far beyond transactional engagements.

COLLABORATION OPPORTUNITIES:

Influencer collaborations can be important in expanding your reach and achieving business goals in our highly connected world. While reviews are a common way to collaborate with influencers, there are many other opportunities to explore that can bring a fresh and exciting twist to your partnership. Here are some creative collaboration ideas to consider:

Host Joint Events: Organize live or virtual events with influencers that bring together your brand and their audience. This could include workshops, product launches, webinars, or even exclusive meetups. By combining your knowledge and the influencer's influence, you can create an engaging experience that benefits both parties and offers value to your target audience.

Participate in Live Interviews: Arrange interviews, Q&A sessions, or panel discussions with influencers in which you can discuss relevant industry topics or product-related discussions. This helps to establish your brand's authority, sparks meaningful conversations, and provides valuable insights to your audience.

Create Exclusive Content Together: Collaborate with influencers to create co-branded content, such as blog posts, videos, or podcasts. This lets you tap into the influencer's unique style and knowledge, while also giving them an opportunity to showcase their creativity. By pooling your resources and skill sets, you can produce high-quality content that appeals to both your audiences and maximizes exposure.

Take Over Social Media Accounts: Offer influencers the opportunity to take over your brand's social media accounts for a day or a specific campaign. This lets them engage with your audience directly and share their unique perspective, while also giving your brand a fresh voice and increased visibility within their community.

Host Influencer Challenges or Contests: Create challenges or contests in collaboration with influencers, where participants can showcase their creativity, skill, or knowledge related to your brand. This not only generates user-generated content that can be shared on social media, but also helps to build a sense of community and loyalty among your audience.

Co-Create Products or Services: Explore the possibility of developing co-branded products or exclusive services with influencers. This lets their creativity and expertise be directly integrated into your offerings, making it more appealing to their audience and strengthening the partnership further.

Remember, when considering collaboration opportunities with influencers, it's essential to choose influencers whose values align with your brand and have an audience that matches your target market. By thinking outside the box and exploring these creative collaboration ideas, you can establish a more meaningful connection with influencers, amplify your brand's message, and achieve mutually beneficial outcomes.

EXPRESSING GRATITUDE:

Expressing gratitude is an important skill that helps strengthen relationships and shows appreciation for someone's support and influence. Whether it's an influencer who has helped you grow your business, provided guidance, or simply inspired you, acknowledging their efforts publicly is a great way to show your gratitude.

One way to express gratitude is by sharing the influencer's content. This not only shows you value their work, but also helps increase their reach and visibility. When you come across an influencer's post, article, or video that resonates with you, take a moment to share it on your own social media platforms. Add a thoughtful caption explaining why you appreciate their work and tag them so they can see your message. This act of sharing not only exposes the influencer but also helps build a sense of reciprocity and gratitude.

Another way to show appreciation is by acknowledging their efforts publicly. When an influencer helps you, whether it's through mentoring, collaborations, or simply providing valuable insights, take the time to publicly thank them. This could be as a post on your social media platforms, a blog post featuring them, or even a shoutout during a webinar or conference presentation. By publicly acknowledging their contributions, you not only express your gratitude but also enhance their reputation and influence.

Sending personalized thank-you messages is also a powerful way to show your appreciation. Taking the time to craft a thoughtful message that highlights how the influencer has affected your life or business can leave a lasting impression. Whether it's a handwritten note, an email, or a direct message on social media, the key is to make it personal and sincere. Be specific about how their support has been valuable to you and how it has made a positive difference.

Expressing gratitude for influential figures in your life is important for fostering relationships and showing appreciation. By acknowledging their efforts publicly, sharing their content, or sending personalized thank-you messages, you can make a lasting impact and show your gratitude for their support and influence.

∿

MAXIMIZING THE IMPACT:

UTILIZING INFLUENCERS IN ONGOING MARKETING EFFORTS:

INFLUENCERS HAVE BECOME powerful marketing tools for brands looking to expand their reach and engage with their target audience in our highly connected environment. Integrating influencer mentions into your ongoing marketing efforts can be a highly effective strategy to amplify your brand message and drive conversions. To maximize the impact of influencer collaboration, it is important to understand how to seamlessly integrate influencer mentions into different marketing channels. This includes social media campaigns, email newsletters, and website promotions.

Social Media Campaigns:

Social media is often the first point of contact between brands and their audience. Incorporating influencer mentions in your social media campaigns can help you leverage their credibility and following to increase brand awareness. Consider these tips:

- Collaborate with influencers who align with your brand values and target audience. Their followers should be potential customers who resonate with your products or services.
- Create engaging and authentic content that incorporates influencer mentions. This can be as product reviews, tutorials, endorsements, or simply featuring them in your brand's posts.
- Use hashtags and tagging features to ensure your influencer mentions reach a wider audience and increase the chances of your content being discovered.

EMAIL NEWSLETTERS:

Email newsletters are a powerful tool for maintaining communication with your existing customer base. Integrating influencer mentions in your newsletters can enhance engagement and drive conversions. Here are best practices:

- Include influencer quotes, testimonials, or endorsements in your newsletters to highlight their positive experiences with your brand.
- Collaborate with influencers on exclusive deals or promotions you can offer to your loyal subscribers. This provides a real benefit to the influencer's audience more likely to engage with your brand.
- Feature influencer-generated content in your newsletters, such as user-generated photos or reviews, to showcase the credibility and trust that influencers bring to your brand.

WEBSITE PROMOTIONS:

Driving traffic to your website is important for expanding brand visibility and driving sales. Integrating influencer mentions into your website promotions can boost credibility and increase conversions. Consider these strategies:

- Create dedicated landing pages featuring influencer collaborations. This lets visitors directly engage with influencer content and learn about their experiences with your brand.
- Incorporate influencer testimonials and endorsements on relevant product or service pages to build trust and provide social proof.
- Offer exclusive discount codes or promotions tied to influencer collaborations. This not only incentivizes the influencer's audience but also lets you track the success of the campaign through referral codes.

To ensure a seamless integration of influencer mentions across your marketing channels, it is essential to establish clear communication with influencers. Convey your brand messaging, campaign goals, and content guidelines to ensure a cohesive and authentic representation of your brand. Using influencers in ongoing marketing efforts, you can amplify your brand message, drive engagement, and ultimately increase conversions.

TRACKING AND ANALYZING RESULTS:

Tracking and analyzing results is an important part of any influencer collaboration campaign for your book. It helps you understand the impact of these collaborations and provides valuable insights to refine your strategies. Here are reasons tracking and analyzing results is important:

Measure campaign effectiveness: By tracking and analyzing the results, you can determine the effectiveness of your influencer collaborations. You can measure metrics like engagement, click-through rates, website traffic, book sales, and social media followers gained because of the collaborations. This data will help you gauge which collaborations generate the best results.

Identify successful strategies: Tracking results lets you identify the strategies that are most successful in promoting your book. For example, you may find that collaborations with influencers with a specific target audience, or a particular content format generate higher engagement and sales. By analyzing these successful strategies, you can build on them for future campaigns.

Understand audience preferences: Analyzing the impact of influencer collaborations provides insights into your target audience's preferences and behaviors. You can gain a better understanding of what type of content resonates with them, which influencers they engage with the most, and how they discover and buy books. This knowledge can inform your future collaborations and marketing efforts.

Optimize budget allocation: Tracking and analyzing results can help you optimize your budget allocation. By identifying which collaborations yield the highest return on investment, you can give more resources toward those influencers or platforms. This ensures you are maximizing your marketing budget and targeting the right audience effectively.

Adjust and refine strategies: Results analysis enables you to adjust and refine your strategies based on data-driven insights. If certain collaborations or tactics are not yielding desired results, you can make informed decisions to pivot and try different approaches. This continuous optimization makes sure your influencer collaborations evolve and improve.

Tracking and analyzing the impact of influencer collaborations is important for understanding what works best for promoting your book. By measuring campaign effectiveness, identifying successful strategies, understanding audience preferences, optimizing budget allocation, and refining strategies, you can develop more effective influencer collaborations and achieve better results with your book marketing efforts.

· · ·

Building relationships with influencers can significantly increase your book's visibility and reach. By understanding the value of influencers, investing in genuine connections, and implementing effective outreach strategies, you can create long-lasting partnerships that propel your book to new heights. Use this guide as a roadmap to establish influential relationships and watch as your book garners mentions, reviews, and features that help position it on recommended reading lists.

USING SOCIAL MEDIA AND ADVERTISING:

AS AN AUTHOR, it is important to use social media and advertising strategies to increase the chances of your book appearing on suggested reading lists and also-boughts. These platforms provide a massive audience, letting you reach your target readers and maximize exposure. By leveraging social media and running effective advertising campaigns, you can significantly affect the success of your book.

Identify your target audience: Before diving into social media and advertising, it is essential to understand who your target audience is. Determine their demographics, interests, and online behavior. This information will help you tailor your campaigns to reach the right people.

Create engaging content: Develop valuable and engaging content related to your book. This can include blog posts, videos, interviews, and excerpts. Share this content on your social media channels to build anticipation and generate interest in your book.

Leverage social media platforms: Utilize platforms like Facebook, Instagram, Twitter, and LinkedIn to promote your book. Develop a strong presence on these platforms by regularly posting updates, sharing relevant content, and engaging with your audience. Create a community around your book, interact with readers, and encourage them to share their thoughts and reviews.

Use targeted advertising campaigns: Social media platforms offer highly effective targeting options for advertising. You can narrow your audience by factors such as age, location, interests, and reading preferences. Craft compelling ad copy and use eye-catching visuals to capture users' attention and entice them to click through to your book's landing page or sales page.

Collaborate with influencers: Collaborating with social media influencers in the book blogging and reviewing community can increase your book's visibility. Contact influential bloggers or reviewers and offer them a copy of your book in exchange for an honest review or feature on their platform. This can help generate buzz and increase the chances of your book appearing on suggested reading lists.

Use hashtags: Hashtags are a powerful tool for increasing discoverability on social media platforms. Research and use relevant hashtags related to your book's genre, themes, and target audience. Encourage readers to use these hashtags when they share and talk about your book, further expanding its reach and visibility.

Engage in online communities: Join online book clubs, forums, and communities that align with your book's genre or themes. Engage in discussions, offer valuable insights, and subtly promote your book when appropriate. Proving yourself to be an active and knowledgeable member of these communities can lead to increased exposure and recommendations from fellow readers.

Track and analyze results: Regularly track and analyze the performance of your social media and advertising campaigns. Social media platforms provide analytics tools that show impressions, clicks, engagement rates, and conversions. Analyze this data to identify what is working and what needs improvement. Adjust your strategies to optimize your book's exposure and reach.

Using social media and targeted advertising campaigns, you can effectively appear on suggested reading lists and also-boughts. Leverage these platforms to reach your target audience, build a community around your book, and generate buzz and excitement. With consistent effort and analysis, you can maximize exposure and increase the success of your book.

TRACKING RESULTS AND MAKING ADJUSTMENTS:

TRACKING data and analytics have become essential tools for authors to measure the effectiveness of their marketing efforts in the evolving world of publishing. By understanding the importance of these metrics and learning how to interpret them, authors can make informed decisions and changes to their book's marketing approach. This not only improves performance but also increases the chances of getting on suggested reading lists and also-boughts, which can significantly boost book sales and visibility.

Tracking data and analytics provide valuable insights into the performance of various marketing channels. By tracking metrics such as website traffic, email open rates, social media engagement, and conversion rates, authors can determine which strategies are generating the most interest and engagement from potential readers. This data helps them identify the most effective channels and give their resources.

Interpreting these metrics requires careful analysis and pattern recognition. For example, if an author's website receives a high volume of traffic but has a low conversion rate, it could show that the website is not optimized for conversions or that the book's sales page needs improvement. But if a specific social media platform drives a significant number of book sales, it might be worth investing more time and effort into that platform.

Additionally, tracking metrics related to reader engagement can provide important information about the effectiveness of different marketing strategies. Tracking metrics such as click-through rates, time spent on the book's landing page, and user feedback can reveal how well the book resonates with its target audience. Authors can use this information to refine their messaging, adjust their targeting, or change the book's cover and blurb to better appeal to potential readers.

Another essential part of tracking results is tracking book sales and rankings. By keeping an eye on sales data, authors can identify trends and patterns, such as the impact of different promotions or advertising campaigns. This information lets them replicate successful strategies, tweak underperforming ones, and adjust their overall marketing approach to maximize sales and visibility.

Making changes based on the insights gained from tracking data and analytics is important to improving marketing performance. By continuously tracking and analyzing results, authors can fine-tune their marketing efforts to reach a wider audience, attract positive reviews, and increase the likelihood of getting their book recommended or appearing in also-boughts on online platforms.

When adjusting marketing strategies, it's important to experiment and test different approaches. For example, authors can try running A/B tests for book covers or ad copy to see which version resonates better with their target audience. They can also experiment with different advertising platforms, promotional strategies, or even book genres to broaden their reach and discover untapped markets.

Finally, it's important to note that tracking data and adjusting should be an ongoing process. As the publishing landscape evolves and reader preferences change, authors must adapt their marketing strategies. By staying informed and continuously tracking and analyzing data, authors can stay ahead of the curve, make informed decisions, and increase their chances of success in a competitive market.

Tracking data and analytics play an important role in measuring the effectiveness of marketing efforts for authors. By interpreting these metrics and adjusting their marketing approach, authors can improve performance, increase visibility, and enhance their chances of getting on suggested reading lists and also-boughts. Embracing data-driven decision-making and continuously refining marketing strategies are important steps toward succeeding the ever-changing world of publishing.

MONETIZING YOUR WRITING BEYOND BOOK - EXPLORING ADDITIONAL REVENUE STREAMS FOR AUTHORS:

AUTHORS ARE INCREASINGLY EXPLORING additional revenue streams beyond traditional book sales, adapting to the changing dynamics of the publishing industry. While writing a book can provide a strong foundation for building a writing career, there are countless opportunities to leverage your skills and knowledge to generate income in other creative ways. This chapter aims to guide authors in monetizing their writing beyond books by exploring alternative revenue streams that can both enhance their earnings and expand their reach.

FREELANCE WRITING:

One of the most accessible and lucrative paths for authors to monetize their writing talents is through freelance work. Many publications, websites, and businesses constantly need quality content. By offering freelance writing services, authors can tap into a broader client base and diversify their income streams. Whether it's crafting articles, blog posts, website copy, or even ghostwriting for other aspiring authors, freelancing allows writers to showcase their knowledge while earning a steady income.

CONTENT CREATION FOR ONLINE PLATFORMS:

With the rise of digital media and online platforms, authors can leverage their writing skills to create content specifically tailored for these spaces. This could include writing scripts for podcasts, creating video content for YouTube channels, or even producing written content for social media platforms. By adapting their writing to various media formats, authors can expand their audience reach and tap into the growing demand for online content.

Speaking Engagements and Workshops:

Authors with a deep understanding of their subject matter and have a strong presence can monetize their knowledge through speaking engagements and workshops. Many conferences, seminars, and events are seeking knowledgeable and engaging speakers to talk to their audience. By leveraging their writing experience, authors can offer captivating presentations, share their insights, and earn speaking fees. Offering writing workshops or coaching services can also be a lucrative revenue stream, letting authors share their craft with aspiring writers while earning more income.

ONLINE COURSES:

In an increasingly digital world, online learning has become a popular and convenient way for individuals to acquire new skills. Authors can create and sell online courses centered on their writing knowledge. These courses can cover various aspects of the writing process, such as character development, plot construction, or marketing strategies. By monetizing their knowledge and providing valuable content, authors can not only generate passive income but also prove themselves to be authority figures in their respective niches.

MERCHANDISE AND BRANDING:

Authors who have built a strong personal brand can explore opportunities to monetize their audience's loyalty through merchandise sales.

This could include merchandise related to their books, such as t-shirts, mugs, or bookmarks featuring memorable quotes or book cover designs. Additionally, authors can explore partnerships with relevant brands or collaborations with artisans to create unique and limited edition items that appeal to their readership.

While writing books remains a fundamental part of an author's career, it is important to explore additional revenue streams to enhance earning potential and maximize the impact of their writing talents. By delving into freelance writing, content creation for online platforms, speaking engagements, workshops, online courses, and merchandise sales, authors can create multiple income streams that not only boost their finances but also expand their creative reach and establish a more sustainable writing career. With a combination of creativity, adaptability, and entrepreneurial spirit, authors can thrive in the ever-evolving publishing landscape.

SECTION FIFTEEN KEY TAKEAWAYS AND ACTION ITEMS

KEY TAKEAWAYS:

1. **Amazon Page Optimization:**
2. A compelling title, subtitle, and professional cover are critical.
3. Craft a persuasive book description with keywords.
4. Encourage and engage with reader reviews.
5. Use relevant categories and keywords.
6. Use Amazon Author Central effectively.
7. Implement Amazon Advertising strategically.
8. Optimize pricing and promote through various channels.
9. **Advertising and Promotion:**
10. Choose the right pricing strategy based on market analysis.
11. Create impactful sales pages with clear CTAs.
12. Use targeted advertising on social media and other platforms.
13. Measure and optimize campaign performance continuously.
14. **Effective Book Promotions:**
15. Define your target audience and tailor promotions.
16. Leverage social media and connect with influencers.
17. Use book review sites and bloggers.

18. Organize giveaways and collaborate with other authors.
19. Engage with readers and participate in literary events.
20. **Suggested Reading Lists:**
21. Research and target appropriate reading lists.
22. Engage with influencers who create reading lists.
23. Collaborate with bookstores and libraries.
24. Create your own suggested reading list.
25. **Also-Boughts:**
26. Understand and leverage the influence of Also-Boughts.
27. Use data to optimize book listings.
28. Analyze customer behavior to enhance discoverability.
29. Build strategic partnerships based on Also-Bought insights.

Action Items:

1. **Optimize Your Amazon Page:**
2. Update your book's title, subtitle, and cover if necessary.
3. Revise your book description with SEO in mind.
4. Start a campaign to encourage more reviews.
5. Reassess and adjust your book's categories and keywords.
6. **Enhance Advertising Efforts:**
7. Analyze current pricing and adjust for competitiveness.
8. Redesign sales pages to be more compelling.
9. Plan and execute a targeted advertising campaign.
10. Set up tools for tracking and analyzing advertising results.
11. **Boost Book Promotions:**
12. Define and research your target audience.
13. Increase social media activity and outreach to influencers.
14. Contact book review platforms for your genre.
15. Plan a giveaway or a collaboration with another author.
16. Schedule reader engagement activities, like Q&A sessions.
17. **Get Featured on Reading Lists:**
18. Identify influential reading lists and understand their criteria.

19. Reach out to influencers and offer your book for consideration.
20. Partner with local bookstores and libraries for promotions.
21. Curate and promote a reading list that includes your book.
22. **Maximize Also-Bought Potential:**
23. Review and optimize your book's Amazon metadata.
24. Analyze Also-Bought data for insights into reader preferences.
25. Consider strategic partnerships with authors in your Also-Boughts.
26. Continuously track your book's performance and adjust strategies.

In our next Section…

In our next section, we'll delve into the practical application of the insights and action items discussed previously, focusing on real-world implementation for maximum impact. Our primary objective will be to explore how businesses, particularly in the publishing and marketing sectors, can effectively use data analytics, sales tracking tools, and market research to refine their strategies and optimize performance. This involves a detailed look at using platforms like Amazon KDP (Kindle Direct Publishing) and IngramSpark for comprehensive sales tracking, leveraging tools like Google Analytics for campaign effectiveness, and the importance of consistent data tracking for sustainable growth. By integrating these tools and techniques, businesses can enhance their decision-making processes, better understand their audiences, and significantly improve sales and marketing outcomes.

Additionally, we'll examine case studies of successful authors and publishers who have used data-driven approaches, providing practical examples and actionable insights. These real-life success stories will illustrate how adapting to market trends, using effective promotional strategies, and maintaining a focus on reader engagement can lead to a lot of improvements in book sales and overall business success. The section will emphasize the importance of staying adaptable and responsive to changing market conditions, using automated data collection for efficiency, and the continuous refinement of marketing strategies based on tracked data. By the end of this section, readers will have a comprehensive understanding of how to apply these key take-aways and action items in their own business contexts, leading to long-term growth and success.

SECTION SIXTEEN: LEVERAGING ANALYTICS FOR MARKETING SUCCESS

UNDERSTANDING AND USING ANALYTICS TO GUIDE MARKETING DECISIONS. OVERVIEW:

ANALYTICS HAS BECOME an essential tool for marketers in today's data-driven world. The ability to collect, analyze, and interpret data provides valuable insights that can guide marketing decisions and drive business success. Understanding and effectively using analytics helps marketers understand their target audience, measure the effectiveness of marketing campaigns, and make informed decisions to optimize their marketing strategies.

One of the key benefits of using analytics is gaining a deeper understanding of the target audience. By analyzing data collected from various sources, marketers can identify trends, preferences, and demographics of their audience. This knowledge lets them tailor their marketing efforts to better meet the needs and expectations of their customers. Whether it is refining product offerings, developing personalized messaging, or determining the most effective channels to reach their target audience, analytics plays an important role in this process.

Another powerful use of analytics in marketing is tracking the performance and impact of marketing campaigns. With the ability to track and measure key performance indicators (KPIs), marketers can evaluate the success of their campaigns and make data-driven decisions to optimize their strategies. Whether it is tracking website traffic, email open rates, conversion rates, or social media engagement, analytics provides insights into what is working and what needs improvement. By analyzing these metrics, marketers can make informed decisions on budget allocation, content creation, and campaign changes to maximize their ROI (return on investment).

Analytics can help marketers identify opportunities and anticipate market trends. By analyzing historical data and market trends, marketers can identify new market segments, emerging trends, and potential areas for growth. This information enables them to develop strategies that capitalize on these opportunities and stay ahead of the competition.

To effectively use analytics, marketers must have a strong foundation in data analysis and interpretation. They should be able to identify relevant KPIs, collect and manage data effectively, and draw meaningful insights from the data. Additionally, marketers must stay up to date with the latest analytics tools and technologies to ensure they are leveraging the full potential of the available data.

Understanding and using analytics to guide marketing decisions is important in today's competitive business landscape. By harnessing the power of analytics, marketers can gain a deeper understanding of their target audience, measure the effectiveness of their campaigns, and identify opportunities for growth. By making data-driven decisions, marketers can optimize their marketing strategies and drive business success.

TOOLS AND RESOURCES TRACKING BOOK SALES AND ROI:

IN THE COMPETITIVE world of book publishing, it is important to track sales and ROI to gauge the success of your publishing efforts. This section aims to provide a comprehensive guide to the tools and resources available for effectively tracking book sales and measuring your ROI. Whether you are an aspiring author, self-published writer, or part of a publishing team, this section will equip you with the knowledge and tools needed to make data-driven decisions and maximize your profits.

PART 1: UNDERSTANDING THE IMPORTANCE OF TRACKING SALES AND ROI

Exploring the significance of tracking book sales and ROI

Tracking book sales and ROI is important for authors and publishers as it lets them measure the success and profitability of their work. By exploring the significance of tracking book sales and ROI, we can understand the advantages it brings and how it can inform future decision-making.

Measuring Success: Tracking book sales enables authors and publishers to measure the success of their books. It helps in determining whether the book is reaching its target audience and if it is meeting sales expectations. This information is essential for assessing the effectiveness of marketing strategies and understanding which parts of the book resonate with readers.

Understanding Market Trends: By tracking book sales, authors and publishers can gain valuable insights into market trends. They can identify which genres or themes are popular, letting them tailor their future publications according to readers' preferences. It helps them stay ahead of the competition and make informed decisions on what types of books to invest in.

Identifying Revenue Streams: Through tracking book sales, authors and publishers can identify the most profitable revenue streams. They can determine which formats (e.g., hardcover, paperback, ebook) or distribution channels (e.g., online retailers, brick-and-mortar bookstores) generate higher sales and better ROI. This information is valuable for optimizing revenue generation and reducing costs.

ROI Evaluation: Tracking book sales alongside the associated costs lets authors and publishers calculate the return on investment. This analysis helps them understand the financial implications of publishing a book, including printing costs, marketing expenses, and author royalties. By comparing revenue with investment, they can assess whether the book has been a profitable endeavor or not.

Planning and Decision-making: The data obtained from tracking book sales and ROI lets authors and publishers make informed decisions about future projects. They can identify which genres or themes are more likely to generate sales, which marketing strategies are effective, and which distribution channels offer better returns. This information enables them to strategize book releases, set realistic goals, and allocate resources effectively.

Negotiating with Publishers and Agents: For authors seeking deals with publishers or literary agents, tracking book sales and ROI can be useful during negotiations. Concrete sales data and ROI figures show the potential profitability of a book, making authors more attractive to publishers and agents. It gives them leverage and helps secure better publishing contracts or representation.

Tracking book sales and ROI is significantly important to authors and publishers. It lets them measure success, understand market trends, identify revenue streams, evaluate ROI, and make informed decisions. By harnessing this data, authors and publishers can optimize their strategy, increase profitability, and ensure their future literary endeavors are well-aligned with market demands.

The Benefits of Data-driven Decision Making:

Data-driven decision making is a business strategy that involves using quantitative data and analysis to inform decision making processes. This approach has gained popularity in recent years due to its many benefits. Here are some advantages of data-driven decision making:

Accuracy and reliability: Data-driven decision making eliminates guesswork and reduces the risk of deciding based on subjective opinions or biases. By relying on factual data and analysis, businesses can make more accurate and reliable decisions.

Improved decision making: Data-driven decision making lets businesses gain insights into various parts of their operations, such as customer behavior, market trends, and operational efficiency. These insights help organizations make well-informed decisions with a higher probability of success.

Cost efficiency: By analyzing data, businesses can identify areas where they can reduce costs and improve efficiency. For example, they can identify processes consuming excessive resources and streamline or eliminate them. Data-driven decision making helps companies make cost-effective choices.

Competitive advantage: In today's highly competitive business environment, staying ahead of the competition is important. Data-driven decision making enables organizations to identify new market opportunities, understand customer preferences, and adapt their strategies. This gives them a competitive edge over their rivals.

Enhanced customer experience: Data-driven decision making lets businesses analyze customer data and gain insights into their preferences, needs, and behaviors. By understanding their customers better, companies can tailor their products, services, and marketing efforts to meet their specific needs, resulting in an improved customer experience.

Risk mitigation: Making decisions based on data helps businesses reduce risks and make more informed choices. Data analysis can identify potential risks, anticipate market trends, and highlight potential issues before they become major problems. This enables organizations to take proactive measures to mitigate risks and enhance their overall risk management strategy.

Measurable outcomes: Data-driven decision making provides a measurable approach to evaluate the success of decisions. By setting clear goals and using data to track progress, businesses can objectively measure the outcomes of their decisions. This lets them assess their performance, identify areas for improvement, and adjust as necessary.

Data-driven decision making empowers businesses to make informed choices based on objective facts and analysis. This leads to more accurate decision-making, improved efficiency, enhanced customer experience, and a competitive advantage. Using data-driven strategies, organizations can optimize their operations, reduce costs, and achieve sustainable growth.

PART 2: ESSENTIAL TOOLS FOR TRACKING BOOK SALES

There are several online platforms for authors and publishers to track book sales, track revenue, and gain valuable insights into the performance of their published works. Some popular platforms include:

Amazon KDP: One of the most widely used platforms, Amazon KDP gives authors real-time data on their eBook and paperback sales. It offers detailed reports on units sold, royalties earned, and Kindle Unlimited pages read. Additionally, it provides sales data broken down by region, marketing promotions, and advertising campaigns.

IngramSpark: IngramSpark lets authors distribute their books to various online retailers, bookstores, and libraries worldwide. It provides comprehensive sales reports, including print-on-demand (POD) sales, eBooks, wholesale, and retail distribution. The platform displays data on units sold, revenue, discounts, and a breakdown of sales by format and location.

Barnes & Noble Press: As a self-publishing platform for Barnes & Noble, it offers authors access to sales data through their online dashboard. Authors can track their eBook and print sales, measure their royalties, and track performance across different geographical regions.

BookBub Partners: BookBub is primarily known for its email marketing service, but it also provides a strong dashboard for authors to track eBook sales. It offers insights into sales from BookBub promotions, affiliate links, third-party retailers, and can even provide information about other titles that have been cross promoted.

Draft2Digital: Draft2Digital is a distribution platform that helps authors publish their eBooks across multiple platforms such as Amazon, Apple Books, Kobo, Barnes & Noble, and more. While it does not provide data on individual book sales, it aggregates sales data from different retailers, letting authors view their total sales, royalties earned, and trends.

Smashwords: Smashwords is an eBook distribution platform that helps authors distribute their works to major online retailers. The platform offers sales and royalty reporting, enabling authors to track their sales performance across various channels.

These platforms play an important role in tracking book sales and providing authors and publishers with the data to evaluate their success, make informed marketing decisions, and optimize their book distribution strategies.

Spreadsheet Templates and Software for Sales Tracking:

Sales tracking is an essential part of managing a business. Using spreadsheet templates and software can help streamline the process and ensure correct and organized sales data. Below are examples of spreadsheet templates and software that can be used for sales tracking:

Microsoft Excel:

Excel is a popular spreadsheet software that offers a variety of templates for sales tracking. These templates include pre-designed tables, charts, and formulas to track sales data, such as revenue, units sold, and profit margins. Excel also allows customization based on specific business needs.

Google Sheets:

Google Sheets is a cloud-based spreadsheet software similar to Excel but with the advantage of being accessible from anywhere with an internet connection. It offers various sales tracking templates that can be easily shared with team members for real-time collaboration.

Salesforce:

Salesforce is a comprehensive Customer Relationship Management (CRM) software that includes sales tracking capabilities. It lets businesses track leads, opportunities, and closed deals, as well as generate reports and forecasts. Salesforce also integrates with other tools and platforms to provide a complete sales tracking solution.

HubSpot:

HubSpot is another popular CRM software that offers sales tracking features. It lets businesses manage contacts, track deals, and automate sales processes, providing insights into sales activities and performance. HubSpot also integrates with marketing automation tools, making it a comprehensive solution for sales and marketing alignment.

Zoho CRM:

Zoho CRM is a cloud-based CRM software that offers sales tracking functionalities. It helps businesses track leads, manage sales pipelines, and generate reports. Zoho CRM also provides automation features, such as email and workflow automation, to streamline sales processes.

Pipedrive:

Pipedrive is a CRM software designed specifically for sales teams. It offers an intuitive interface and visual sales pipeline, making it easy to track deals and track progress. Pipedrive also provides features like activity reminders, document tracking, and goal setting to enhance sales tracking and performance.

Insightly:

Insightly is a CRM software that includes sales tracking capabilities. It lets businesses manage contacts, track leads and opportunities, and track sales activities. It also offers project management features, making it a suitable choice for businesses that need both sales and project tracking capabilities.

When choosing a spreadsheet template or software for sales tracking, it is important to consider the specific needs and size of your business. Evaluate the features, ease of use, and integration capabilities to find the best fit for your sales tracking requirements.

Sales Tracking Apps and Tools:

There are several sales tracking apps and tools available in the market that can help businesses effectively manage and track their sales activities. Here are popular options:

Salesforce: Salesforce is one of the most widely used sales tracking apps that provides a comprehensive platform for managing sales, marketing, and customer relationships. It offers features like lead management, pipeline tracking, sales forecasting, and real-time analytics.

HubSpot CRM: HubSpot CRM is a free tool that lets businesses track their sales activities, manage contacts, and monitor deals. It also offers sales reporting, deal management, and email tracking features to help sales teams stay organized and focused.

Zoho CRM: Zoho CRM is a strong sales tracking tool that offers features like lead and pipeline management, sales automation, and performance tracking. It lets businesses create custom reports, track sales goals, and integrate with other business applications.

Pipedrive: Pipedrive is a sales-focused CRM tool that provides a visual sales pipeline to help businesses track deals and sales activities. It offers features like deal tracking, contact management, sales activity dashboards, and goal setting capabilities.

Insightly: Insightly is a CRM platform that offers sales tracking features to help businesses manage leads, contacts, and sales opportunities. It provides functionalities such as email tracking, task management, sales reporting, and integration with popular business tools.

Salesflare: Salesflare is an easy-to-use sales tracking app that automates contact and pipeline management. It offers features like email tracking, deal tracking, follow-up reminders, and data enrichment to ensure accurate and up-to-date customer information.

Freshsales: Freshsales is a sales CRM tool that helps businesses track leads, track sales activities, and manage customer relationships. It offers features like lead scoring, email tracking, pipeline management, and sales reporting.

Pipedrive: Pipedrive is a sales CRM tool that provides a visual sales pipeline to help businesses track deals and sales activities. It offers features like deal tracking, contact management, sales activity dashboards, and goal setting capabilities.

These are a few examples of sales tracking apps and tools available in the market. Each tool has its own unique features, so evaluate your specific needs and consider factors like price, scalability, and integration capabilities before choosing the best sales tracking app for your business.

PART 3: ANALYZING BOOK SALES DATA

Metrics to Consider When Analyzing Book Sales Data:

When analyzing book sales data, there are several metrics to consider to gain insights into the performance and success of a book. These metrics can include:

Unit Sales: This metric measures the number of books sold within a specific period. It indicates the popularity and reach of a book.

Revenue: Revenue refers to the total income generated from sales. It is an essential metric that helps determine the financial success of a book.

Royalties: Royalties are the author's share of the revenue earned from book sales. Tracking royalty payments provides insights into the financial compensation authors receive based on their book's performance.

Average Selling Price: This metric calculates the average price at which a book is sold. It can help understand the pricing strategy and its impact on sales and revenue.

Sales by Format: Analyzing sales by format, such as hardcover, paperback, ebook, or audiobook, helps identify the preferred reading formats among consumers. This information can help in deciding on format variations and marketing strategies.

Sales by Genre: Analyzing sales by genre provides insights into consumer preferences and trends. It helps identify popular genres and specific genres performing well or struggling.

Sales by Region: Evaluating sales by region provides information about regional preferences and potential target markets. It helps identify regions where the book is in high demand and regions that can be further explored.

Sales by Channel: This metric analyzes sales by different distribution channels, such as brick-and-mortar bookstores, online retailers, direct sales, or specialty stores. It provides insights into the effectiveness of various sales channels and helps in optimizing distribution strategies.

Conversion Rate: Conversion rate measures the percentage of potential readers who actually buy the book. It helps track the effectiveness of marketing strategies, cover design, book descriptions, and other factors that influence readers' purchasing decisions.

Bestseller Rankings: Tracking bestseller rankings, such as those on platforms like Amazon, indicates a book's popularity and visibility. It allows for benchmarking against competitors and helps understand the book's performance in relation to others in the same category.

By analyzing these metrics, publishers, authors, and marketers can make better-informed decisions, optimize marketing efforts, and identify growth opportunities in the book industry.

Interpreting Sales Patterns and Trends:

Interpreting sales patterns and trends is an essential part of identifying and understanding the performance of a business. By analyzing these patterns, businesses can make informed decisions about their marketing strategies, inventory management, and overall operations.

One of the first steps in interpreting sales patterns and trends is to gather relevant data. This data typically includes sales figures, customer demographics, product categories, and geographical information. This information lets businesses segment their sales data and identify patterns specific to certain customer groups or product lines.

Once the data is collected, businesses can begin analyzing the sales patterns and trends. Several key factors are worth considering during this analysis:

Seasonality: Sales patterns often show seasonal fluctuations, influenced by factors such as holidays, weather, or cultural events. By recognizing these recurring patterns, businesses can plan their marketing campaigns and inventory management.

Trend Analysis: Tracking sales trends over an extended period helps businesses identify long-term patterns and predict future performance. It involves analyzing sales data over a specified time frame (monthly, quarterly, or yearly) to identify growth or decline patterns.

Product Performance: Analyzing sales patterns at a product level is important to understand which products are selling well and which are underperforming. This analysis helps businesses decide on product development, inventory management, and pricing strategies.

Customer Segmentation: Segmenting sales data by customer demographics, such as age, gender, or location, lets businesses identify specific consumer behavior patterns. This information helps tailor marketing and sales strategies to meet the unique needs and preferences of different customer segments.

Comparative Analysis: Comparing sales patterns against competitors can provide valuable insights into a business's market position and performance. This analysis can uncover opportunities for improvement, highlight competitive advantages, or reveal gaps.

Data Visualization: Representing sales patterns and trends visually through graphs, charts, or dashboards simplifies complex data analysis. Visual presentations make it easier to identify patterns, correlations, and outliers, aiding in decision-making processes.

Interpreting sales patterns and trends is an ongoing process that requires regular tracking and analysis. By focusing on these patterns, businesses can identify areas of growth, optimize their operations, and adapt to changing market conditions. It also helps create data-driven strategies that lead to increased sales and improved overall performance.

Identifying Target Markets and Reader Demographics:

Identifying target markets and reader demographics is an important step in understanding and connecting with your audience. By understanding the features and preferences of your target market, you can tailor your marketing efforts and content to effectively engage with your readers. Here are steps to help you identify target markets and determine reader demographics:

Define your product or service: Start by clearly defining what you offer. What problem does your product or service solve? What are its features and benefits? This will help you identify the primary group of people likely to need your offering.

Research the market: Conduct market research to gather data and insights about your industry and potential customer base. Look for existing market reports, analyze trends, and study the competition.

This information will give you a broader understanding of who your target market might be.

Create customer profiles: Develop detailed profiles of your ideal customers, also known as buyer personas. Consider demographics such as age, gender, location, education level, income, occupation, and lifestyle. Additionally, examine psychographics like interests, values, hobbies, and personality traits. This will help you build a clear image of the individuals who would help most from your product or service.

Conduct surveys and interviews: Consider conducting online surveys and interviews with your current customers or target audience. This direct interaction will provide valuable insights into their preferences, needs, and motivations. Ask questions about their demographics, buying behaviors, and communication preferences. This data will confirm or refine your understanding of your target market.

Analyze website and social media analytics: Dive into the analytics of your website and social media platforms to gain insights into who is consuming your content and engaging with your brand. Look at metrics like page views, bounce rate, time on site, and demographics (when available). This data will help you understand the features of your current readership and identify any gaps between your target market and actual audience.

Test and refine: Use the information you have gathered to develop targeted marketing campaigns and content strategies. Implement A/B testing to refine your targeting and messaging based on what resonates best with your target market. Continually track and analyze your results, making changes as needed.

Remember that identifying target markets and reader demographics is an ongoing process. Regularly engage with your audience, collect feedback, and adapt your strategies as your market evolves. By understanding your target market and their specific needs, you can craft compelling content and build a loyal readership.

PART 4: MEASURING RETURN ON INVESTMENT (ROI)

Understanding the Concept of ROI for Book Publishing:

ROI is an important concept to understand in the context of book publishing. It lets publishers evaluate the financial success of their publishing endeavors by comparing the money they have invested in a particular book project to the returns they have generated from it.

ROI is calculated by dividing the net profit from a book by the total investment cost and expressing it as a percentage. The net profit is calculated by subtracting all the expenses involved in publishing, marketing, distributing, and promoting the book from the revenue generated through book sales. The total investment cost includes all the costs associated with publishing and marketing the book, such as printing, editing, cover design, marketing campaigns, author advances, and royalties.

Understanding ROI is important for publishers for several reasons. First, it helps them determine the financial viability of a book project before committing significant resources to it. By analyzing the potential ROI, publishers can assess whether the projected returns justify the investment.

Additionally, ROI analysis can help publishers make informed decisions about pricing, marketing strategies, and distribution channels. For example, if the ROI for a particular genre of books is consistently higher than others, publishers may allocate more resources to that genre or focus their marketing efforts in that direction.

ROI analysis lets publishers track the performance of their catalog and make strategic decisions about future acquisitions. By assessing the ROI of earlier publications, publishers can identify trends, genres, or authors that consistently generate high returns and replicate their success. But they can identify books or genres that consistently underperform and adjust their strategies.

ROI analysis is not only important for publishers but also for authors. It helps authors understand the financial impact of their book and make informed decisions about marketing, pricing, and self-publishing options. By clearly understanding ROI, authors can better negotiate royalties and advances, evaluate different publishing offers, and optimize their marketing efforts to maximize their returns.

Understanding the concept of ROI is crucial for book publishers to assess the financial viability of their projects, make strategic decisions, and track the overall performance of their catalog. By analyzing ROI, publishers can make informed decisions about pricing, marketing strategies, and distribution channels, ultimately leading to more successful and profitable book publishing endeavors.

Determining the cost and potential revenue of book production

Determining the cost and potential revenue of book production involves various factors related to the production process, distribution, marketing, and sales. Let's break down the key elements involved in assessing these costs and revenue potential.

Cost of Production:

a. Writing and editing: Consider the cost of author fees, editors, proofreaders, and researchers involved in creating the book's content.

b. Design and layout: Determine expenses for cover design, interior layout, and formatting services.

c. Printing and binding: Calculate costs related to printing physical copies if applicable.

d. Illustrations and graphics: If the book includes illustrations or graphics, factor in the cost of hiring artists or buying stock images.

e. ISBN and copyright: Consider the expenses associated with acquiring an International Standard Book Number (ISBN) and copyright registration.

f. Marketing and promotion: Include costs related to book trailers, website development, author events, and promotional materials.

Distribution Costs:

a. Printing and delivery: If you are publishing physical copies, calculate printing costs and expenses for shipping and warehousing.

b. Ebook distribution: Factor in any distribution fees, such as those charged by online marketplaces like Amazon KDP or Apple Books.

c. Inventory management: Consider any costs associated with managing and tracking inventory.

Marketing and Sales:

a. Advertising and promotions: Budget for online advertising, social media promotions, book launch events, and other promotional activities.

b. Public relations: Determine expenses for hiring a publicist or participating in book fairs and literary festivals.

c. Book reviews: If you plan to get professional book reviews, allocate costs for review copies and associated fees.

d. Author royalties: Calculate the amount to be paid to the author as a percentage of each book sold.

Revenue Potential:

a. Pricing: Determine an appropriate price for the book, considering factors like genre, target audience, production costs, and market trends.

b. Sales projections: Evaluate the potential demand for the book based on market research, competition analysis, and any pre-launch marketing efforts.

c. Sales channels: Assess distribution channels like online marketplaces, physical bookstores, and direct sales through the author's website.

d. Royalties and profit: Estimate potential income from book sales based on the royalty percentage and projected number of copies sold.

Remember that the cost and revenue potential of book production can vary significantly depending on factors like genre, book format (print or ebook), marketing efforts, author platform, and market conditions. Thorough research and careful planning are important for determining accurate costs and revenue projections.

Calculating ROI Using Various Models and Formulas:

Calculating ROI is an important element in evaluating the profitability and effectiveness of investment opportunities. There are various models and formulas that can calculate ROI, including the basic ROI formula, the net present value (NPV) model, the payback period method, and the internal rate of return (IRR) model.

Basic ROI Formula:

The most straightforward way to calculate ROI is by using the basic ROI formula, which is:

ROI = (Net Profit / Cost of Investment) * 100

This formula measures the ROI as a percentage, based on the ratio of net profit to the cost of investment.

Net Present Value (NPV) Model:

The NPV model is commonly used for evaluating investment opportunities over a longer time horizon. It considers the time value of money, as it discounts future cash flows to their present value. The formula for calculating NPV is:

NPV = $\sum$ (Cash Flow / $(1 + r)$^t)

Where:

$\sum$ denotes the summation of cash flows over a specific time period

Cash Flow represents the expected cash flow at a particular time period

r denotes the discount rate or the required rate of return

t represents the time period

. . .

A positive NPV indicates a profitable investment opportunity, while a negative NPV indicates a loss.

Payback Period Method:

The payback period method calculates the time required to recover the initial investment. It provides a quick measure of the investment's profitability. The formula for calculating the payback period is:

Payback Period = Initial Investment / Annual Cash Flow

The shorter the payback period, the quicker the investment is expected to be recovered.

Internal Rate of Return (IRR) Model:

The IRR model calculates the discount rate at which the present value of cash inflows equal the present value of cash outflows. It indicates the profitability and potential rate of return of a project. The formula to calculate IRR is derived by setting the NPV equal to zero:

$$0 = \sum (\text{Cash Flow} / (1 + \text{IRR})^t)$$

Where:

$\sum$ denotes the summation of cash flows over a specific time period

Cash Flow represents the expected cash flow at a particular time period

IRR represents the internal rate of return

t denotes the time period

The IRR percentage is the discount rate at which the NPV equals zero. Higher IRR values show better investment opportunities.

Different investment models and formulas might be suitable for different scenarios and investment types. It is recommended to use multiple approaches for comprehensively evaluating an investment opportunity.

PART 5: MARKETING AND PROMOTIONAL TRACKING

Tools for tracking the effectiveness of marketing campaigns (social media analytics, website traffic, etc.)

Tools for tracking the effectiveness of marketing campaigns are crucial for businesses to measure and evaluate the impact of their marketing strategies. Here are some commonly used tools:

Google Analytics: This widely-used web analytics tool provides insights into website traffic, user behavior, conversion rates, and more. It helps businesses track visitor sources, popular content, and engagement metrics to evaluate the success of their marketing efforts.

Social media analytics platforms: Tools like Hootsuite, Sprout Social, and Buffer offer comprehensive analytics for social media marketing campaigns. These platforms track engagement, reach, and impressions across various social media platforms, letting businesses measure the effectiveness of their social media campaigns.

Customer Relationship Management (CRM) software: CRM platforms like Salesforce and HubSpot incorporate marketing automation and reporting modules. These can help track lead sources, conversion rates, customer acquisition costs, and customer lifetime value, providing insights into the performance of marketing campaigns.

Email marketing software: Tools like Mailchimp, SendinBlue, and Constant Contact offer analytics features that enable businesses to track email open rates, click-through rates, and conversion rates. These insights help measure the effectiveness of email marketing campaigns.

Heatmap and user testing tools: Services like Hotjar and Crazy Egg provide heatmaps and user recordings to analyze how users interact with a website. These tools visualize user behavior, clicks, and scrolling patterns, helping businesses optimize their marketing campaigns for better conversion rates.

Call tracking software: Platforms like CallRail and Invoca enable businesses to track phone call conversions from marketing campaigns. This is useful for measuring offline conversions generated through marketing efforts.

A/B testing tools: A/B testing platforms such as Optimizely and Google Optimize let businesses test different versions of webpages or marketing materials. By analyzing conversion rates and user behavior, these tools help identify the most effective marketing strategies.

Surveys and feedback tools: Tools like SurveyMonkey and Google Forms help with the collection of customer feedback and measure customer satisfaction. These insights help evaluate the effectiveness of marketing campaigns from a customer perspective.

By using these tools, businesses can gain valuable insights into the impact of their marketing campaigns, identify areas for improvement, and make data-driven decisions to optimize their marketing strategies.

Assessing the impact of different promotional strategies on book sales

Promotional strategies play an important role in driving book sales and reaching the target audience effectively. This chapter, aims to assess the impact of different promotional strategies on book sales, exploring various methods such as advertising, social media marketing, book signings, and book reviews.

Advertising

Advertising is a traditional yet effective promotional strategy for books. Print ads in newspapers, magazines, and book-related publications help raise awareness among potential readers. However, the impact of these ads may vary depending on the target audience and the publication's readership. Television and radio ads also offer a broader reach but are often more expensive. Digital platforms, including online banners and paid search ads, can target specific demographics and yield measurable results. Analyzing the ROI of various advertising methods can help publishers refine their strategies and allocate budget effectively.

Social Media Marketing

In the digital age, social media has become a powerful tool for promoting books. Platforms like Facebook, Instagram, Twitter, and Goodreads allow authors and publishers to engage directly with readers. Building a strong online presence, through regular updates, author interviews, and engaging content, can generate buzz and lead to increased book sales. Book trailers, behind-the-scenes videos, and sneak peeks can create anticipation among readers. Additionally, collaborations with popular social media influencers and book bloggers can extend the reach and impact of promotional campaigns.

Book Signings and Events

Book signings and events allow authors to connect directly with readers and create a personal connection. These events can be held at bookstores, libraries, literary festivals, and book clubs, among other venues. Hosting engaging discussions, author readings, and Q&A sessions can generate interest and attract potential readers. Limited edition copies, signed bookplates, and promotional giveaways during such events can incentivize book purchases. The success of book signings depends on factors such as the author's popularity, the event's organization, and effective promotion to the target audience.

Book Reviews and Influencer Endorsements

Positive book reviews greatly affect book sales, as readers often rely on recommendations before making a purchase. Professional book reviewers, both online and offline, play an important role in providing critical analysis and driving reader engagement. Positive reviews in reputable publications can significantly boost book sales. Additionally, endorsements from influential individuals, such as well-known authors or celebrities, can attract a wider audience. Collaborating with book clubs or online communities dedicated to specific genres can also amplify exposure and generate word-of-mouth recommendations.

Assessing the impact of different promotional strategies on book sales is important for publishers and authors looking to optimize their efforts and reach a wider audience. While advertising through various mediums remains effective, social media marketing provides a cost-effective way to engage with readers directly. Book signings and events also have a personal touch that can drive sales and foster a loyal fan base. Finally, book reviews and influencer endorsements help build credibility and entice potential readers. By implementing a combination of these strategies and analyzing their outcomes, publishers and authors can maximize their promotional efforts and achieve higher book sales.

Tracking Reader Engagement and Reviews:

Tracking reader engagement and reviews is an essential task for any author, publisher, or content creator. Understanding how readers are engaging with your content and what they think of it can help you make informed decisions to improve your work and connect with your audience. Here are effective ways to track reader engagement and reviews:

Social media tracking: Keep an eye on social media platforms where readers might discuss your work, such as Twitter, Facebook, Instagram, or Goodreads. Set up alerts or use social listening tools to track mentions and conversations related to your content.

Website analytics: Utilize tools like Google Analytics to track website traffic, bounce rates, time spent on specific pages, and click-through rates. This data can help you gauge reader engagement and understand which articles or sections are more popular.

Email marketing metrics: If you send out newsletters or promotional emails, pay attention to metrics like open rates, click-through rates, and conversion rates. These metrics can provide insights into the engagement levels of your readers.

Bookstore reviews and ratings: Regularly check popular online bookstores like Amazon, Barnes & Noble, or Goodreads for reader reviews and ratings of your work. Note both positive and negative feedback to gain a holistic understanding of reader sentiment.

Surveys and polls: Create short surveys or polls on your website or through social media to gather direct feedback from readers. Ask questions about their favorite parts of your content, areas of improvement, or any specific topics they would like to see covered. Encourage readers to leave detailed comments to gain deeper insights.

Engage with readers directly: Respond to comments on your blog, social media posts, or book reviews to foster engagement and build a relationship with your audience. Engaging in conversations lets you better understand reader perspectives and address any concerns or questions.

Collaborate with influencers and bloggers: Partner with influencers and bloggers who have a relevant audience and ask them to review your work. Track their reviews and the discussions generated to see how readers are responding to their content and recommendations.

Track sales and downloads: Keep track of sales figures and download counts for your content. Analyze trends and patterns to see if certain promotional efforts or changes in content have affected reader engagement positively or negatively.

Remember to track these metrics regularly and consistently to identify trends and patterns. Analyzing and interpreting the data will help you make data-driven decisions to enhance reader engagement and improve your content.

PART 6: INTEGRATING DATA FROM MULTIPLE PLATFORMS

Consolidating Data from Various Sales Channels and Platforms:

Consolidating data from various sales channels and platforms is an important process for businesses looking to gain a comprehensive view of their sales performance. With the proliferation of multiple online platforms, social media channels, retail stores, and more, it becomes essential to bring all the sales data together in a centralized system for analysis and decision-making.

Here are the steps involved in consolidating data from various sales channels and platforms:

Identify all sales channels and platforms: Begin by identifying all the channels and platforms through which the company makes sales. This could include ecommerce platforms, social media channels, retail stores, marketplaces, etc.

Evaluate data compatibility: Assess the data format and compatibility of each sales channel or platform. Determine whether they provide data in a structured format that can be easily integrated and combined with data from other sources. If not, extract and transform the data into a compatible format.

Select a centralized system or data integration tool: Choose a centralized system or data integration tool that can handle the data consolidation process. This system should be capable of integrating data from various sources, automating the data extraction process, and combining the data into a unified format.

Extract data from each channel: Set up the automation tools or interfaces to extract data from each sales channel or platform. This may involve integrating APIs, using web scraping techniques, or exporting data files in a specified format.

Clean and transform data: Once the data is extracted, it may be necessary to clean and transform it to ensure consistency and accuracy. This may involve removing duplicate entries, standardizing formatting, and applying data cleansing techniques.

Map data fields: Map the data fields from each sales channel or platform to ensure uniformity across all sources. This step helps to consolidate similar data attributes under a single category or variable.

Consolidate data: Use the chosen centralized system or data integration tool to consolidate all the cleaned and transformed data into a single database or data warehouse. This consolidation will enable cross-channel analysis and reporting, providing a comprehensive view of sales performance.

Regularly update and reconcile data: Establish a regular schedule for updating and reconciling the consolidated data. This makes sure the data remains accurate and up to date as new transactions occur across various channels and platforms.

Analyze and report on consolidated data: Utilize data analytics and reporting tools to generate insights and reports based on the consolidated data. This analysis can help identify trends, patterns, and opportunities for business growth.

Make data-driven decisions: Finally, use the consolidated data and the insights gained from analysis to make informed, data-driven decisions. This includes formulating marketing strategies, optimizing inventory, targeting specific customer segments, and improving overall sales performance.

Consolidating data from various sales channels and platforms is an ongoing process that requires regular tracking and maintenance. By implementing these steps, businesses can gain valuable insights from their sales data and improve their overall operations.

Data analysis and visualization tools for holistic book sales tracking

Data analysis and visualization tools are essential for tracking and analyzing book sales in a holistic way. These tools help in extracting meaningful insights from data and presenting them in a visual format, making it easier for publishers, authors, and marketers to make informed decisions. Here are popular tools that can be used for book sales tracking:

Microsoft Excel: Excel is a versatile tool that lets users organize and analyze data effectively. It offers various features like pivot tables, charts, and formulas that can track book sales. Excel is widely used due to its simplicity and availability.

Tableau: Tableau is a powerful data visualization tool that enables users to create interactive dashboards and reports. It can connect to various data sources, including spreadsheets and databases, making it convenient for tracking book sales across different platforms. Tableau allows for the creation of visually appealing charts and graphs, helping with better data analysis.

Google Analytics: Google Analytics is primarily used for web analytics but can also track book sales on online platforms. It provides detailed information about website traffic, conversion rates, and user behavior, which can help authors and publishers understand how their books are performing online.

Python with libraries like pandas, Matplotlib, and Seaborn: For more advanced data analysis and visualization, Python can be used along with libraries like pandas for data manipulation and analysis, Matplotlib for creating static visualizations, and Seaborn for creating statistical graphics. Python offers flexibility, scalability, and the ability to automate repetitive tasks.

Power BI: Power BI is a business analytics tool by Microsoft that lets users create interactive visualizations and reports. It can connect to multiple data sources, including spreadsheets and databases, enabling users to track and analyze book sales data effectively. Power BI provides many pre-built visualizations and is highly customizable.

Adobe Analytics: Adobe Analytics is a comprehensive analytics solution that provides insights into various parts of book sales. It offers real-time reporting, advanced segmentation, and predictive analytics capabilities. Adobe Analytics lets users track book sales across different channels, optimize marketing campaigns, and improve overall sales performance.

These tools provide different functionalities and capabilities, and the choice of tool depends on the specific requirements and preferences of users. By leveraging these data analysis and visualization tools, book sales can be effectively tracked and analyzed, leading to better decision-making and improved marketing strategies.

Automation Techniques for Streamlined Data Collection and Analysis:

Automation techniques for streamlined data collection and analysis have become increasingly important in today's data-driven world. They help businesses and organizations collect, process, and analyze large volumes of data efficiently and accurately. Here are some key automation techniques for streamlined data collection and analysis:

Data Integration and Extraction: Integration and extraction tools automate gathering data from various sources such as databases, APIs, websites, and files. These tools allow for the seamless collection of data into a centralized data repository, eliminating the need for manual data entry and ensuring accuracy.

Robotic Process Automation (RPA): RPA involves software robots or 'bots' to automate repetitive and rule-based tasks. Bots can be programmed to collect and update data from different systems and applications, reducing manual effort and minimizing human error.

Data Cleansing and Transformation: Data cleansing involves the identification and correction of errors, inconsistencies, and discrepancies in the collected data. Automation tools can automatically clean and transform data, ensuring its quality and consistency before analysis.

Artificial Intelligence and Machine Learning: AI and ML algorithms can automate data analysis tasks, such as pattern recognition, anomaly detection, and predictive modeling. These techniques can help streamline the data analysis process by reducing the time and effort required by analysts.

Real-time Data Streaming: With the increasing availability of IoT devices and sensor technologies, data is being generated in real-time. Automation techniques can be used to collect, process, and analyze streaming data, enabling businesses to make timely and informed decisions based on up-to-date information.

Dashboard and Reporting Automation: Automation tools can generate interactive dashboards and reports that provide real-time insights from the collected and analyzed data. These dashboards can be customized to meet specific business requirements and shared with stakeholders, automating the reporting process.

Workflow and Task Automation: Workflow automation tools can streamline the entire data collection and analysis process by automating the flow of data and tasks between different systems and departments. This makes sure the right data reaches the right people at the right time, increasing efficiency and reducing manual errors.

Data Governance and Security Automation: Automation techniques can also enforce data governance policies and ensure data security. This includes automated data access controls, encryption, and compliance tracking, helping maintain data quality and protect sensitive information.

By leveraging these automation techniques, businesses and organizations can streamline their data collection and analysis processes, reduce human error, increase efficiency, and make more informed decisions based on accurate and timely insights.

PART 7: LEVERAGING INSIGHTS FOR BOOK SALES OPTIMIZATION

Using tracked data to refine marketing strategies and target audiences effectively

In today's digital world, businesses have access to a wealth of tracked data that can refine marketing strategies and effectively target specific audiences. By analyzing this data, businesses can gain valuable insights into consumer behavior, preferences, and buying patterns, letting them tailor their marketing efforts. Here are keyways in which tracked data can refine marketing strategies and target audiences effectively.

First, tracked data can give businesses a deep understanding of their target audience. By collecting and analyzing demographic information such as age, gender, location, and interests, businesses can identify their ideal customers and tailor their marketing messages to resonate with them. This enables them to create highly targeted campaigns that effectively reach the right audience and drive better results.

Tracked data can help businesses identify which marketing channels are most effective in reaching their target audience. By analyzing data on customer engagement and conversion rates across different channels such as email, social media, search engines, and websites, businesses can identify which channels are delivering the best ROI. This lets them allocate marketing budgets more efficiently and focus their efforts on channels most likely to drive results.

In addition, tracked data can provide insights into consumer buying behavior and preferences. By analyzing data on product page views, click-through rates, and buy history, businesses can gain a better understanding of which products or services are most popular among their target audience. This information can refine product offerings, develop personalized marketing messages, and cross-sell or upsell relevant products to customers.

Tracked data can help businesses identify trends and patterns in consumer behavior. By analyzing data on customer interactions, businesses can gain insights into when and how customers engage with their brand. This can help them optimize marketing campaigns by scheduling content at peak times, tailoring messages to specific times of the year, or using personalized retargeting strategies to reach customers who have shown interest in their products or services.

Leveraging tracked data for marketing strategies must comply with ethical guidelines and privacy regulations. Businesses must make sure data is collected and used in a transparent and secure manner, with proper consent from customers.

Tracked data gives businesses valuable insights into consumer behavior, preferences, and purchasing patterns. By harnessing this data, businesses can refine their marketing strategies and effectively target specific audiences. From understanding the target audience and identifying the most effective marketing channels to analyzing buying behavior and identifying trends, using tracked data can greatly enhance marketing efforts and lead to improved results and returns on investment.

Identifying underperforming titles and making changes to improve sales

When identifying underperforming titles and making changes to improve sales, there are a few key steps that can be taken. These steps involve analyzing sales data, conducting market research, making strategic changes to the product, and tracking the impact of those changes. Here's a step-by-step guide on how to go about it:

Analyze sales data: Start by scrutinizing sales data to identify titles or products underperforming. Look for trends and patterns such as declining sales, inventory buildup, or low customer ratings. Closely examine factors like release date, price point, marketing efforts, and customer feedback to get a clear understanding.

Conduct market research: Once you have identified the underperforming titles, conduct thorough market research to understand the customer preferences, emerging trends, and competitive landscape. Analyze both your target audience and potential customer segments to gain insights into the reasons behind the underperformance.

Identify the problem: Based on sales data and market research, identify the specific problem areas for the underperforming titles. This could include a lack of visibility or awareness, ineffective marketing strategies, pricing issues, poor packaging, or outdated content.

Develop a plan to address the issues: Create a detailed plan to address the identified problems. This might involve various strategies such as rebranding, marketing campaign redesign, changing the cover design, adjusting the pricing strategy, or updating the content of the book. Each solution should be tailored to the specific problem identified.

Make the changes: Take action to make the changes outlined in your plan. Execute marketing campaigns, update product packaging or design, adjust pricing, or make any other necessary changes to improve the performance of the underperforming titles.

Monitor and measure the impact: Continuously monitor the sales and performance of the titles after making the changes. Keep an eye on key performance indicators, such as sales volume, customer reviews, and market share, to evaluate the effectiveness of the implemented changes. If the desired results are not achieved, reassess the situation and make more changes as needed.

Iterate and improve: Use the insights gained from tracking the impact of changes to further refine your strategies. Continuously gather customer feedback, stay updated on market trends, and be willing to adapt your approach to further improve sales performance.

By following these steps, businesses can effectively identify underperforming titles and make changes to boost sales. It is important to remain proactive, conduct regular reviews, and adapt to changing market dynamics to stay competitive and continually enhance performance.

Case studies of successful authors and publishers using data-driven approaches

Amazon Publishing: Amazon Publishing has been leveraging data-driven approaches to identify and publish successful books. They analyze customer reading habits, purchase history, and user-generated data to identify emerging trends and reader preferences. By understanding what readers want, Amazon Publishing can make data-driven decisions when acquiring and marketing books, increasing the likelihood of success.

J.K. Rowling and Pottermore: J.K. Rowling, the author of the Harry Potter series, partnered with data analysts to create Pottermore, an interactive website for fans. Through this platform, Rowling collected data on readers' preferences, behaviors, and engagement with the franchise. This data let her tailor her content and marketing strategies leading to increased sales and engagement.

Wattpad: Wattpad is a digital platform that offers a vast collection of user-generated stories. Using data analytics, Wattpad tracks user engagement, reads, and comments to identify popular stories and genres. They then leverage this data to connect successful authors with publishing opportunities and book deals, increasing their chances of becoming successful authors.

Penguin Random House: Penguin Random House uses data analytics to understand reader behavior, market trends, and competitor analysis. By analyzing sales data, book reviews, and social media sentiments, they identify patterns and preferences, helping them with better book curations, targeted marketing, and personalized recommendations. This data-driven approach makes sure their published titles align with the interests and demands of readers, ultimately leading to success.

Neil Gaiman: Neil Gaiman, a renowned author, has embraced data-driven approaches to expand his reach and engage with his audience. By tracking online platforms, social media conversations, and blog engagements, Gaiman gains valuable insights into his readers' interests, letting him tailor his content and engage with his fans more effectively. This data-driven approach has helped him grow his fanbase, improve book sales, and create a loyal following.

In all these case studies, successful authors and publishers have recognized the value of data-driven approaches in understanding and connecting with their readers. By analyzing reader preferences, behaviors, and market trends, they can make informed decisions about book acquisitions, marketing strategies, and audience engagement, increasing the likelihood of success in the highly competitive publishing industry.

PART 8: BEST PRACTICES FOR LONG-TERM TRACKING AND GROWTH

Establishing a sustainable tracking system is an essential step in managing resources, reducing waste, and improving overall efficiency in various industries. Whether it is tracking the movement of goods in a supply chain, tracking energy consumption in a building, or tracking the performance of employees in an organization, a sustainable tracking system helps in making informed decisions and driving positive change.

Here are key steps to establish a sustainable tracking system:

Set clear goals: Begin by defining the goals of your tracking system. Identify the specific areas where you want to track and monitor data to improve sustainability. It could be related to resource utilization, waste reduction, emissions control, or any other relevant part within your organization.

Identify key performance indicators (KPIs): Once the goals are defined, identify the key performance indicators that will help measure progress toward those goals. For example, if you want to reduce energy consumption, KPIs could include energy usage per square foot or the percentage of renewable energy used.

Choose appropriate technology: Selecting the right technology to track and monitor data is important. Consider using sensors, meters, data loggers, or software solutions that best suit your tracking needs. Make sure the technology selected provides accurate and real-time data to enable prompt action and decision-making.

Collect and analyze data: Implement a data collection mechanism that captures the relevant information for your tracking system. This can include automated data collection through sensors or manual inputs from employees. Analyze the data to identify patterns, trends, and areas for improvement.

Establish benchmarks and targets: Establish benchmarks and targets based on industry standards, best practices, or organizational goals.

Use the collected data to set achievable targets for sustainability performance. Regularly track progress against these targets to identify areas that need improvement.

Implement feedback loops: A sustainable tracking system is not just about collecting data; it should also give feedback to relevant stakeholders. Regularly communicate the performance data to employees, management, and other stakeholders to raise awareness, encourage accountability, and promote a culture of sustainability.

Continuous improvement: In order to create a sustainable tracking system, it is important to continuously monitor, evaluate, and improve the system itself. Take feedback from stakeholders and collect data on the effectiveness of the system. Make necessary changes, integrate new technologies, and update processes to ensure the system remains relevant and effective.

Regular reporting and transparency: Establish a reporting system that provides periodic reports on the performance of the tracking system. Transparently communicate the results internally and externally to show the organization's commitment to sustainability and help with informed decision-making.

By following these steps, authorpreneurs can establish a sustainable tracking system that enables them to measure, track, and improve their environmental, social, and economic performance. This system not only helps in achieving sustainability goals but also enhances the overall efficiency, productivity, and competitiveness of the organization.

Adapting to Changing Market Trends and Technologies:

Adapting to changing market trends and technologies has become important for the success and sustainability of any organization, given the dynamic nature of the business world. To stay competitive, businesses need to identify and embracing emerging trends and technologies, rather than being reactive and playing catch-up with their competitors. Here are strategies for adapting to changing market trends and technologies:

Stay informed: Keep a close eye on industry news, market research reports, and technological advancements. Subscribe to relevant newsletters, follow influential thought leaders, and attend conferences or webinars to stay updated on the latest trends and technologies. Knowledge is power, and being well-informed helps you respond quickly to any changes.

Conduct market research: Regularly conduct market research to gather insights into customer preferences, behaviors, and expectations. This will help you identify shifts in market trends, emerging customer needs, and potential opportunities. Use various research methods like surveys, focus groups, and social media listening to get a holistic understanding of the market.

Foster a culture of innovation: Encourage employees to be creative and think outside the box. Create a culture that embraces change and rewards new ideas. Establish channels for employees to contribute their innovative ideas and provide resources and support to implement them. Encouraging a culture of innovation will help your organization adapt and stay ahead of the curve.

Build strategic partnerships: Collaborate with industry partners, startups, and technology companies to tap into their expertise and gain access to new innovations. Partnerships can help you accelerate your adoption of new technologies and enable you to quickly respond to market trends. Seek mutually beneficial collaborations that align with your business goals.

Invest in training and development: Provide your employees with the necessary training and development opportunities to enhance their skills and knowledge in emerging technologies. This will help build a workforce equipped to meet the demands of a changing market. Offer workshops, online courses, and mentorship programs to cultivate a culture of continuous learning and development.

Be agile and adaptable: Create a flexible organizational structure and processes that enable quick decision-making and implementation. This includes adopting agile methodologies, empowering cross-functional teams, and decentralizing decision-making authority. Being agile and adaptable lets you respond rapidly to market trends and leverage new technologies effectively.

Embrace digital transformation: Embrace the digital revolution by integrating technology into your business processes. Use cloud computing, artificial intelligence, data analytics, and other digital tools to streamline operations, improve customer experiences, and extract valuable insights from data. Embracing digital transformation enables you to stay competitive in an increasingly digital world.

By implementing these strategies, businesses can effectively adapt to changing market trends and technologies. Through ongoing innovation, strategic partnerships, and a focus on employee development, organizations can position themselves as leaders in their industry and thrive in the ever-changing business landscape.

Maintaining Consistent Data Tracking Practices for Continuous Growth:

Maintaining consistent data tracking practices is important for ensuring continuous growth in any organization. By tracking and analyzing relevant data regularly, businesses can identify areas for improvement, make informed decisions, and monitor progress toward their goals. Here are key steps for maintaining consistent data tracking practices:

Define clear goals and metrics: Start by defining specific goals and the key metrics that align with those goals. This will help in identifying what data needs to be tracked and how to interpret it effectively.

Standardize data collection and storage: Establish standardized methods for collecting and storing data across all relevant departments or systems. This ensures consistency and makes it easier to analyze and interpret data accurately.

Implement robust data management systems: Invest in tools and systems that help with data management, such as CRM systems and data analytics software. These systems can help automate data collection, streamline processes, and provide real-time insights.

Train and educate employees: Provide adequate training and education to employees involved in data tracking and analysis. They should understand the importance of data integrity, how to collect data consistently, and how to interpret it effectively.

Establish data validation processes: Create processes to confirm and verify the accuracy and integrity of data regularly. This may include cross-referencing data, performing audits, or using error-checking algorithms.

Regularly analyze and report on data: Schedule regular data analysis sessions to identify trends, patterns, and areas for improvement. Create comprehensive reports to communicate findings to relevant stakeholders and make sure the insights are acted on.

Continuously improve data tracking practices: Regularly review data tracking practices to ensure they remain effective and aligned with organizational goals. Stay updated with new advancements in data tracking technologies and best practices and implement any necessary changes.

Foster a data-driven culture: Nurture a culture that values data-driven decision-making. Encourage employees to rely on data when making choices, and reward those who use data effectively to drive growth and success.

Track and adjust data tracking processes: Continuously track the performance of data tracking processes to identify any inefficiencies or gaps. Adjust as needed to ensure data is tracked consistently and accurately.

By following these steps and maintaining consistent data tracking practices, organizations can gain valuable insights, make informed decisions, and achieve continuous growth.

Tracking book sales and ROI is not only crucial for measuring success but also for strategically planning future endeavors. This book has provided an extensive overview of tools, techniques, and best practices for effective sales tracking and ROI measurement. By implementing these insights, authors and publishers can make informed decisions, optimize sales strategies, and ultimately meet their publishing goals.

ANALYZING SOCIAL MEDIA ENGAGEMENT:

ANALYZING social media engagement is important for businesses and individuals to understand the impact and effectiveness of their online presence. It involves examining various metrics and data to evaluate the level of audience interaction, reach, and overall performance of social media platforms.

The first step in analyzing social media engagement is to identify the key metrics to measure. This can include likes, shares, comments, clicks, reach, impressions, and conversion rates. Each metric provides valuable insights into how well a post or content is performing and resonating with the target audience.

Next, it is important to track the engagement level over time to identify trends and patterns. By comparing the data from different periods, one can determine the effectiveness of certain strategies or content types and make appropriate changes. For example, if there is a noticeable increase in engagement after changing the posting frequency or content style, it indicates that the new approach is resonating well with the audience.

Another important part to consider is the demographic data of the engaged audience. Analyzing the age, gender, location, and interests of those who engage with the content provides valuable insights into the target market. This information can help tailor future content to better suit the interests and preferences of the engaged audience.

Additionally, sentiment analysis can be conducted to understand how people feel about the content posted. This can be done manually by analyzing comments and feedback, or using sentiment analysis tools that automatically categorize responses as positive, negative, or neutral. This analysis enables businesses to identify the topics or types of content that generate the most positive sentiment and those that need improvement.

Comparing engagement metrics across different social media platforms can provide valuable insights into which platforms are most effective in reaching and engaging with the target audience. It is essential to evaluate each platform individually, considering their unique features, algorithms, and user behavior patterns. By understanding the strengths and weaknesses of each platform, businesses can optimize their social media strategy.

Analyzing social media engagement is essential for evaluating the success and effectiveness of online presence. By tracking metrics, identifying trends, understanding the target audience, analyzing sentiments, and comparing across platforms, businesses can refine their social media strategies to maximize engagement and meet their goals.

TRACKING WEBSITE TRAFFIC AND CONVERSION

TRACKING website traffic and conversion is essential for any business aiming to optimize their online presence and increase customer engagement. This process involves analyzing data and metrics generated by website visitors, tracking their behavior, and measuring the effectiveness of various marketing strategies. A well-designed tracking system enables businesses to identify opportunities for improvement, refine marketing efforts, and ultimately, enhance conversions.

Here are key steps to effectively track website traffic and conversion:

Set up an analytics tool: Start by selecting a reliable web analytics tool, such as Google Analytics, which offers comprehensive data on website performance. Install the relevant tracking code on your website to begin collecting data.

Define conversion goals: Determine the specific actions you want visitors to take on your website, such as making a purchase, filling out a contact form, or subscribing to a newsletter. Set up conversion tracking in your analytics tool to measure these goals and track their performance.

Analyze website traffic: Monitor the overall website traffic by tracking metrics such as the number of visits, unique visitors, page views, and bounce rate. Analyze this data to identify trends, peak periods of activity, and potential areas for improvement. Regularly review traffic sources to determine which channels are driving the most visitors to your site, such as organic search, social media, or paid advertising.

Track user behavior: Use website analytics to gain insights into how visitors interact with your site. Track metrics such as time on site, pages per visit, and click-through rates to understand user engagement levels. Identify popular pages, entry points, and exit points to optimize user flow and increase conversion rates.

Track conversion rates: Measure how effectively your website is converting visitors into customers or achieving other defined goals. Analyze conversion rate metrics across different pages, devices, and traffic sources to identify areas that need improvement. Experiment with various strategies, such as A/B testing, to optimize landing pages, forms, or CTAs.

Engage in funnel analysis: Understand the customer journey from the first interaction to conversion. Use analytics tools to track visitor flow throughout the website and identify any bottlenecks or drop-off points. Optimize your funnel by identifying areas where users are abandoning the process and making necessary changes to improve conversion rates.

Regular reporting and tracking: Set up regular reporting intervals to track website performance on an ongoing basis. Create customized dashboards or reports that summarize key metrics and goals. Regularly review these reports to identify trends, track progress, and make data-driven decisions to enhance website performance and conversion rates.

Continuously improve and optimize: Use the insights gained from website tracking to make changes and improvements. Test and refine strategies, website design elements, and marketing campaigns based on data-backed insights. Continuously track and analyze performance to make sure your efforts are yielding positive results.

By carefully tracking website traffic and conversion, businesses can gain a deeper understanding of their audience, refine their marketing strategies, and improve their overall online performance. This tracking process is ongoing that requires regular analysis, testing, and optimization to optimize conversions and drive business growth.

ADJUSTING AND OPTIMIZING MARKETING STRATEGIES:

ADJUSTING and optimizing marketing strategies is a crucial part of ensuring success in the ever-evolving business landscape. As consumer behaviors, preferences, and technology continue to change, businesses must continuously adapt their marketing strategies to stay relevant and meet their target audience's needs. Here are key steps to effectively adjust and optimize marketing strategies:

Review and analyze data: Start by gathering and analyzing data about your current marketing efforts. Use tools such as web analytics, social media insights, and customer surveys to evaluate the performance of your campaigns. Identify areas of strength and weakness, including key metrics like conversion rates, customer engagement, and ROI.

Understanding target audience: Take the time to understand and segment your target audience. Analyze their demographics, behaviors, interests, and pain points. This will help you tailor your marketing messages and tactics to effectively engage and convert your audience. Consider conducting market research or creating buyer personas to gain deeper insights into your customers.

Keep up with industry trends: Stay up to date with industry trends and changes. Follow thought leaders, join industry groups, and attend conferences or events to stay informed about the latest marketing strategies, technologies, and best practices. Being aware of emerging trends will help you to identify potential opportunities and adjust your strategies.

Use digital marketing channels: Nowadays, marketing primarily takes place online, so take advantage of digital marketing channels such as social media, SEO, email marketing, and content marketing. Explore new digital platforms and trends that might align with your target audience's preferences and behaviors.

Experiment with new ideas: Don't be afraid to test and experiment with new marketing ideas or strategies. Set aside a budget for experimentation and try out different approaches to see what works best for your brand. This could involve A/B testing, running different ad campaigns, or partnering with influencers. Track the results closely and iterate based on the outcomes.

Foster relationships with customers: Building strong relationships with customers is key to maintaining brand loyalty and repeat business. Focus on engaging and interacting with your target audience through various channels, including social media, email newsletters, and personalized communication. Listen to their feedback, address their concerns, and show appreciation for their support.

Continuous learning and improvement: Marketing strategies should be viewed as an ongoing process rather than a one-time effort. Regularly evaluate the effectiveness of your strategies, adapt to changing market conditions, and optimize your campaigns based on data-driven insights. Keep an open mindset and be willing to learn from both successes and failures.

Adjusting and optimizing marketing strategies is essential for any business seeking sustained success. By reviewing data, understanding the target audience, keeping up with industry trends, using digital marketing channels, experimenting with new ideas, fostering customer relationships, and continuously learning and improving, businesses can better align their marketing efforts with their goals and drive growth.

SECTION SIXTEEN KEY TAKEAWAYS AND ACTION ITEMS

1. **Analytics for Audience Insight**: Analytics provide deep insights into the target audience, revealing preferences and demographics essential for tailored marketing.
2. **Campaign Evaluation via Analytics**: Tracking KPIs through analytics is key to assessing marketing campaign effectiveness and optimizing strategies for improved ROI.
3. **Spotting Market Opportunities**: Analytics enable the identification of new market segments and emerging trends, important for staying ahead in the competitive landscape.
4. **Essential Data Analysis Skills**: Marketers must have skills in data analysis, interpretation, and be updated with current analytics tools and technologies.
5. **Importance of Sales Tracking Tools**: Platforms like Amazon KDP and IngramSpark offer comprehensive sales reports, aiding in strategic decision-making.
6. **Using Spreadsheets and CRM Software**: Tools like Microsoft Excel and CRM software are important for efficient sales tracking and data analysis.

7. **Benefits of Sales Tracking Apps**: Apps like Salesforce and HubSpot CRM offer insights into sales effectiveness and customer behavior.

8. **Analyzing Book Sales Data**: Focusing on metrics like unit sales, revenue, and royalties is important for strategic publishing decisions.

9. **Understanding Sales Trends**: Regular assessment of sales patterns is necessary for comprehending market dynamics and consumer behavior.

10. **Target Market Identification**: Conducting detailed market research and using direct feedback are key to identifying and understanding target markets.

11. **ROI Calculation Methods**: Using various models like ROI formula and NPV model helps in evaluating investment profitability.

12. **Effectiveness of Marketing Campaign Tracking**: Tools like Google Analytics provide essential insights into the impact of marketing campaigns.

13. **Impact of Promotional Strategies**: Different promotional strategies like advertising and social media marketing significantly affect book sales.

14. **Reader Engagement Tracking**: Monitoring reader engagement through social media and website analytics is important for effective content strategies.

15. **Data Consolidation Importance**: Integrating data from multiple sales channels provides a comprehensive view of sales performance.

16. **Visualization Tools for Insightful Sales Tracking**: Tools like Tableau aid in visualizing sales data for better decision-making.

17. **Data Collection Automation**: uUing techniques like RPA and AI enhances efficiency and accuracy in data collection and analysis.

18. **Refining Marketing with Data**: Tracked data is invaluable in tailoring marketing strategies and targeting audiences effectively.

19. **Tactics for Improving Underperforming Titles**: Identifying and making strategic changes are key to enhancing the sales of underperforming titles.

20. **Learning from Successful Case Studies**: Analyzing successful authors and publishers who used data-driven approaches provides valuable learning opportunities.

21. **Sustainable Tracking System Setup**: Establishing a sustainable tracking system with clear goals and standardized data collection is fundamental for long-term success.

22. **Adaptability to Market Trends**: Staying informed and adaptable to changing market trends and technologies is essential for businesses.

23. **Consistency in Data Tracking**: Regular and consistent data tracking fosters continuous growth and informed decision-making.

Action Items:

1. **Leverage Analytics:** Use analytics tools to gain insights into your audience and evaluate marketing campaigns.

2. **Stay Updated with Market Trends:** Regularly research and adapt to new market trends and technologies.

3. **Use Sales Tracking Tools:** Implement platforms like Amazon KDP and IngramSpark for detailed sales tracking.

4. **Employ Data Analysis Tools:** Use Microsoft Excel, CRM software, and sales tracking apps for comprehensive sales analysis.

5. **Track Sales Metrics:** Keep a close watch on unit sales, revenue, and royalties to make informed publishing decisions.

6. **Conduct Market Research:** Regularly gather and analyze market data to identify and understand your target audience.

7. **Calculate ROI:** Use various models to assess the profitability of your investments.

8. **Track Marketing Campaigns:** Implement tools like Google Analytics to measure the effectiveness of marketing campaigns.

9. **Evaluate Promotional Strategies:** Assess the impact of different promotional strategies on book sales.

10. **Engage with Readers:** Monitor and engage with readers through social media and website analytics.

11. **Consolidate Sales Data:** Integrate data from multiple sales channels for a holistic view of sales performance.

12. **Use Visualization Tools:** Implement tools like Tableau for effective sales data visualization.

13. **Automate Data Collection:** Apply automation techniques for efficient data collection and analysis.

14. **Refine Marketing Strategies:** Use tracked data to optimize marketing strategies and audience targeting.

15. **Improve Underperforming Titles:** Analyze and strategize to enhance the sales of underperforming titles.

16. **Learn from Successful Examples:** Study case studies of successful data-driven approaches in publishing.

17. **Implement a Tracking System:** Set up a sustainable tracking system with standardized processes.

18. **Continuously Track Data:** Maintain consistent data tracking practices for ongoing growth and improvement.

In our next Section...

As we wrap up our discussion on long-term strategies for authorpreneurial success, it's important we also consider how to stay resilient in the face of the inevitable challenges any business owner faces. Maintaining motivation and adapting to changing market conditions are critical skills for any entrepreneur or creative professional.

In the following section, we'll explore best practices for staying motivated in your work, embracing change, continuously learning, seeking feedback, building support networks, celebrating small wins, and more. We'll also discuss tips for taking calculated risks to spur growth while reviewing and adapting your strategies based on business metrics.

Finding harmony between creative fulfillment and business growth is another key topic we'll cover. By clearly defining your goals, developing a strategic plan, fostering collaboration, staying connected with your community, and remaining flexible, you can build a fulfilling and financially sustainable creative business.

Whether you're an author, artist, or other type of creative professional, our next section will provide invaluable advice for achieving long-lasting success on your journey.

SECTION SEVENTEEN: SUSTAINING YOUR AUTHORPRENEUR JOURNEY

LONG-TERM STRATEGIES FOR AUTHORPRENEURIAL SUCCESS AND EXPANDING YOUR AUTHOR BRAND:

As an authorpreneur, your long-term success relies not only on the quality of your writing but also on your ability to establish and expand your author brand. Here are six strategies that can help you achieve authorpreneurial success and expand your author brand over the long term:

Define your author brand: Before you can expand your author brand, you need a clear understanding of what it represents. Identify your unique voice, themes, and values as an author. This will help you attract a loyal fan base who resonates with your work.

Build an online presence: Having a strong online presence is important. Create an author website that showcases your work, includes your bio, and provides a way for readers to connect with you. Maintain an active presence on social media platforms relevant to your target audience, such as Facebook, Instagram, Twitter, or LinkedIn. Engage with your readers, share behind-the-scenes content, and promote your books.

Consistent content creation: As an authorpreneur, you must consistently create valuable content to maintain and grow your author brand. This can include writing blog posts, sharing excerpts or short stories, recording podcasts, or creating videos about your writing process. Regularly give your audience fresh and engaging content that keeps them coming back for more.

Develop a strong email list: Email marketing is an effective tool for building a loyal community of readers. Offer incentives, such as a free book or exclusive content, to encourage readers to sign up for your mailing list. Regularly communicate with your subscribers by sending newsletters, updates, and special offers. Use your email list to keep readers engaged and informed about your new releases and upcoming events.

Collaborate and network: Expand your author brand by collaborating with other authors, bloggers, influencers, or experts in your genre. This can include participating in joint author events, guest blogging, or hosting podcast interviews. Building connections within the writing community can expose you to new audiences and expand your reach.

Diversify your revenue streams: While book sales may be the primary source of income for most authors, consider diversifying your revenue streams to ensure long-term success. Explore opportunities such as public speaking engagements, teaching writing workshops, offering consultancy services, or creating merchandise related to your books. By diversifying your income, you can increase your financial stability and expand your author brand through different channels.

Remember, building a successful author brand takes time and effort. Stay consistent, adapt to changes in the industry, and always focus on providing value to your readers. With these long-term strategies, you can prove yourself to be a successful authorpreneur and expand your author brand.

~

STAYING MOTIVATED AND ADAPTING TO MARKET CHANGES:

Staying motivated and adapting to market changes is essential for success in any business. As an entrepreneur or professional, you may face various challenges and uncertainties that can easily dampen your motivation. However, with the right mindset and strategies, you can stay motivated and navigate through market changes effectively. Here are tips to help you:

Set clear goals: Define your short-term and long-term goals, and make them specific, measurable, attainable, relevant, and time-bound (SMART goals). This will give you a clear direction and purpose, keeping you motivated and focused.

Embrace change: Markets are dynamic, and change is inevitable. Instead of resisting change, embrace it as an opportunity to learn and grow. Stay updated on market trends, consumer preferences, and technological advancements to adapt your strategies.

Continuous learning: Invest in your knowledge and skills to stay relevant in the market. Attend industry conferences, workshops, and webinars. Join professional associations or networking groups to learn from others' experiences. Acquire new skills and stay up to date with industry best practices.

Seek feedback: Regularly seek feedback from customers, clients, and industry experts. This will help you understand their preferences, expectations, and any necessary changes needed in your products or services. Analyze the feedback and make necessary changes to stay competitive.

Build a strong support network: Surround yourself with like-minded individuals, mentors, or a mastermind group. Connect with people who share your goals and values, who can provide guidance and support during challenging times. Collaborate with others and learn from their experiences and insights.

Celebrate small wins: Acknowledge and celebrate your achievements, no matter how small they may seem. This will help you maintain a positive attitude and keep your motivation high. Break down your goals into smaller milestones and celebrate each milestone achieved along the way.

Take care of your well-being: Your physical and mental well-being play an important role in staying motivated and adapting to market changes. Focus on self-care activities such as exercise, healthy eating, and getting enough rest. Practice mindfulness or meditation to reduce stress and improve focus.

Maintain a positive mindset: Challenges are inevitable, but maintaining a positive mindset can help you overcome obstacles. Surround yourself with positive influences, visualize success, and reframe setbacks as learning opportunities. Believe in your abilities and stay resilient in the face of adversity.

Take calculated risks: The market landscape is ever evolving, and sometimes taking calculated risks is necessary for growth. Conduct market research, assess potential risks, and make informed decisions. Be willing to step out of your comfort zone and adapt your strategies.

Review and adapt your strategies: Continuously evaluate the effectiveness of your strategies and make necessary changes. Monitor market trends, competitors, and customer feedback to stay ahead. Be willing to change course if needed and embrace innovation to stay competitive.

Remember, staying motivated and adapting to market changes requires perseverance, flexibility, and a growth mindset. By incorporating these tips into your daily routine, you will be better equipped to navigate through uncertainties and achieve long-term success.

BALANCING CREATIVE FULFILLMENT WITH BUSINESS GROWTH:

As an artist or creative individual, it can often be a challenge to balance the pursuit of creative fulfillment with the need for business growth. On one hand, you want to create art that speaks to you and fulfills your creative vision. But you also need to consider the practical parts of running a business and making a living from your art. However, balancing these two parts is not impossible, and with the right approach, you can find a harmonious middle ground.

It's important to define your goals and priorities. Ask yourself what you want to achieve with your art. Is it purely creative fulfillment, or do you also want to grow your business and make a living from your art? Understanding your own goals will help you shape your approach to balancing creativity and business growth.

Once you have clarity on your goals, it's time to develop a plan. Consider dividing your time and energy between creative pursuits and business-related tasks. Dedicate specific hours or days to focus only on creating art, giving yourself the freedom to explore your creativity without distractions. During these periods, allow yourself to experiment, take risks, and follow your intuition.

Simultaneously, set aside dedicated time for business-related tasks such as marketing, networking, and financial planning. Treat these tasks as an essential part of your artistic practice but remember not to let them overshadow your creativity. Be strategic in your approach, identifying the most effective channels for promoting your work and connecting with potential clients or customers.

Collaboration is another valuable tool for balancing creative fulfillment and business growth. Seek opportunities to collaborate with other artists, organizations, or businesses that align with your values. Collaborations can give you a chance to explore new creative territories and expand your network, all while promoting your work and generating business opportunities.

Additionally, never forget the importance of staying inspired and staying connected to your artistic community. Surround yourself with like-minded individuals who understand and support your creative journey. Go to workshops, conferences, or art events where you can learn from others, share experiences, and find new sources of inspiration.

Last, be open to evolving and adapting your approach along the way. The balance between creative fulfillment and business growth is not a static idea and may shift. Allow yourself the freedom to explore new avenues, push your limits, and embrace new opportunities that may arise.

Balancing creative fulfillment with business growth requires a thoughtful approach and a commitment to both parts of your artistic journey. By setting clear goals, developing a plan, fostering collaboration, staying inspired, and remaining adaptable, you can achieve a harmonious balance that lets you thrive both creatively and commercially. Remember that each artist's journey is unique, so listen to your own instincts and intuition as you navigate this delicate balance.

SECTION SEVENTEEN KEY TAKEAWAYS AND ACTION ITEMS

Key Takeaways:

1. **Defining Your Author Brand**: Understand and articulate your unique voice, themes, and values to attract and retain a loyal fan base.
2. **Online Presence**: Develop a strong digital footprint through an author website and active social media engagement, catering to your target audience.
3. **Content Creation**: Regularly provide fresh, engaging content like blog posts, stories, podcasts, or videos to keep your audience interested.
4. **Email Marketing**: Build and maintain a robust email list to foster a community of readers, using newsletters and special offers to engage subscribers.
5. **Collaboration and Networking**: Expand your reach by collaborating with other authors, bloggers, and influencers within your genre.
6. **Diversifying Income**: Explore various revenue streams beyond book sales, like speaking engagements, workshops, or merchandise.

7. **Goal Setting**: Establish SMART goals to maintain focus and motivation while adapting to market changes.
8. **Embracing Change**: Stay informed about market trends and consumer preferences to effectively adapt strategies.
9. **Continuous Learning**: Invest in personal and professional development to stay relevant in the market.
10. **Feedback Implementation**: Actively seek and incorporate feedback for continuous improvement and competitiveness.
11. **Support Networks**: Build a network of mentors, peers, and collaborators for guidance and support.
12. **Well-being and Positivity**: Prioritize physical and mental health to maintain resilience and a positive mindset.

Action Items:

1. **Craft Your Brand Narrative**: Take time to clearly define what your author brand stands for and how it differentiates you.
2. **Develop a Digital Strategy**: Regularly update your website and social media profiles with engaging content tailored to your audience.
3. **Content Calendar**: Create a schedule for consistent content creation and stick to it.
4. **Grow Your Email List**: Implement strategies like offering free content to encourage email sign-ups.
5. **Seek Collaborative Opportunities**: Actively look for networking events and collaboration opportunities within the literary community.
6. **Research Additional Revenue Options**: Explore and experiment with different income-generating activities related to your work.
7. **Regular Goal Reviews**: Periodically review and adjust your goals as needed to align with your growth and market changes.

8. **Stay Informed**: Dedicate time each week to research market trends and new opportunities.
9. **Educational Investment**: Enroll in courses or attend workshops to enhance your skills.
10. **Gather and Analyze Feedback**: Use surveys or direct communication to collect reader feedback and implement necessary changes.
11. **Nurture Your Network**: Regularly engage with your support network for shared learning and encouragement.
12. **Self-care Routine**: Establish and maintain a self-care routine to support your physical and mental well-being in a demanding career.

CONCLUSION: THE EVOLVING WORLD OF AUTHORPRENEURSHIP

Embracing **Your Future as an Authorpreneur**

As we draw the curtains on this journey, it's time to take a moment and recognize the incredible stride you've made. You began this journey with a passion for writing and a dream to share your stories with the world. Now, you stand at the precipice of a new era in your career, armed with the knowledge, strategies, and tools to make your mark as an authorpreneur.

Your Transformation into an Authorpreneur

Throughout this book, "Unleash Your Inner Authorpreneur: DIY Marketing Strategies Writers Need Today," we've navigated the dynamic intersection of creativity and commerce. You've learned to blend your artistic vision with a strategic mindset, transforming your writing from a solitary pursuit into a thriving, marketable brand.

The Power of Strategic Marketing and Branding

You've discovered the importance of establishing a unique author brand in a crowded digital space. With insights on optimizing your online presence, engaging with readers, and using analytics to guide your strategies, you're now equipped to elevate your writing career.

The entrepreneurial spirit you've nurtured will be your guide as you navigate the ever-changing landscape of the literary world.

Mastering the Art of Connection and Promotion

We delved into the art of creating content that resonates, fostering discussions, and building a community around your work. Your ability to connect with readers, influencers, and industry professionals is no longer a dream but a real skill you have.

Embracing Challenges and Opportunities

Remember, the path of an authorpreneur is filled with both challenges and opportunities. Stay dedicated, gather feedback, and don't hesitate to take calculated risks. Your journey is unique, and every step, every setback, every triumph brings you closer to realizing your full potential.

The Journey Ahead

As you step into the future, remember that your journey as an author-preneur is a continuous process of growth, learning, and adaptation. Embrace the changes, celebrate your achievements, and never lose sight of your passion for writing.

Your New Beginning

This isn't just a conclusion; it's a commencement of your thrilling expedition in the world of authorpreneurship. With the strategies and insights from this guide, you are now poised to soar into new realms of success and fulfillment.

Take Flight on Your Authorpreneurial Journey

It's time to spread your wings and take flight. As you start this exciting phase, let your passion for storytelling, combined with your newfound marketing skills, guide you. The world is waiting for your stories, your insights, your voice.

. . .

I wish you all the best as you start this transformative journey. Go forth with confidence and courage, and let the world witness the rise of an authorpreneur ready to make an indelible impact. Your story isn't just to be written; it's to be lived. Embrace your path and may your author-preneurial journey be as rewarding as it is inspiring.

Rae A. Stonehouse

Authorpreneur

ABOUT THE AUTHOR

Rae A. Stonehouse is an author, speaker, and self-publishing consultant dedicated to helping others embrace constant improvement and overcome challenges. With over 40 years of experience as a Registered Nurse in psychiatry and mental health, Rae brings a wealth of knowledge and passion for self-development to his writing and presentations.

As a 30 year member of Toastmasters International, Rae has systematically built his communication abilities and self-confidence to share his insights as an author and speaker. His self-help books and personal development presentations aim to have conversational one-on-one connections with readers and audiences.

Rae is known for his wry sense of humor and sage advice delivered in a relatable coaching style. After four decades as a nurse, Rae has rewired rather than retired, actively writing and pursuing public speaking. He strives to share lessons learned to help others achieve personal and professional growth.

To learn more about Rae and his approach to constant improvement, visit his website at https://raestonehouse.com or to learn more about his publications visit https://liveforexcellence.store

ALSO BY RAE A. STONEHOUSE

VISIT HTTPS://LIVEFOREXCELLENCE.STORE/ for a selection of personal/professional self-development books by Rae A. Stonehouse.

If you have found this book to be helpful, please leave us a warm review wherever you purchased it.

~

You may be interested in books in *The Successful Self-Publisher Series: How to Write, Publish and Market Your Book Yourself.*

Book One: Writing & Publishing as a Business

Self-publishing can be frustrating to learn, but author Rae A. Stonehouse's Successful Self-Publisher Series offers advice on writing, publishing, and marketing your own book. The series covers topics such as:

- organizing your content, formatting your manuscript, and creating book titles that sell.

Book Two: Self-Publishing for Fun and Profit in The Successful Self-Publisher Series, by author Rae A. Stonehouse, offers advice on self-publishing, covering topics such as:

- proofreading,

- pricing,

- royalties,

- and digital rights management.

Book Three Content Marketing Strategies That Work

Writing a book can take up to 30% of your time, while marketing can take up to 130%. However, marketing your content is achievable with basic and advanced strategies, as highlighted in the book "Content Marketing Strategies That Work" by author Rae A. Stonehouse.

All three books are available in ebook, paperback and audio versions.

Visit our Live For Excellence online store at https://liveforexcellence.store/product-category/self-publishing/ for more details.

www.ingramcontent.com/pod-product-compliance
Lightning Source LLC
Chambersburg PA
CBHW061132120626
46546CB00005B/1748